*Wilderness and the Heart*

# *Wilderness*
### AND THE *Heart*

Henry Bugbee's Philosophy
of Place, Presence, and Memory

EDITED BY *Edward F. Mooney*

THE UNIVERSITY OF GEORGIA PRESS

ATHENS & LONDON

© 1999 by the University of Georgia Press
Athens, Georgia 30602
All rights reserved
Designed by Erin Kirk New
Set in 10 on 13 Fairfield Light by G&S Typesetters
Printed and bound by Maple-Vail Book Manufacturing Group
The paper in this book meets the guidelines for
permanence and durability of the Committee on
Production Guidelines for Book Longevity of the
Council on Library Resources.

Printed in the United States of America
03  02  01  00  99  C  5  4  3  2  1
03  02  01  00  99  P  5  4  3  2  1

Library of Congress Cataloging in Publication Data
Wilderness and the heart : Henry Bugbee's philosophy of place,
presence, and memory / edited by Edward F. Mooney.
   p.    cm.
   Includes bibliographical references and index.
   ISBN 0-8203-2070-6 (alk. paper). — ISBN 0-8203-2098-6 (pbk. :
alk. paper)
   1. Bugbee, Henry Greenwood, Jr.   Inward morning.
2. Philosophy.   I. Mooney, Edward F., 1941– .
B945.B7631538   1999
191—dc21                                                    98-26779

British Library Cataloging in Publication Data available

Frontispiece: Henry Bugbee. Photo no. 74097-22, K. Ross Toole
Archives, The University of Montana—Missoula.

*Dedicated to Henry and Sally*
*who radiate a quiet joy to all about them*

## *In Celebration of Henry Bugbee*

Henry came to Harvard in 1947 for five years as assistant professor. Thirty-seven years later, in *The Time of My Life,* I described him as "lean, contemplative, and best visualized in leather jacket with pipe, rod, reel, and creel. He had a mystical sense of the pure poetry of being."

Henry is the ultimate exemplar of the examined life. He walks and talks slowly and thoughtfully, for he is immersed— a Bugbee word—in the wonders of the specious present. *The Inward Morning,* true to form, is a day-by-day compilation of his philosophical reflections, each fresh that day. His thoughts conform to the discreetness of the concrete, eschewing the factitious continuity of abstraction. His is an atheistic mysticism, free of mythical trappings. Like mystics before him, he is drawn to the mountains and wilderness. In and about Missoula he found the ideal blend of academe and wilderness, and after some forty years I made my way there as Henry Bugbee Lecturer.

He was the authentic Henry Bugbee for all his years, and we walked and talked along the banks of a trout stream flanked by the Rockies and the Bitter Roots in their autumn splendor.

W. V. QUINE

*The highest merit we ascribe to Moses, Plato, and Milton is that they set at naught books and traditions, and spake not what men but what they thought. A man should learn to detect and watch that gleam of light which flashes across his mind from within, more than the luster of the firmament of bards and of sages.*—Ralph Waldo Emerson, "Random Musings"

These words apply to Henry Bugbee's work. It must be read as his alone, even as he accepts help.

JOHN M. ANDERSON

# Contents

Foreword  ALASDAIR MACINTYRE  xiii
Preface  xxi
Acknowledgments  xxiii

1. *Introduction*  1

    Answering the Call of the Wild: Walking with Bugbee and Thoreau  DANIEL W. CONWAY  3

    Melt the Snowflake at Once! Toward a History of Wonder  DAVID ROTHENBERG  18

    Presence, Memory, and Faith: Passages from a Notebook on *The Inward Morning*  STEVEN E. WEBB  32

2. *Wilderness and Experience*  73

    Wilderness as Wasteland and Paradise  GEORGE HUNTSTON WILLIAMS  75

    Zen Existentialism: Bugbee's Japanese Influence  ANDREW FEENBERG  81

    The Inward Wild  DAVID STRONG  92

3. *Finality, Responsibility, and Communion*  113

    Bugbee on Philosophy and Modernity  ALBERT BORGMANN  115

Autonomy and Authenticity
GORDON G. BRITTAN JR.    129

A Burden Tender and in No Wise Heavy
MICHAEL D. PALMER    150

4. *Faith, Love, and Lyric Evocation*    165

As We Take Things, So We Have Them: Reflections on the Fragility of Nature    DAVID TOOLE    167

Henry Bugbee's Interpretation of the Book of Job
JOHN LAWRY    184

On Starting with Love    ORVILLE CLARKE    196

When Philosophy Becomes Lyric
EDWARD F. MOONEY    204

5. *Celebrations: Human Voice and Moving Waters*    227

Henry Bugbee as Teacher    CYRIL WELCH    229

Henry Bugbee as Mentor    GARY WHITED    236

Five Henry Stories    DAVID JAMES DUNCAN    245

Contributors    261

Index    263

# Foreword

We all of us forget too easily how remarkably various the literary expressions of philosophy are: Wittgenstein's *Tractatus* and Sartre's *La Nausée,* Quine's *Word and Object* and Nietzsche's *Also Sprach Zarathustra,* Simone Weil's *Cahiers* and Derrida's essays. All these works resist paraphrase: how they are written and what they say are to be grasped together or not at all. Henry Bugbee's *The Inward Morning* in this respect belongs in their company. The unique quality of the author's voice and the distinctiveness of what the author has to communicate and how he communicates it are inseparable.

Someone may respond: These comparisons invidiously exaggerate the importance of *The Inward Morning.* A classic it may be, but at most a minor classic, one that in philosophical achievement clearly does not rank with Wittgenstein or Sartre or Quine or Nietzsche or Weil or Derrida. To which I reply: "Yes, yes, of course, but . . ." And it is what follows the "but" that matters. For what can be learned from *The Inward Morning* is not primarily a set of philosophical theses and arguments—although such theses and arguments are to be found in it—but rather something of the first importance about the place that philosophical theses and arguments might have in our lives, the relevance to our lived experience of the reading of philosophical texts. Someone who has learned what *The Inward Morning* has to teach will from then on be a different kind of reader of Wittgenstein, Sartre, Quine, Nietzsche, Weil, Derrida and the rest. How so?

Twenty years before *The Inward Morning* was published Gabriel Marcel wrote that "the act of thinking cannot be represented and must be grasped as such" and that to grasp what the act of thinking is involves learning to understand every representation of thinking as essentially inadequate.[1] Marcel thereby rejected a view of philosophy often taken for granted among analytic philosophers. Philosophy on this analytic view is a second-order activity, that of reflecting and reporting upon such first-order activities as doing and thinking. What such philosophy aspires to afford is an account of what thinking is, a representation of thinking. Marcel claims that this project is bound to break down. What thinking is can be *shown* in and through concrete examples. But the attempt to abstract from such examples and, by so doing, to provide a set of sound philosophical arguments and true philosophical theses about thinking is bound to result in an impoverished and inadequate representation of the act of thinking.

It is not necessary to accept Marcel's conclusions to understand the force of his challenge: present to yourself the activity involved in reflective thought in all its concrete detail and heterogeneous variety, then ask yourself whether what you have understood can be communicated through the medium of an abstract conceptual account. I myself do not share Marcel's conviction that such a philosophical account of thinking *must* involve misrepresentation and falsification. I am inclined instead to agree with those who have argued that although such an account will be of little value, unless grounded in and understood by reference to a series of detailed, insightful descriptions of acts of thought, it can be so grounded and understood in a way that takes us beyond the examples. But whether we accept Marcel's conclusions, or this latter view, or some standard analytic conception of second-order philosophical accounts of thinking must in the end depend on discovering what it is that such philosophically illuminating descriptions are able to disclose to us about the nature of thinking. And before we can hope to make this discovery, we will first have to find examples of such descriptions. It is at this point that the singular importance of *The Inward Morning* becomes evident.

For Bugbee excels in providing just the kinds of description that we need. It is not surprising that Marcel should have been so impressed, first by his conversations with Bugbee in August 1955 and then by *The*

*Inward Morning*. For although Marcel had himself experimented with writing philosophy in the form of a journal, had warned his readers against the dangers of abstraction, and had summoned them to a respect for the concrete and the particular, he himself had done all this in a remarkably abstract way. His writing remains for the most part incurably academic. But Bugbee practiced what Marcel preached, something that requires an unusual combination of literary and philosophical gifts.

It is crucial for the integrity of *The Inward Morning* that it is not a novel, that the journal is not the work of a fictional character, as the journal of Antoine Roquentin is in Sartre's *La Nausée*. Sartre uses the novelist's art to conceal himself behind Roquentin. Bugbee uses much of the same art not to conceal, but to disclose. *The Inward Morning* is in part about the relationship of the writer to his words, posing the question: What makes them *his* words, so that he takes and is understood to take responsibility for them? And Bugbee's answer to this question has to be communicated not only by what he says but also by the way in which he shows us how he makes himself responsible for what he says, by the disclosure of his presence in the writing. Sartre, as he reports in *Les Mots,* both was and was not Roquentin. Bugbee has to avoid this doubleness, so characteristic of the artfulness of literature.

At the same time he has in mind readers to whom he is extending an invitation to rethink their thoughts and make them, if they will, their own. So it would have violated the purpose of this journal if it had been an exhibition of the author's personality, an advertisement of idiosyncracies. It is instead a quietly reflective work that invites an equally reflective reading.

Reflection runs in two directions in *The Inward Morning*. There is the movement through which a range of experiences elicits from the author philosophical responses. And to this movement it is almost irrelevant that the author is or has been or will be an academic philosopher by profession. The experiences are those that may occur to anyone who has kept a night watch at sea or navigated in a storm or rowed or chopped wood or walked in the mountains. I say "may" and not "will" because without openness to experience there will be no cause for reflection. Openness to experience involves absorption in and by what is experienced, the kind of absorption that expresses a commitment to the activity and that may well leave no room for reflection about the activity—as contrasted with thought embodied in the activity—until after the event.

Reflection after the event pursues answers to such questions as "What is the difference between activity to which I am committed and activity that is mine, but from which nonetheless I am distanced or distance myself in some way?" "What is the difference between the directed thoughtfulness involved in committed activity and the free-ranging reflection about that thoughtfulness that may take place after the event?" In eliciting such questions from his readers Bugbee also directs them toward answers, just by describing carefully how such questions are elicited, that is, how reflection on everyday experience becomes philosophy.

There is however quite another direction taken by reflection in *The Inward Morning*. Its author presents himself as a professional academic teacher of philosophical texts, someone engaged in giving a course on ethics. He is a reader of Plato, Aristotle, Eckhart, Spinoza, Hume, Kant, Kierkegaard, Sartre, and C. I. Lewis, not to mention Pindar, Shakespeare, Proust, and Faulkner. So the author can scarcely avoid responding to the questions, arguments, and assertions presented in philosophical texts. But it is not difficult for a teacher to contain those responses within a curricular framework, to treat philosophy's questions, arguments, and assertions as one more disciplinary subject-matter, a proper concern for the classroom or the seminar, but something that can and perhaps should be left behind when we emerge from those peculiarly academic contexts. We "do philosophy," on this view, when we teach our class on Plato or Descartes between 9:00 and 10:00 A.M. on Mondays, Wednesdays, and Fridays, or when we prepare our classes, or when we write those articles for professional journals, the publication of which is a necessary step for professional success. And we cease to do philosophy when we walk out of the classroom or put on one side our philosophical writing. But what this conception of philosophical activity evades is the question of how I am related to my vocation, of how I stand to my philosophical words, of what it is to appropriate for myself this or that text or thesis or argument. Philosophy is always more than a set of propositions. "Even the rationale of coherent thinking seems to involve 'something' which is indispensable to the *de jure* force of a system of coherent propositions which cannot be reduced to a mode of relationship between the propositions explicitly entertained."[2] What is omitted is a particular mind's relationship to both the propositions and the immanent reality.

A variety of philosophical attitudes can prevent us from recognizing this omission. "The demand for proof can always take the form of an insistence on abstraction." And the wrong sort of adversarial stance can have the same effect. "An argumentative attitude, as we know, is as inflexible and unrealistic as can be."[3] But we may also encounter philosophical doctrines that systematically conceal this omission: "where Rationalism and Empiricism seem in essential agreement is in the reportorial vein in which they proceed. . . . The reportorial attitude is just that of one who claims to be looking and telling you what is going on, what is there, without editing or interpretation; you can leave him out of it. He is being objective, no more and no less. . . . [A] philosopher must get over thinking that what he wants to talk about can ever be reduced to something lying before him, which he merely talks about as a reporter might, leaving himself and his mode of involvement in reality out of account."[4] So the question of the philosopher's mode of involvement in reality becomes central.

We make a mistake, however, if we suppose that our mode of involvement is primarily a matter of our choices. Our fundamental commitments are at a level quite other than that at which we make our choices. Choices "are made at the level of the optional, or of the problematic and technical. . . . Choice involves alternatives reduced to the terms in which we can represent them to ourselves; and though it means taking up mutually exclusive alternatives one at a time, it does not preclude shifting from one alternative to another without threat to a person's integrity."[5] William James failed to understand this. For James, beliefs, including fundamental beliefs, are acquired through choices: "beliefs are treated as tools with which we enter upon action, to be chosen and shaped for their efficacy." And Bugbee responds: "The give-away in James, to me, is his conception of the *optional* character of fundamental belief, as if what were fundamentally believed might be the sort of thing one could understand well enough, but for which one sees that he must lack substantiating or disconfirmatory evidence."[6]

Pragmatism, because of its "concern to find reason for action in future attainment," loses sight of our "groundedness in present action." But if such groundedness is not a matter of our choices, and if it is prereflective, how is it to be characterized? Heidegger at this point offers us a philosophical theory. But no theory could provide the kind of answer toward which the questions of *The Inward Morning* direct us. For it is no accident that we are pointed toward answers but in the end left only with reformulated questions. The answers to *these* questions are not going to be found through reading any philosophical work, but only in reflection upon the activity of a self-aware agent by that agent her- or himself. Consider in this light what Bugbee has to say about necessity.

We encounter features of our situation of which we *cannot but* take account. We find ourselves part of a course of events in which we *have to* reckon with how things must be. "Can we understand things in their necessity apart from acting on that necessity as it governs us?"[7] Here Bugbee introduces his readers to a topic notably absent from the discussions of most moral philosophers—with one notable exception whom I shall notice presently—that of what it is to which we give expression, when we say not "I ought . . ." but "I must . . ." or "I cannot do otherwise." "I must . . ." is never the conclusion of an argument, for "there is no demonstrable necessity about any course of action which we can represent to ourselves." It is only insofar as we think about necessity "from the standpoint of unconditional concern" that we can avoid misunderstanding. "We can only bear witness to the necessity of what we do, and through that action which is necessary, rather than through showing how what we do fulfills specifiable conditions by virtue of which it must be acknowledged as necessary."[8] My activity, that is to say, is not to be understood in terms of some representation, some rule or precept to which it conforms; when I act because I must, the "I *must*" takes its sense from the mode of unconditional commitment and concern to which it gives expression. And what this mode is can be learned only by learning how to act from such commitment and to become aware of what distinguishes this mode of activity from others. But does this mean that there is no way in which we can achieve even a minimally adequate theoretical understanding of the kind of commitment involved? Can we go no further beyond experience and activity than the kind of reflective description provided in *The Inward Morning* will take us?

How we might go further is suggested in *The Inward Morning* by Bugbee's criticisms of Hume and Kant. Hume's failure to understand how necessity can govern action is ascribed to his adopting the standpoint of an external observer. Where the ethical is construed in terms of utility and agreeableness, "an idea of necessity that can be believed in is not to be expected."[9] And Kant is criticized for a conception of categorical imperativeness that is inadequate, at least in part, because of his failure to relate it to the experience of finality touched upon in the *Critique of Judgment*. Hume has, on Bugbee's account, a conception of our interests that excludes our unconditional concerns; Kant, a conception of imperativeness that does not recognize the interests that are at stake for us in acting from imperative necessity. My question is, Through these negative criticisms of Hume and Kant have we not been brought very close to a positive account, a representation of what it is for an agent to recognize necessity?

One recent philosopher who has taken "I must" seriously is Bernard Williams. In *Shame and Necessity* Williams considers the "I must" uttered by some of Sophocles's characters, notably Ajax and Oedipus, and connects the utterance of "I must" with the expression of a sense of shame, shame being here a response to the expectations and attitudes of some other whose judgment upon us we take with great seriousness.[10] There is here a sharp contrast with what is said in *The Inward Morning*. The necessity that concerns Bugbee is not Sophoclean necessity as characterized by Williams, in that it is a matter not of our relationship to some other but of our relationship to ourselves. Yet in drawing this contrast we can learn something more: that in taking responsibility for our actions we have made our faithfulness in doing what we must a measure of ourselves, and that commitment is not a matter of willed decision but of standing by that measure and continuing to judge ourselves by it.

What I am suggesting then is that from the dialogues between

Bugbee and other philosophers that recur in *The Inward Morning* there begins to emerge a possibility of doing what Marcel believed could not be done. But it matters very much that this possibility emerges from a reflective and descriptive mode that allows Bugbee and his readers to avoid being prematurely entangled within those kinds of abstract philosophical constructions that conceal from view the realities of enacted experience. In so doing Bugbee has shown us something about the kind of life that we have to lead if our reading and teaching of philosophical texts is not to be sterile. It is in this rare achievement that the classic quality of *The Inward Morning* becomes evident.

The essays in this volume celebrate the work of Henry Bugbee. I am honored to be even in this small way part of that celebration.

ALASDAIR MacINTYRE

## Notes

1. Gabriel Marcel, *Metaphysical Journal* (Chicago: Henry Regnery 1964), entry for 2 February 1933.
2. Henry Bugbee, *The Inward Morning: Philosophical Explorations in Journal Form* (1958; reprint, with a new introduction by Edward F. Mooney, Athens: University of Georgia Press, 1999), 98–99.
3. Ibid., 99.
4. Ibid., 98.
5. Ibid., 68.
6. Ibid., 205.
7. Ibid., 148.
8. Ibid., 153.
9. Ibid., 150.
10. Bernard Williams, *Shame and Necessity* (Berkeley: University of California Press, 1993).

# Preface

Forty years after its first publication in 1958, Henry Bugbee's philosophical journal *The Inward Morning* continues to speak to our deepest human concerns. It speaks to our need for stable ground and sense of place, to our need to know, when the day is done, the shape a worthy, reflective life can take, to our need for communion with others and with natural things, and for alertness to the wonders of our world. In Bugbee's writing, the lessons of a dwindling wilderness become an essential key to these concerns, needs as old and young as philosophy itself.

Bugbee calls *The Inward Morning* "a philosophical exploration in journal form." It is an exploration that encourages others to push ahead in their own distinctive ways, on their own paths. As the reflections collected in this volume vividly attest, his journal has won appreciation from writers across a range of philosophical styles and temperaments. Whether his thought is characterized as philosophy in wilderness, as Zen existentialism, or as a phenomenology of place, what matters is the specific strands of thought that he pursues and a record of those strands that set another thinker on a shared venture of discovery. The present volume assembles this record, providing contributions to our understanding of responsibility and reflective action, to our grasp of the restorative power of natural things and place, to our appreciation of the fine structure of generosity, gratitude, and compassion, and to our vision of the meaning of our vulnerability to suffering and inevitable perishing.

The essays are arranged in five sections, each opened by short prefatory remarks. The progress is from a set of relatively broad overviews of Henry Bugbee's thought to several groups of essays that explore specific themes he addresses in the journal—wilderness, experience, responsibility, faith—and finally to closing thoughts on Henry Bugbee as a teacher, a mentor, and a friend at home reflecting on the wild.

# Acknowledgments

Many thanks to each contributor, to Dan Conway and Andrew Feenberg, who helped hatch the idea, and to Gary Whited and Steve Webb, who stayed with it, to Bert Dreyfus, Ray Lanfear, Walt Gulick, Joan Stanbaugh, and Glen Martin for their part, to Sally Moore for her unstinting effort, to Henry for his exemplary presence, and to Penny DeWind for hours of support. Thanks also to David Rothenberg and to the dedicated and professional staff at the University of Georgia Press, especially Barbara Ras.

# 1

# *Introduction*

Henry Bugbee characterizes his reflective philosophical task as a "meditation of the place," a task that links him to Thoreau. Daniel Conway responds by reminding us of Thoreau's late essay "Walking," with its image of a westward path opening fresh vistas and new dawns. Both Bugbee and Thoreau require a writer's desk but also seek attunement to their setting that is gathered through the rhythm of attentive walking and is then refined through memory and reflection. Such mobile meditation invites us to a place among the things of creation, *our* place, an inward morning.

David Rothenberg pursues these thoughts in terms of wonder, the wonder, say, that things exist at all in their splendor, simple presence, or outright terror. Wonder stills the restless mind; the stance of fixing things or problem solving retreats, as when great seascapes, music, or poetry speak. We are grasped in an epiphany, something closer to a Buddhist than to a Rationalist enlightenment.

In the last of these initial explorations, Steven Webb traces the faith underlying Henry Bugbee's openness to wilderness. We respond, as Bugbee has it, to the "voice" of things, their vivid presence amplified in memory. This tunes and readies receptivity, giving access to "the essential truth of things," a sense of place and spiritual repose. But if redwood trees or streams call on our wonder and respect, what can we make of postures of indifference or of Sartre's renowned inverted view that seeing life straight-on occasions stomach-turning emptiness? Webb asks what grounds Henry Bugbee's affirmative, compassionate response to unbounded wild things.

# Answering the Call of the Wild

## Walking with Bugbee and Thoreau

DANIEL W. CONWAY

> So we saunter toward the Holy Land, till one day the sun shall shine more brightly than ever he has done, shall perchance shine into our minds and hearts, and light up our whole lives with a great awakening light, as warm and serene and golden as on a bankside in autumn.
> —Henry David Thoreau, "Walking"

> I weighed everything by the measure of the silent presence of things, clarified in the racing clouds, clarified by the cry of hawks, solidified in the presence of rocks, spelled syllable by syllable by waters of manifold voice, and consolidated in the act of taking steps, each step a meditation steeped in reality. What this all meant, I could not say, kept trying to say, kept trying to harmonize with the suggestions arising from the things I read.
> —Henry Bugbee, *The Inward Morning*

It is no coincidence that many of the greatest philosophers have also been prodigious walkers. Thales is known to us not only for launching the tradition of Western ontology but also for stumbling, absent-mindedly, into a well. The formidable ironist Socrates is praised by Alcibiades not only for his unironic barefoot exploits on the battlefield but also for his martial swagger. Even Plato, about whom we know little else, apparently voted with his feet when invited to his teacher's macabre farewell party. Aristotle is well known for his peripatetic lectures, which, we can only hope, were accurately recorded by his doubtlessly fatigued auditors. David Hume, whose corpulence usually ruled out strenuous physical exertion, was able to waddle purposively when nearing the vicinity of a hospitable Paris *salon*. If we can believe the rascal Heine, Kant's metronomic walks were so regular that the good citizens of Königsberg solemnly synchronized their chronometers to his dutiful strides. Nietzsche claims to have been seized by the adventitious idea of eternal recurrence while walking, as was his wont, in the Upper Engadine near Sils Maria. Heidegger's pioneering work in ontology took shape in the course of his explorations of the *Holzwege* that meander through his beloved *Schwartzwald* homeland.

Especially in light of the popular caricature of philosophy as a sedentary, detached, abstract, and other-worldly enterprise, this fondness for walking deserves further scrutiny and comment. Indeed, whence the value to metaphysicians and ontologians of this telltale concession to their earthbound existence? As a means of securing a preliminary purchase on this question, I wish to investigate a distinct lineage of philosophical ambulation, as practiced by American philosophers against the horizon of their western frontier. In particular, I wish to address the walking habits of two prominent American thinkers, Henry David Thoreau and Henry Bugbee. This "tale of two Henrys" will propose walking as an indispensable catalyst for the particular type of personal, immanent immersion in reality that is the hallmark of American philosophy.

Toward this end, I begin by excavating the Thoreauvian roots of Bugbee's perennial study *The Inward Morning*. In addition to furnishing insight into the psychology underlying Bugbee's forays into Nature, Thoreau helps us to understand the distinctly moral dimension of Bugbee's philosophical explorations. Although Bugbee and Thoreau walk primarily to stoke the dying flame of wilderness within their own souls, their personal immersions in Nature also reverberate with undeniably public repercussions. While the philosopher's journey of self-discovery remains essentially "private," its sumptuary residue enters the public sphere as an invitation and temptation to others. This is the "inward morning" of which both Thoreau and Bugbee speak, the daybreak of wilderness within a soul ordinarily benighted by the domestic routines of culture and commerce.

Bugbee's "inward morning" thus generates both light and heat. It not only reveals his ownmost place within the "energy circuit" of Nature but also inflames within him those embers of wilderness that alone make civil society meaningful and tolerable. The daybreak of this inward morning furthermore instructs his readers to explore the forgotten wilderness that thrives both within and without themselves. Like Thoreau before him, that is, Bugbee involuntarily invites his readers to receive—and to answer—the call of wild.

I

While the weight of Thoreau's influence on Bugbee is perhaps indisputable, the gravity of my attention to the theme of walking may not be so readily conceded. Although Bugbee refers on various occasions throughout *The Inward Morning* to lapidary insights he has gleaned from Thoreau, these references all cite *Walden,* which comprises, in large part, Thoreau's paean to the sedentary (or at least stationary) life. Moreover, Bugbee himself has precious little to say in *The Inward Morning* about walking, apparently preferring to describe his experiences in nature's wilds rather than on the way to them.[1]

Despite this admitted lack of overt textual evidence, I nevertheless wish to trace the provenance of *The Inward Morning* to marching orders issued by Thoreau. Bugbee learned to walk from Thoreau, even heeding the latter's gnostic advice to cleave to a westward course: "Every sunset which I witness inspires me with the desire to go to a West as distant and as fair as that into which the sun goes down. He appears to migrate westward daily, and tempt us to follow him. He is the Great Western Pioneer whom the nations follow."[2]

In fact, whereas Thoreau's walks rarely led him beyond the woods west of Concord, Bugbee migrated to a western frontier celebrated, but unvisited, by Thoreau. Reprising the occidental trajectory that Thoreau ascribes to the flight of nature's arrow, Bugbee settled in Montana in 1957, where he established himself as a leading heir to the Thoreauvian tradition in American philosophy. Notwithstanding its obvious debts and contributions to twentieth-century European phenomenology, *The Inward Morning* stands as an unmistakably American philosophical achievement, a testament to the mysterious, fructifying powers of our westward frontier.

It is my contention, then, that a Thoreauvian conception of walking operates as the catalyst of Bugbee's realism, as the condition of his immersion in the "sense of place" that he receives from his philosophical explorations. While he devotes only a few entries in *The Inward Morning* to the pedestrian theme of ambulation, his occasional references nevertheless confirm the centrality of walking to his larger project of exploration. The following passage, for example, conveys the importance of walking for the execution of Bugbee's unique phenomenological methodology:

> During my years of graduate study before the war I studied philosophy in the classroom and at a desk, but my philosophy took shape mainly on foot. It was truly peripatetic, engendered not merely while walking, but *through* walking that was essentially *a meditation of the place*. And the balance in which I weighed the ideas I was studying was always that established in the experience of walking in the place.[3]

As this passage clearly indicates, the relationship between Bugbee's philosophizing and his walking is not merely accidental. He does not walk simply to clear his mind, tone his musculature, quicken his pulse, organize his jumbled thoughts, or replenish the supply of oxygen to his brain. Walking is not merely a calisthenic propaedeutic to the heroic labors of philosophizing. Rather, walking functions as the engine of immersion, which enables him to take the phenomenological measure of the wild place he temporarily inhabits. As Bugbee himself puts it, walking thus engenders *a meditation of the place,* a meditation he describes as "steeped in reality," whereby he situates himself phenomenologically within the immanence of the place whose reality he wishes to experience.

As this rich passage also suggests, walking involves for Bugbee (as for Thoreau) a regimen of receptivity, whereby the peripatetic philosopher readies himself to accept the intimations of reality that Nature promiscuously and amorally transmits. By forging a link between the wilderness without and the wilderness within oneself, walking reveals the reality of the place, of Nature, and *a fortiori,* of one's own character and relationship to Nature. Walking thus delivers one to the sheer, immanent reality of the place in which one aimlessly wanders, thereby restoring, if only briefly, one's ownmost voice.

Walking thus constitutes a preferred means of receiving (and as we shall soon see, of responding to) the call of the wild. Echoing Thoreau on this point, Bugbee thus maintains, "But here is an essential point: Nothing can be truly given to us except on the condition of active receptiveness on our part. Our capacity for estrangement from reality, in all its permutations, is to be marked in all our indecision, our insistence to have things on our own terms."[4] One walks, that is, not to arrive at any particular geographical destination, but to advance the progress of a private project of self-transformation. While perambulating in the manner of Bugbee and Thoreau, one becomes a particular type of human being, divested of one's cumbersome "agency" and renewed in one's primordial attunements to the reality within and without oneself.

*Fluency* is a concept of central importance to Bugbee's realism, and *The Inward Morning* is accurately appraised as "a *plunge* into reality." Indeed Bugbee's evocative prose favors images and metaphors of fluidity, and he is at his suggestive best when portraying the plenteous economy of Nature as a grand circulatory network.[5] Effectively doubling the texture of this constellation of images, Bugbee overlays his painterly account of pristine mountain watersheds with a metaphysical invocation of the invisible flows of energy that lattice and traverse the intricate circuitry of Nature. Uniting these twin sets of images is the theme of walking, for the fluency of Nature, it turns out, is best appreciated on foot.

And why not? Walking is itself a fluid endeavor, especially if one walks with no particular destination or goal in mind, in step not with the regimented rhythm of commerce but with the rambling rhythm of Nature. In order to describe this nonpurposive mode of ambulation, Thoreau recommends the quaint term *sauntering*:

> I have met with but one or two persons in the course of my life who understood the art of Walking, that is, of taking walks—who had a genius, so to speak, for *sauntering*, which word is beautifully derived "from idle people who roved about the country, in the Middle Ages, and asked charity, under pretense of going *a la Sainte Terre*," to the Holy Land, till the children exclaimed, "There goes a *Sainte-Terrer*," a Saunterer, a Holy-Lander. They who never go to the Holy Land in their walks, as they pretend, are indeed mere idlers and vagabonds; but they who do go there are saunterers in the good sense, such as I mean.[6]

Thoreau thus dispenses sage advice to prospective, latter-day saunterers: Those who actually reach the Holy Land are those who set out with no predetermined destination in mind. It is as if the sanctity of this Holy Land would be besmirched by the consequentialist designs of mercenary crusaders. Those who would recover the Holy Grail, or the tomb of Jesus, or whatever object crudely symbolizes the fruition of one's ownmost spiritual quest, would do well to follow their hearts rather than the maps furnished by generals and priests.

Even on this Thoreauvian model of sauntering, however, walking is not to be confused with flying, gliding, soaring, or any other airborne mode of travel. The saunterer always proceeds with at least one foot planted firmly on the ground, continually connected to the earth by a steady rhythm of meandering footfalls. Bugbee thus reminds us that "[i]t is all very well to image our proper independence as responsible beings by talking of standing on our own feet. But this image, by itself, leaves us hanging in air. Let us not neglect to think of the ground being under our own feet; and let us not talk as if we placed the ground under our own feet. A ground which our *feet* do not *discover* is no ground."[7]

Sauntering thus affords one a modest exercise of freedom within the ubiquitous, multivalent constraints of nature, an expression both of one's connection to the natural cycle and of one's discernment of this cycle. To walk after the fashion of Thoreau and Bugbee is to join in an ancient, chthonic dance in which one invites Nature to dictate the rhythm and tempo of one's quotidian existence. Although the intrepid saunterer sets out with no destination or goal in mind, he is often rewarded for his *naiserie* with a homecoming of sorts, which can be achieved only in the event that it is not sought. Walking leads one back to oneself, to the wildness within, to the "inward morning" that reflects one's daybreak in Nature.

Thus described, walking transcends a dramatic reversal in the economy of the sauntering soul. Whereas the guiding aims of civil society require us to act, to form, to impress our stamp onto things, Nature teaches us to wait, to observe, to receive things as they present themselves to us in their reclusive reality. Bugbee thus reminds us to shed our preconceptions and illusions about Nature as we set out to walk: "To love things as modes is to avoid idolatry, and it is to love *them*, nonetheless; and to love them *for what they are*. Yet what they are, their meaning, is only defined as we realize our own existence."[8]

Under the tutelage of Nature, the aimless saunterer learns (or recollects) the art of receptivity, of opening his soul to the immeasurable density of reality. Walking thus obliterates the artificial, consequentialist frame of temporality, slowing the flight of time's arrow to the dawdling, squandering, inefficient pace of Nature itself: "There have been times when I waited expectantly to hear the song, only to find that I had mistaken the whole matter. Truly heard, the song comes upon one in a readiness to hear that has nothing to do with getting set in expectation. Such is the clarification of the eternity of things."[9]

As Thoreau persuasively argues, walking thus frees the civilized soul from the constraints of its civil liberties, thereby reacquainting the intrepid saunterer with the ancient, primitive wilderness that is his atavistic heritage: "If you are ready to leave father and mother, and brother and sister, and wife and child and friends, and never see them again—if you have paid your debts and made your will, and settled all your affairs, and are a free man—then you are ready for a walk."[10]

This is not to proclaim, of course, that the ceaseless activity of civil society is either evil or demeaning; in some very basic forms, in fact, this activity is required for our very survival. Like Thoreau, Bugbee walks not to slough the skins of civilization and renew a life of noble savagery, but to rekindle the primordial fire that civilization both steals, protects, and occasionally threatens to extinguish.

For in addition to the busy activity required for commerce and civil society, we always also partake, consistently if unconsciously, of a measure of fugitive wilderness. It is this residual wilderness that allows us to tolerate the inevitable indignities of civil society, that obliges us to orient even our most impersonal commercial affairs against the horizon of our finitude. Civilization need not be the enemy of wilderness, but if left unchecked it will suffocate even the most resilient flame of wilderness within us.

2

In taking his marching orders from Thoreau, Bugbee learned to receive the subtle intimations of reality that are transmitted throughout the boundless, amoral economy of Nature. As Thoreau reminds us, and as Bugbee's philosophical explorations demonstrate, the key to adopting a posture of nonanticipatory receptivity lies in one's attunement to the call of the wild.

Unlike Thoreau, Bugbee makes no "extreme statement" in favor of "absolute freedom and wildness, as contrasted with a freedom and culture merely civil."[11] Bugbee nevertheless attests to the centrality to his own realism of a galvanizing experience of wilderness: "Things exist in their own right; it is a lesson that escapes us except as they hold us in awe. Except we stand on the threshold of the wilderness, knowingly, how can our position be true, how can essential truth be enacted in our hearts?"[12]

By virtue of his own example, then, Bugbee seconds Thoreau's motion to celebrate wilderness. The posture of receptivity that he wishes to recommend to his fellow travelers is attainable only within the context of an immersion in wilderness. He consequently recommends the upbuilding power of wilderness to those who can attend carefully to its subtle teachings: "And it was there in attending to this wilderness, with unremitting alertness and attentiveness, yes, even as I slept, that I knew myself to have been instructed for life, though I was at a loss to say what instruction I had received."[13]

The wilderness that galvanizes the soul is not the prehistoric instinctual life of the primal horde, made both topical and taboo by Freud. Like Thoreau, Bugbee experiences wilderness primarily in the aesthetic, spiritual terms favored by the American transcendentalists. In describing the instruction he has received from his immersion in wilderness, he speaks not of a harrowing journey into the savage heart of darkness, but of merging seamlessly with a serene, late-autumn landscape: "It was in the fall of '41, October and November, while late autumn prevailed throughout the northern Canadian Rockies, restoring everything in that vast region to a native wildness. Some part of each day or night, for forty days, flurries of snow were flying. The aspens and larches took on a yellow so vivid, so pure, so trembling in the air, as to fairly cry out that they were as they were, limitlessly."[14]

This is not to imply, of course, that wilderness is not *also* raw, brutal, inhospitable, and occasionally lethal. Although the temptation to romanticize nature is perhaps greater than Bugbee generally allows, he is primarily concerned here with the galvanizing, aesthetic role of wilderness in his philosophical explorations of reality. As uniquely directed to *him,* the call of the wild emanates not from the savagery and blood lust that also characterize Nature, but from a transfigurative moment of sublime beauty and solemnity in the Canadian Rockies.

According to Thoreau, the carefree saunterer does not happen upon wilderness entirely by accident. Nature resonates with the call of the wild, which, though imperceptible to the civilized ear, entices the attentive walker to blaze his ownmost trail: "What is it that makes it so hard sometimes to determine whither we will walk? I believe that there is a subtle magnetism in Nature, which, if we unconsciously yield to it, will direct us aright. It is not indifferent to us which way we walk. There is a right way; but we are very liable from heedlessness and stupidity to take the wrong one."[15]

Where Thoreau alludes to the "subtle magnetism" of Nature, to which the carefree saunterer cheerfully yields, Bugbee figures Nature as a vast energy circuit, through which the vital current of wilderness ceaselessly circulates. Reminiscent of Aldo Leopold's suggestive image of an energy circuit, Bugbee observes that "[i]n our experience of things as presences, reality conveys itself and permeates us as a closed electrical circuit in which we are involved with things; the circuit is charged with finality. But in so far as we take things, and think of them, as placed over against us, i.e., objectively, we break the circuit. It is inevitable then that we can find no purchase in things for the thought of finality in them, and fall back upon some conception of intrinsic value as a property of ourselves, or as we are apt to say (objectifying 'experience'), as a property of our experience."[16]

One walks, that is, to reintegrate oneself—if only temporarily—within the timeless flow of the energy circuit of Nature. Man resumes his "natural" place within the energy circuit only when he allows its native wilderness to replenish the fugitive wilderness within his own soul. Bugbee thus accepts Thoreau's imperative "to regard man as an inhabitant, or a part and parcel of Nature, rather than a member of society."[17]

Here it is important to note, however, that receptivity alone is insufficient to secure one's reintegration into the energy circuit of Nature. The peripatetic philosopher must not only receive the call of the wild; he must respond to it as well. And in order to answer the call of the wild, one must allow oneself to be re-formed, even transfigured, by Nature itself. That is, the invitation to return to wilderness must be reciprocated with an invitation to wilderness to reclaim possession of one's soul. In order to establish a contrast with the customary, "passive" modality of receptivity, Bugbee introduces the seemingly oxymoronic term "active receptiveness," by which he means to describe the condition that both enables and manifests the philosopher's immersion in reality.[18] This appeal to "active receptiveness" thus suggests a condition that we might call patiency, whereby the sauntering philosopher, having received the call of the wild, now invites wilderness to express itself through him.

Patiency should not be confused with passivity. As Bugbee's reference to "active receptiveness" suggests, the attainment of patiency requires the philosopher both to acknowledge and to reclaim his basic embeddedness in the sprawling plenum of Nature. Having rendered himself receptive to the call of the wild, the philosopher accedes to a condition of patiency by actively resigning his agency, which is so beloved of and misappraised by orthodox metaphysicians. This gesture of forfeiture effectively closes the artificial (albeit prophylactic) distance between man and Nature, thereby embedding the philosopher in the reality of the place on which he meditates.

The immersion in Nature that Bugbee describes is thus attained not by dint of any mode of "doing," but only by a "letting be," by allowing one's orientation to the place to be determined by the current and flow of the primordial energy circuit: "I think of immersion as a mode of living in the present with complete absorption; one has the sense of being comprehended and sustained in a universal situation. The absorption is not a matter of shrunken or congealed attention, not a narrowing down or an exclusion. One is himself absorbed into a situation, or by it, and the present which is lived in does not seem accurately conceivable as a discrete moment in a series."[19]

The achievement of this condition of patiency thus suggests the transformation of the receptive philosopher into a medium, conduit, or vessel of Nature itself. While bound in the thrall of patiency, the ambulatory philosopher no longer merely witnesses, observes, or deduces the defining habits of wilderness. He *becomes* wilderness incarnate and thereby resumes his rightful place within the energy circuit of Nature. The "active receptiveness" of patiency restores one to wilderness, which in turn renews the wilderness within oneself. In bidding footloose ramblers to become patients of wild Nature, Bugbee clearly evinces—and honors—his philosophical debt to Thoreau.

Bugbee's signal accomplishment here is to suggest, via implication, a novel definition of wilderness: wilderness as patiency. In leading us beyond the walls of civil society, walking also deranges the artificial limitations imposed on us by conventional models of agency. An attunement to the reality of things in nature thus presupposes the suspension of one's hubristic agency, of one's "privileged" status within the natural world. Wilderness dissolves the cumbersome armor of human agency, returning the responsive saunterer to a primal state of patiency, wherein nature might impress upon him its indelible stamp. After describing a stranger's brush with death in the rapids of a wild, freely flowing river, Bugbee thus remarks, "Not a word passed between us. As nearly as I can relive the matter, the compassion I felt with this man gave way into awe and respect for what I witnessed in him. He seemed absolutely clean. In that steady gaze of his I met reality point blank, filtered and distilled as the purity of a man."[20]

No longer the causally efficient originator of action, the patient walker stands naked before the rest of wild nature, finally prepared to receive the intimations of reality that are presaged in the call of the wild.

Similar accounts of the transition from agency to patiency are scattered throughout the history of philosophy: Socrates's rendition of Diotima's speech in the *Symposium*; the communion of the Stoic sage with the fatality of Nature; the uneasy inhabitation by Hegel and Marx of dialectical nodes of world-historical transformation; Nietzsche's transfigurative experience of eternal recurrence, which leads him to profess his undying *amor fati*; and Heidegger's recommendation of a posture of anticipatory releasement (*Gelassenheit*) toward the destinal sending of Being itself. What lends a distinctly American inflection to the "active receptiveness" praised by Bugbee is his tacit appeal to the fructifying power of the western frontier. Following Thoreau, Bugbee conceives of the frontier as the crucible of philosophical attunement, as the irreplaceable arena for any immersion in reality. In short, it is the western frontier that transforms the receptive walker into a patient of wilderness—hence the importance for both Thoreau and Bugbee of sauntering along a westerly course.

As the backdrop for the uniquely spiritual vocation of American philosophy, the western frontier is commonly viewed (and revered) as the source, ground, or home of wilderness. To plot a westward course is to renew the wilderness within and without oneself. Bravely squinting into the glare of the afternoon sun, one tests one's mettle in the forge of Nature while divesting oneself of the conquest prosthesis furnished by civilization. To follow the sun's inexorable path is both to receive and to answer the call of the wild. Thus accounting for his own occidental proclivities, Thoreau insists that "The West of which I speak is but another name for the Wild; and what I have been preparing to say is, that in Wildness is the preservation of the World."[21]

Tracking the westward flight of nature's arrow, the Thoreauvian saunterer is thus delivered to his unknown, unanticipated Holy Land: the primordial wilderness of the American frontier. And, as Thoreau insists, the frontier of the wild West shelters our ultimate experience of freedom: "Eastward I go only by force; but westward I go free.... I believe that the forest which I see in the western horizon stretches uninterruptedly toward the setting sun, and there are no towns nor cities in it of enough consequence to disturb me. Let me live where I will, on this side is the city, on that the wilderness, and ever I am leaving the city more and more, and withdrawing into the wilderness."[22]

In comparison, Horace Greeley's famous exhortation to aspiring adventurers seems measured and avuncular: Nature herself bids us to occident ourselves to the American frontier. Those who would march westward to the frenetic beat of commerce or trade are destined not only to arrive empty-handed on the sun-kissed shores of the Pacific, but also to overlook the reality they carelessly inhabit along the way.

The frontier plays an undecidably dual role in Thoreau's transcendentalism. Just as we are literally drawn westward by the solar trajectory of our manifest destiny, so a philosophical voyage of discovery figuratively transports us to the frontiers of reality and intelligibility. In either sense of the frontier, we find ourselves dispatched to a wild, untamed place, be it the terra incognita that lies beyond the sheltering walls of civilization or the fugitive wilderness we carry within ourselves. In either event, the frontier functions as a gateway to the undiscovered country of wilderness, wherein resides, as Thoreau reminds us, the Holy Grail of the *Sainte-Terrer*. Poised precariously on the western frontier, the peripatetic philosopher finds himself, paradoxically, *at home*.

Like Thoreau, Bugbee conceives of walking as cultivating a spiritual homecoming. Eschewing the voluntaristic conceit of so much contemporary philosophy, Bugbee insists that there is no need for humankind to fashion a home for itself in nature. We already have a home in the wilderness that links the microcosm of the human soul to the macrocosm of Nature. Bugbee thus advocates a radical reversal of one of the hoary aims of traditional philosophy: "Philosophy is not a making of the home for the mind out of reality. It is more like learning to leave things be: restoration in the wilderness, here and now."[23]

As Thoreau himself was inclined to put it, the condition of homelessness is therefore unknown to the savvy saunterer: "Some, however, would derive the word from sans terre, without land or a home, which, therefore, in the good sense, will mean, having no particular home, but equally at home everywhere. For this is the secret of successful sauntering. He who sits still in a house all the time may be the greatest vagrant of all; but the saunterer, in the good sense, is no more vagrant than the meandering river, which is all the while sedulously seeking the shortest course to the sea."[24]

Walking thus enables a homecoming of the soul, wherein the sauntering philosopher recovers his ownmost voice and calling. We must always beware, of course, of romanticizing wilderness, of discounting the native perils of this uncanny vocation. The call of the wild may summon our souls homeward, but wilderness characteristically exhibits no discernible attunement to the "civilized" plans and goals that define the ambit of our agency. On this point Thoreau uttered a truth more universal than he was willing to allow:

> For my part, I feel that with regard to Nature I live a sort of border life, on the confines of a world into which I make occasional and transient forays only, and my patriotism and allegiance to the state into whose territories I seem to retreat are those of a moss-trooper. Unto a life which I call natural I would gladly follow even a will-o'-the-wisp through bogs and sloughs unimaginable, but no moon nor firefly has shown me the causeway to it.[25]

Although we are born of wild nature, we are also born to forsake our native wilderness for the peace and security of civilization. Nature is simultaneously our home and our Holy Land, and we must therefore content ourselves to shuttle incessantly between wilderness and civilization. Having answered the call of the wild, that is, we must inevitably turn a deaf ear to its siren song and return to stoke anew the Promethean fires of civilization.

With respect to this restlessly ambivalent destiny, this forcible wrenching of the spirit from its wilderness home to the alienated security of civilization and back again, it is perhaps appropriate to reserve the last word for the last words of *The Inward Morning*: "I am not content with what I have worked out; but I have worked out enough, perhaps, to be content to consider more carefully as I move along, and to welcome all manner of thinking other than my own."[26]

## Notes

1. A notable exception, I am pleased to observe, is found in Bugbee's acknowledgments, in which he thanks my retired colleague John M. Anderson for "those days in the late Thirties when we began to walk and talk it out together in the Berkeley Hills." Henry Bugbee, *The Inward Morning: A Philosophical Exploration in Journal Form* (1958; reprint, with a new introduction by Edward F. Mooney, Athens: University of Georgia Press, 1999), 13–14.

2. Henry David Thoreau, *Walden and Other Writings of Henry David Thoreau* (New York: Modern Library, 1950), 609.

3. Bugbee, 139.

4. Ibid., 133–34.

5. Invoking a similar set of images, Thoreau explains that "He who sits still in a house all the time be the greatest vagrant of all; but the saunterer, in the good sense, is no more vagrant than the meandering river, which is all the while sedulously seeking the shortest course to the sea" (592–93).

6. Ibid., 597.

7. Bugbee, 111.

8. Ibid., 137.

9. Ibid., 194.

10. Thoreau, 598.

11. Ibid., 597.

12. Bugbee, 164.

13. Ibid., 140.

14. Ibid., 139.

15. Thoreau, 606–7.

16. Aldo Leopold, *A Sand County Almanac, with Essays on Conservation from Round River* (New York: Ballantine Books, 1970), especially, 237–64. While proposing his controversial "land ethic," Leopold explains: "Land, then, is not merely soil; it is a fountain of energy flowing through a circuit of soils, plants, and animals. Food chains are the living channels which conduct energy upward; death and decay return it to the soil. The circuit is not closed, . . . but it is a sustained circuit, like a slowly augmented revolving fund of life" (253). Bugbee, 167–68.

17. Thoreau, 597.
18. Bugbee, 135.
19. Ibid., 60.
20. Ibid., 172.
21. Thoreau, 613.
22. Ibid., 607.
23. Bugbee, 155.
24. Thoreau, 597
25. Ibid., 625.
26. Bugbee, 232.

# Melt the Snowflake at Once! Toward a History of Wonder

DAVID ROTHENBERG

## 1. The Walk from Philosophy to Poetry

I first took down the name of Henry Bugbee when I noticed how many American philosophers wrote that he was the one whose writing spurred them on into philosophy. Bugbee's name comes up time and again in *Falling in Love with Wisdom,* the collection of essays in which philosophers tell their own stories.[1] The mutual recommendations were enough to encourage me to take a trip down from my cabin in Maine to the Harvard library to pick up a copy of *The Inward Morning* and see for myself what the excitement was all about. Immediately I understood that here was a uniquely American voice in philosophy, one that inspires us not to follow or agree with him, but to engage in our own moving reflection that does not stand still. Bugbee, like Thoreau, needs to be walking in order to be thinking:

> During my years of graduate study before the war I studied philosophy in the classroom and at a desk, but my philosophy took place mainly on foot. It was truly peripatetic, engendered not merely while walking, but *through* walking that was essentially a *meditation of the place.* And the balance in which I weighed the ideas I was studying was always that established in the experience of walking in the place. I weighed everything by the measure of the silent presence of things, clarified in the racing clouds, clarified by the cry of hawks, solidified in the presence of rocks, spelled syllable by syllable by waters of manifold voice, and consolidated in the act of taking steps, each step a meditation steeped in reality.[2]

Ideas come as we move through the world. They come out of a need to question things that happen to us. To ask the meaning of them as we move around and through them. This is not simply literature, telling a good story with resonances of meaning, but it relates to literature as long as it is written beautifully. Philosophy for Bugbee is like poetry for William Carlos Williams, "a structure built upon your own ground."[3] The central question then becomes: how is it different from poetry, or from literature? This is the distinction that Bugbee will wrestle with throughout his work, and it is a conflict that still goes on at the borders of philosophy, as maverick thinkers want to go deep and also be clear, to reach a wider public and still be true to the inquiring stance of the discipline.

Bugbee is impressed when one day he hears Williams read his poetry to an audience: "Relax! relax," the old doctor comforts the crowd. "Do not try to make something of it. . . . Take it as it comes."[4] Poetry is no more than poetry. Philosophy is no more than philosophy. It changes nothing, perhaps because it attends so carefully to all that is already changing.

Bugbee writes in aphorisms. They are not Wittgensteinian aphorisms of cool detachment and careful convolution. They are pithy calls to wake up! to pay attention to all the wonders that are around. Admitting wonder brings so much more reality to any walking, waking life. He worries what all this meditative reflection will do for his career. He does not want to join ranks with the existentialists and the phenomenologists. He will not become a continental philosopher, unless they will let him pick this American island as his continent, no land of deep history and the mass rush to enlightenment. Bugbee finds his answers not in the march of history, but in the clarity of the wild walk home and away from home into the frost-covered hills and back down to the warmth of the hearth.

He looks to Zen techniques for sudden shocks out of our slumber: "What would you say now? . . . A snowflake on a burning stove!"[5] Is it enough to ask and to ask again? Or need we interpret such tales, through years of meditation, or careful analysis?

I can see why Bugbee has so many secret admirers. He is one of a few of our countrymen to demand that philosophy hold on to the sense of astonishment that began it, that astonishment at the color, taste, and richness of the world that wafts on right under our noses, so easy to ignore, so simple to forget. His philosophy arrives in moments, in twists of fate and sudden tales. I can see why he so admires Williams, the poet of everyday life, the doctor who made his patients recover through word and image. (They're all still alive, among us and around.) But there remains a difference between philosophy and poetry. It is not that one seeks to explain, while the other evokes. It is that the former must ask and ask, and keep asking, until our very sense of perplexity becomes exact, complete, not solvable, but a place to contemplate and inhabit through *wonder,* a positive word, a state of grace, an excited way of loving the world.

Meanwhile, poetry captures brief moments of our being, and renders them unforgettable. One should not try to "make something" of the poem, but philosophy exists to be challenged. The challenge should be in the spirit of wonder, not of picayune unmasking. "You have no idea what kind of people study philosophy," cautions the Oxford don in Philip Kerr's Wittgensteinian thriller *A Philosophical Investigation.* He quotes Yeats: "They are the kind who pull off angels' wings."[6]

Sure, philosophers deserve the bad rap. There's a whole school of philosophy of music that asserts that music is not "about" anything but itself. There are schools of linguistic philosophy that proclaim that if we can't say something unambiguously then it shouldn't be said at all. And too many have been afraid of poets and other disreputables because we all "lie too much."

Well, what worth is the truth if it cannot handle the rich ambiguity of reality? Show me a perfect triangle and I'll show you a shape that has no place in our rough, beautiful, tactile, and imperfect world.

The snowflake melts before we can study it. There is no thought-out answer to anything that can hope to stop time. The objects of our contemplation move out of view just as soon as we see them. And yet, and yet. . . . We imagine there can be an explanation, that we can add to the wonder. What is the difference between philosophy and literature? The writer answers: "Does the dawn of a new day have any purpose?" The philosopher: "Why do you want to know?" The answer can be an image or another in a series of endless questions.

One of my graduate school professors thought the following question should be asked to all candidates who should teach aesthetics:

"What is it about a cello that moves us so?" Enough philosophers of music would answer that this is not an appropriate question to be asked, citing historical evidence that music is about music and nothing else, that what is moving or sullen is of no philosophic consequence. The scientist would want to mention pitch, vibration, correlating them to the dimensions and frequency of the human body. The watcher might notice the similarity between the scale and shape of the instrument and the form of a woman. Once I heard a somewhat radical piece of music where the cellist confronts the instrument and stops to ask "who *are* you?"

The writer would tell a story that would evoke the answer. The philosopher would make generalizations about humanity as a whole, making use of the royal "we" and assuming at least at some level that we are all one in agreement.

Despite his fine rhetorical gifts, Bugbee remains a philosopher. He wants to embrace us all with his own thoughts: "We must see to it! We worry. We hurry along. We translate necessity into anxiety and effort, trying to take charge. We are swimmers flailing the water to keep from going down."[7] He is making judgments about the global "we." Who is this great group? All of us? Modern Americans? Anyone who can read the words? All humanity, for all time? Philosophy usually doesn't want to make such distinctions, but instead wants to embrace any and all of its readers in a collective but unidentified group. "One moment we understand, the next we may be lost. One moment we are lifted gratefully along the gentle stream, another we are stranded, gasping and writhing, estranged from the element in which it is given to us to live. The stream comes upon us laden with the twofold aspect of responsibility: *the demand and the capacity to respond;* if we swim with necessity we discover power."[8] Bugbee likes the metaphor of swimming, because moving in the water we cannot forget that the world is thick and in deep flux all around us. See, I want to be a philosopher too. I mention the "we" to give weight to any pronouncement I say. The poet might say "I" instead; the fiction writer might transmute it into a story and claim nothing but the tale itself.

You might say Bugbee's resonant popularity links his method to existentialism. He says "we" but he wants you, the reader, to replace it with "I." You too will be able to experience these things, and can bring the philosophy to life in a way that logic always resists. *Delve* into experience. Articulate it so it will become more of the same, more of itself.

## 2. Essence before Existence?

The popularity of Bugbee's *Inward Morning* might have something to do with the popularity of existentialism as a genre spanning the gulf between philosophy and literature. To embrace existence is to admit that life is a tumult of suffering but realize it is wonderful all the same. Still, it can take a lot of suffering to get the point of wonder. Sisyphus rolls his boulder up the endless mountain *forever* before he starts to enjoy it, and smile during the push. An unforgettable image, but perhaps not all that much fun. It's still an acceptance of traditional religious guilt. Or look at Meursault in Camus's *The Stranger*. He has to kill an Arab for no particular reason, live a life utterly devoid of emotion, be put on trial and convicted and be stuck on death row, and finally the night before his execution he realizes his life has actually been pretty good. Awaiting an inevitable but senseless death, he is finally happy and at peace.

More troubling, but great stories. Literature, not philosophy. Oh? They are both philosophy to the extent that they perfectly convey inexplicable answers to those nagging questions. No analysis can take their crystal qualities away. Literature plays and dances in the face of the hard questions. It laughs at death, smiles at suffering. Philosophy must continue to worry.

Bugbee passes closest to classic existentialism with his experienced tale of the drowning man. Along the North Fork of the Trinity River in northern California, Bugbee saw a man swept into the furious current of the raging stream. Swollen after a storm, the river seemed sure to devour the frightened man. But he grabbed for a willow branch and held on with all his strength. Pulling himself against all odds up on the muddy bank, he seemed safe but shaken when Bugbee reached him:

> Slowly he raised his head and we looked into each other's eyes. I lifted out both hands and helped him to his feet. Not a word passed between us. As nearly as I can relive the matter, the compassion I felt with this man gave way into awe and respect for what I witnessed in him. He

seemed absolutely clean. In that steady gaze of his I met reality point blank, filtered and distilled as the purity of a man. . . .

Some ten or fifteen minutes later, as we lay on the warm sand having a smoke beside the pool, I noticed that this young man had commenced to tremble, and I trembled with him. We had returned to our ordinary estate, and I cannot recall anything unusual about him or the subsequent conversations we had.[9]

So this drowning man knew fear, and he acted, saved himself, and reached a higher state of wonder and the sense of being alive. But the wonder is not only registered in he who suffers but in he who reaches out; Bugbee touches the survivor and meets reality right there, a surge so much greater and more definite than the ceaseless questioning of the musing philosopher. And then, even more remarkable, past the shared trembling, the orgasmic partnership of endurance and empathy, the greatest realization: this was an ordinary man, it could have been any of us who met danger and wanted not to die but to live. The moment fades. We have to write it down. The questions remain.

The eyes lock with the stare into his eyes, the drowning man being carried away by the cascades. The difficulty is to hold onto this closeness, to feel as connected to another, in the thick of any ordinary encounter. Do not wait until something special happens to you before you learn how full of wonder the world is.

What will you refuse to give up *right now?* The master cannot live a day without silence. The writer cannot live a day without the rush of a filigree of words. The philosopher cannot live a day without wonder.

But the problem with existentialism as a life philosophy, beyond its detached morbidity, can be brought home by recalling Vaclav Havel's remarks in a speech to the U.S. Congress. "It's time," he proclaimed, "to put essence before existence," *reversing* Sartre's famous embrace of existence before essence. The problem with those guys, Havel seems to imply, is that their free love of experience led to bad politics. Totalitarian communists or fascists all. They experienced too much and felt no responsibility after a time. That is why their movement became bankrupt. Sooner or later we must own up to the truth: there is no easy answer, and no easy question to counter each question so that they keep moving through philosophy and never rest in literature or rule.

Bugbee knows this. It is never enough for him to exist, but to experience. And in experience comes responsibility. Not "with" experience, but in it. We are required to respond. Nothing happens to us passively, without effort. We look, we listen, we direct our senses, we open them up, and things happen. To me or you. To anyone, whether they care to read this or not.

"What time is it?" they would ask Yogi Berra. He would answer: "You mean right now?" The baseball star had a knack for zenning the question. Time moves. Nothing we can say about something that happened can hold true, as the world moves on. You just have to wonder about this. It's amazing we can do anything at all, that we can say anything at all.

## 3. Catching Zen by the Tail

Reflection is inconclusive. Zen wants us to go beyond it. Bugbee says enlightenment is not swift, but a slow, lumbering progress. Say something *quick,* inhabit this present moment, but then it takes work to make sense of the sacred conundra.

I don't think Bugbee wants years of befuddlement at the foot of a hard master. He wants a personal inhabitation of the deep questions. You will need to walk as you work it out, to make sure the mind does not stay still.

I wrote a version of the one hundred cases of the koan collection *The Blue Cliff Record* to work the rhythms of such puzzles. Here are some jottings of what you may find on the narrow path that climbs the rough hillside:

> Case 46 *Sound of Raindrops*
> On thin ice, running over nails—
> from inside the form of sound,
> he walks above the sound of form.
>
> Outside the gate the raindrops sing.
> *The inversion of beings, losing themselves, following after things.*
> What about you?
> *I almost lose myself.*
> What does that mean?
> *Speaking is easy, expressing the whole* has *to be hard.*

What else can you call the sound of rain?
the chafing of atoms
the drench of the sky
the return of the oceans
the drizzle electric.

It may be a quail hanging upside down.
(The hall is empty but everyone is here.)
There's killing and caring, catch and release,
if ever you say he's let the streams enter.

Clouds brew back of mountains, storing the downpour.
Mark moon with finger, yet finger is not moon.
Your feet tread the ground before you can reach here.

The sky opens up and the snow melts to a freezing rain. Are these observations warm, or cool? Words come flowing out, but the totality evades them. There is no whole picture to be formed out of the cascade of strong insights. This is why Bugbee is stuck with aphorisms, nonplussed by the dream of a whole held together with logic or cement: "For five years I have been writing in an exploratory way, gradually forced to recognize that this was the case and I must accept it, along with its professional consequences. . . . It has been a precarious business."[10] His best insights are often the quickest, single captures out of experience around which he has left enough space so their weight will sink in.

Zen is the ambiguous friend of writer and thinker alike, the cool twist of logic around those things that are almost impossible to say. All it takes is one time to observe these strange but obvious images, then the task is to spend thirty years contemplating their deepest significance, being careful not to reduce them to logic or to symbol. The wonder in the world does not mean anything; but it can take a lifetime to learn how to completely inhabit it.

"What is the difference between belief and discovery?" The writer: "I'll make you trust the unbelievable story." The philosopher: "I will teach you to discover your own unbelievable truth." The master: "What was your original face before your parents were born?"

Out in the high woods there was less than an inch of snow on the ground, not a leaf left on the trees, and the long gentle ridges had hardly been traveled upon as the paths rose up slowly past the distant pond to easy views to the west and the east. A tame but open country. Cold but not too cold to be out of doors; at first it's easier to stay in, then stifling to stay in, obviously clearer in the waning winter light: it was the shortest day of the year.

The return was a whiteblue walk into the orange-bathed sunset. Another easy image. Another exact crispness. Another day in the woods that are not the wilderness, that might have once been the wilderness but only in a time that no one cared to love it and celebrate it, instead dreaming of its civilized possibility.

I learned from the mountains but then I forgot to learn from humankind, said Bugbee. From the mountains he learned that "things say themselves, univocally, unisonously," a fact he found to be of "infinite significance."[11] But there were no people in this world of singing things. A philosopher in this world would only take things in, and seek out experience, but would have no need to act.

Arne Naess, fatherless, looked to the peaks for paternal guidance. He found constancy and responsibility up there. "The smaller we come to feel when compared to the mountain, the nearer we come to participating in its greatness." That's no groveling admission of our place before God as lowly as a worm. And it's not the obvious feeling of conquest, but a sense of the great vastness of the world. And do not let the weight of the world press down on you, and enjoy that comfort in worthlessness. No, use the surrounding greatness. Take it all in. Learn as much as you can and do not be afraid to be shocked out of complacency.

Never mind the snowflake. Put your *hand* on the burning stove, and remember just what it feels like forever. You won't need to do it again and you won't be sorry you did it just once.

## 4. What Use Have We for the Wild?

It can give the lie to it. It can extend, now and then, its elemental emissaries to shores, to suburbs, to the folks downriver, to throngs in airports, to the breadbasket of America, to swaying buildings and empty streets. In pelting downpours, the reach of sky, the weathering willynilly impartial to all, the crawling of ants, the cry of gulls and caw of crows, the rankness of weeds, the silence of snow. . . . Our very dreams might suggest the hidden bulk of the wild which is immolated by our day. And the culture *contrary* to the wild may prove after all, though cloying, to be made of feeble stuff; able to pass itself off only in our waking sleep; some pantomime of life, a common dream, mumbled in unison by an endless crowd.[12]

It is he who lives in the wilderness who forgets the wilderness. The mountain dreamer in the city does not forget, the suburbanite looking for a parking place by the mall, the freeway commuter motionless in a traffic of chrome, sun shades, and cellular phones. The San Gabriels rise over the L.A. smog; the Hudson Highlands are a storied reverie barely visible from the skyscrapers of Manhattan; from Chicago, forgetaboutit, could take you days to reach the realm of trees.

But in any city the wilderness looms in the back of everyone's memory, or imagination, another possibility, another way out, another invented home. But Bugbee knew this wilderness is architecture, not nature. What we want of it is our time's creation, no hint of an original home or primal whiff of the savannah.

I myself have lived for months on end among canyons of concrete, barely seeing the richness of life, and have cried when thrust into a forest of trees. We are adaptable creatures and can be tossed into many strange environments, but at the same time it is amazing how little we forget.

Yet these are the times of doubt and scrutiny. We are taught not to trust our feelings, not to be sure of the primacy of anything. Because we are bombarded by images, creatures of culture, never fully restful at home anywhere. Unexamined life, worthless but happy. The questions, they never go, they're so easy they ask themselves, and no one can stop them unless we choose not to wonder. And wonder, Bugbee reminds us, as any good philosopher reminds us, ought to bring us closer to reality if it is to bring us anywhere at all. "Could we ever understand ourselves in the image of the rocklike island or the stronghold, impervious to what surrounds us, living a life of inner containment, perduring incorruptible in solid singleness, or reigning over ourselves to secure constant excellence and tranquillity within the island of ourselves?"[13] No one is an island. We are not ourselves if we imagine we are alone. All decisions are made in tandem with the world.

"Humans," writes David Abram, "are tuned for relationship." Do not go into the wilderness to be alone, or to find yourself alone, but to connect with the world. A world that fans out from the arena of other people into the peacock spread of the universe. Be attentive to all of it.

## 5. Restoration and the Return

But the world melts down, its beauties fade away in the glass and gray of exacted civilization. What can we recover? Is there anything original that we want? The old ways became the new ways, so there is no point to nostalgia.

Bugbee saw all these problems with looking back, and he anticipated today's environmental movement toward restoration, remaking the wild right in our midst, and he cast it in a certain optimistically spiritual light that I think still gives it a greater meaning than any naive attempt to *construct* wildness:

> It was in the fall of '41, October and November, while late autumn prevailed throughout the northern Canadian Rockies, restoring everything in that vast region to a native wildness. Some part of each day or night, for forty days, flurries of snow were flying. The aspens and larches took on a yellow so vivid, so pure, so trembling in the air, as to fairly cry out that they were as they were, limitlessly. And it was there in attending to this wilderness, with unremitting alertness and attentiveness, yes, even as I slept, that I knew myself to have been instructed for life. . . . Philosophy is not a making of a home for the mind out of reality. It is more like learning to leave things be: restoration in the wilderness, here and now.[14]

Not just ecological restoration, but restoration of something larger, some sense of life and experience, recovery of an openness to wonder. Because it's easy to lose.

I know the lostness he means. So many recent times when I don't want to look out the window, when I won't go outside, when I seek solace in things, the owning of objects when I know inside that they are meaningless. No need to go on when I've already produced things out of experience. I have closed down; I am blasé, no longer open. If philosophy can help me it will have to *restore* wonder. Not only through beautiful words, but in words that inspire wonder.

Philosophy works like the voice-over commentaries you hear in certain films, particularly those speculating works with cascades of images, marked by a single speaking commentary that questions the meaning of the happenings that are observed, albeit at a distance. Chris Marker's *Sans Soleil*. In this 1983 film, a woman is reading letters she has received from a friend who travels to Africa and Japan, a filmmaker who is describing his work to her as the images come over the screen. As the traveler looks up at a place and remarks how it resembles some other place, he can note that down, and he has the film footage to prove it, to demonstrate it, to construct a story. The running commentary seems to me to be philosophy in action, the recording of the happenings around as we move, and the struggle to make sense of it all:

> I remember the images of the month of January in Tokyo, or rather I remember the images I filmed of the month of January in Tokyo. They have substituted themselves for my memory, they *are* my memory. I wonder how people remember things who don't film, don't photograph, don't tape. How has mankind managed to remember! I know, it wrote the Bible. The new Bible will be an eternal magnetic tape of a Time that will have to reread itself constantly just to know it existed. . . . The memory of a precise color in the street bounces back on another country, another distance, another music, endlessly.[15]

Marker is amazed by the links within his own repository of images collected from all over the world, all moods and places and times. He is amazed by the way the future rapidly becomes the past, and we attempt to document our place in time any which way we can. His film is a catalog of wonders, and you leave it seeing the world a new way. It works as philosophy should, to awaken our senses, and builds on the tradition of Bugbee's journalistic form.

This is how philosophy must change the world. Not by giving us reasons to opt for clearer logic, less ambiguous communication, but to celebrate the magic in the very way we see. Wonder itself is what we must restore, and it can be witnessed anywhere, from the wilderness to the city. Nature can awaken it. Time can awaken it. Everything that happens to us can be filled with significance.

I decide it is time to end this essay while reaching moist snowy meadow deep in the Catskills. Down the valley is a view up the rounded peaks of Wittenberg, Cornell, and Slide, and on the ground are tentative tracks of baby bears that have woken up to play in the snow. In the sudden cold the streams have frozen into thin topographic rings of brittle ice, which crackles easy as you step on it through to the rushing water below. A warm mist rises; the temperature will change. Daylight is brief, the slopes soon darken. *What must I do so I don't forget this place?*

The day before, I was in Atlanta, trapped in a cement hotel like so many others in my profession. The fog was so thick some planes circled the airport for hours before a glimpse of the landing lights could coax them down. This mist made the new downtown even more surreal than usual. No one was meant to go outside among these banks and malls, as the buildings are all connected by winding walkways, many stories above the ground. The streets had been declared dead, closed off, inhospitable, and not to be tread upon. Taking the risk to walk outside at night, I gave a homeless man the remains of my Indian dinner, in a styrofoam box. He said he lived in an old warehouse at the edge of the downtown redevelopment district. "Downtown," he mentioned, "you will not find a high class of people. Out in the suburbs, you know, beyond the ring, that's where the better people live."

The city is changed into cold, empty structures. People flee to be far from its center but then not too far. In the wilderness, even farther beyond the ring, glimmers of wind and sky make it seem that restoration might be possible.

The snowflake is already gone. The snow never fell. It is cold and dark some place while it is warm and gray somewhere else. What temperature is it *right now?* There is no right answer, but always a ream of questions. Henry Bugbee taught us how to notice, how to ask. He has set us all on the track of the history of wonder.

## Notes

1. David D. Karnos and Robert G. Shoemaker, eds., *Falling in Love with Wisdom: American Philosophers Talk about Their Calling* (New York: Oxford University Press, 1993).

2. Henry Bugbee, *The Inward Morning: A Philosophical Exploration in Journal Form* (1958; reprint, with a new introduction by Edward F. Mooney, Athens: University of Georgia Press, 1999), 139.

3. Ibid., 33.
4. Ibid., 121.
5. Qtd. in Bugbee, 121.
6. Philip Kerr, *A Philosophical Investigation* (London: Chatto and Windus, 1992), 170.
7. Bugbee, 121.
8. Ibid., 100.
9. Ibid., 172–73.
10. Ibid., 79.
11. Ibid., 141.
12. Henry G. Bugbee Jr., "Wilderness in America," *Journal of the American Academy of Religion* 42, no. 6 (December 1978): 614–20.
13. Bugbee, *Inward Morning*, 72–73.
14. Ibid., 139–40, 155.
15. Chris Marker, "Sunless," [excerpt from script] *Oasis/Semiotexte* 12 (1983): 39.

# Presence, Memory, and Faith

*Passages from a Notebook on* The Inward Morning

STEVEN E. WEBB

Henry Bugbee's philosophical and religious sensibility is centered entirely on the things of this world, or more precisely, on the wonder that things exist, are given, or have presence to us at all. Time and again, in the most diverse forms of expression, Bugbee testifies to his conviction that "the genuine religious mystery" is none other than the existence of things and of ourselves together with them.[1] Bugbee uses the word "existence" in the etymological sense commonly employed by so-called existential philosophers. Unlike most existentialists, however, he does not limit the word's meaning to the defining way human beings *stand out* beyond themselves. In his vocabulary, things too exist, but in their case this means that they stand out *to us* as having real presence in the world we share with them. These different but complementary ways of standing out make up together what Bugbee refers to as "the union existing between ourselves and the whole of nature." The mystery of this union, he tells us, is not subject to intellectual mastery but must be appreciated "as such and in depth."[2] It is mainly in moments of "feeling discernment"—variously called true perception, the experience of presence, experiential finality, and absolute affirmation—that we may come to know with assurance the "eternal meaning in the very existence of finite things."[3] In such moments, "it seems as if the presence of things took root in us, and planted in us an intimation of reality not to be understood exclusively . . . by the ways of explanation." Despite its resistance to discursive thought, the existence, givenness, or presence of things—terms largely interchangeable in Bugbee's text—is the most familiar aspect of our experience, so near to us that it usually eludes our everyday awareness. That is why, whenever it does dawn again, we feel as though we suddenly remember and are astonished that we could have forgotten. Philosophy, in Bugbee's practice, is in part a trying to remember the essential truth of presence; a remembering, when successful, that culminates in wonder, reverence, and gratitude. While philosophy in its narrower analytical sense can help prepare us for the advent of this experiential truth, in the final analysis it is "only as we may be ripe for it in our entirety . . . that reality may dawn on us concretely and anew."[4]

I

To experience the presence of things is to become aware of ourselves as coparticipants with them in one indivisible reality. This experience transcends any interpretation of reality that starts by assuming a wide ontological gulf between things "outside the mind" and things "within the mind." In a passage reminiscent of Wittgenstein, Bugbee urges us to avoid being "taken in" by the "picture" of reality such phrases conjure, and especially by the epistemic divide they interpose between "objective facts" on the one hand and "subjective values" on the other. Neither a realism that affirms the independent reality of things but denies their human significance nor an idealism that affirms the human significance of things but denies their independent reality can approach an adequate appreciation of the mystery of presence in its lived integrity. In Bugbee's words: "Neither theory seems to do justice to things as radically unknown; in neither is the dense presence of things preserved in thought. And our togetherness with things is forgotten, profoundly buried." In contrast to these abstract ways of interpreting reality, Bugbee proposes a reawakening to the pretheoretical givenness of things, a concrete experience that he characterizes as "an understanding of reality as prior to and comprehensive of reality-as-known." This experiential understanding, he explains, "drives us back behind the point at which we fall into a subject-object distinction, and behind the point, if you will, at which we institute a distinction between fact and value."[5]

Bugbee's philosophy might be called "holistic realism" to indicate his adherence both to the independent reality of things *and* to their inherent significance. What distinguishes his realism from the standard scientific or reductive kind, in other words, is his no less emphatic ethical realism. Indeed, his ethical realism ultimately takes the lead in his affirmation of the independent reality of things. Bugbee is deeply moved not to forsake what he experiences as the manifest claim that things make upon his love and respect, and it is his faithfulness to this claim that renders moot any question of their independent reality. If we are truly to know things in their independence, Bugbee tells us, we must allow them to "touch us," which is to say, to summon us to respect and love. "No intimacy: no revelation. No revelation: no true *givenness* of things."[6] For him, the independence of things cannot be interpreted in a hyperrealistic sense that sets things outside or beyond any possible experience we may have of them. Strictly speaking, there are no things we can sensibly refer to in this hyperrealistic sense, and there is no need to go chasing after an independence greater than that which things already have in relation to us. Things are immediately present to our bodies, which means that our perceptual experience of things transpires from our epidermis outward, not from our epidermis inward. We are not insular subjects longing for unmediated contact with an objective reality "outside" ourselves; we already originally exist outside our bodies and there is no additional outside beyond this that need rationally concern us. We exist in "mutual independence" with things in a single dimension of reality that precedes the standard philosophical divisions between inner and outer, subject and object, and mind and matter. Thus the meaning and value of things, their significance in the widest sense, *belong to them,* or in any case to the "milieu of presence" in which they stand directly before us.[7] Because no metaphysical boundary separates things as they are in themselves from things as they are for us, the rigid distinction between their factual nature and their significant nature dissolves as well. Things are directly present to us as independent of us *and* as intrinsically worthy of our respect and love, and in such a way that our very selves participate with them in one reality. This holistic dimension of presence is, for Bugbee, the holy mystery itself, which embraces us and all beings in union.[8]

## 2

Pure theory, Bugbee says, puts us in "the attitude of the non-participant in everyday life," and to that extent it estranges.[9] To appreciate things as they are "in themselves" requires not that we abstract ourselves from them but precisely that we draw nearer to them:

> For concretely, experience of the presence of things is also complete intimacy with them, the opposite of estrangement from them and ourselves. The gift of things in their independence is also the gift of ourselves together with them. . . . In the experience of presence that estrangement between self and other, that tension between self and other, which supports the representation of the other as over against the self, that estrangement and that tension are dissolved. To be aware of the other as a presence in its independence is an experience of participation in reality with the other, and such experience concretely resists the reduction of the independence of the other to the terms of objectivity.[10]

This is why Bugbee so often interrupts his discursive moments to turn to experiences in which the "essential truth" of presence is concretely realized. As an example of what it may mean to bring abstract thought back to concrete reality, Bugbee remarks on the philosophic significance of Sung dynasty landscape painting.[11] By depicting human beings and human things within the encompassing embrace of their natural surroundings, and by representing these surroundings themselves as emanating from a diaphanous background into the clarity of distinct forms, Chinese landscapes convey something of the quiet wonder of our co-emergence with things into the milieu of presence. This dimension into which all things emerge together, the scrolls suggest, is luminous with significance and may be experienced by the receptive soul as a constant call for response and involvement. For Bugbee, intimacy with things is a matter of having utter respect for their individuality, of making them the focus of a detailed and loving regard. Only when our attention is directed to the individuality of things may the mystery of their presence as such dawn on us. But we must somehow let the mystery itself elicit the right response. As Bugbee expresses it:

> [T]he attempt to be thoroughly specific in one's characterization of something *may* plunge one into quite a different mode of appreciation of it, namely, that it exists, just as it is, no matter how far short we fall of saying just what it is. But if the existence of things does not echo through one, searching out, evoking, his utmost responsiveness, as a matter to have a reckoning with from within himself, how can he hope to bring his thought into accord with finding anything ultimate?[12]

## 3

When true perception dawns, ordinary things spring to our attention with a clarity so arresting that we feel ourselves coming alive, awakening, or being reborn to reality itself. The milieu of presence, if we attend to things with proper diligence, may be experienced as charged with divine significance. "The *presence* of things in their definiteness," Bugbee stresses, "is bound up with understanding reality in its absoluteness." From which it follows: "To perceive something truly is to be alive to it in its sacredness."[13] The sacred is not found in a disillusioned flight to the supernatural, but in the active reception of this present world as metaphysically final. In contrast to philosophies of despair and otherworldly escape, Bugbee's philosophy is a constant call to throw off sleep and to realize ourselves in our natural element.

> Those who speak of experience in which man may find conclusive meaning as if this meaning was not a completion of our experience of things and a revelation of them, seem to speak more as men who dream than as men who are awake. Awakening is not finding things illusory, but awakening from illusions into the very reality of things; it is finding finality in them....
> 
> To take that which exists as existing, and not as a symbol for something else; to find something to which one gives full heed, and not merely to push right through it in search of a beyond . . . is to experience containment in reality. But the agile mind and the distraught soul militate against true perception; for true perception requires stillness in the presence of things, the active, open reception of the limitless gift of things.[14]

In view of such statements, Bugbee's frequent use of traditional metaphysical predicates such as "absolute," "infinite," and "eternal" may seem puzzling. For him, however, these terms never refer to a realm beyond the relative, the finite, and the temporal. Rather they refer to "an unanticipated precipitation of meaning" that may from time to time supervene upon our ordinary experience of things. This precipitate of meaning is a nondiscursive mode of intelligibility that enables an unconditional affirmation of the finitude of all things, including ourselves. When at one point Bugbee exclaims of things, "They *are, are,* eternally *are,*" he is obviously not referring to their longevity, but to the ultimate significance that true perception discerns in their finite standing forth as the definite or "defined" things they are. To put this somewhat differently, "conclusive significance" is a concretely realized value appreciated in intimate association with finite presence as such. To know things and oneself as finite beings standing forth in "the light of eternity" is to receive "the ultimate gift of things in their finality, in a universal significance which embraces them, and which, in embracing us, transfigures us and renders us whole."[15]

## 4

Bugbee's appeal to us to adhere to things and find finality in them is so persistent that one can read *The Inward Morning* and quite overlook the invisible principle that grounds the possibility of our affirmation of them. This principle—existence, givenness, presence—might be characterized as the very "withinness" of this one and only world, the "holy place" in which we find ourselves quite literally standing forth with all beings. Presence, while not reducible to things, cannot be separated from them either; it never makes an appearance on its own but is precisely the appearing of whatever does appear. In other words, presence is more like something that *happens* to things, their being admitted into the ambiance of the given, rather than a thing in its own right. Because it never shows up as something we might contemplate by itself, it has the peculiar quality of always referring us away from itself to the things that stand forth vividly in it. It does not eclipse things or shine through them or lure us away from them. We might think of its invisibility as a kind of self-effacing in infinite deference to things, as if this giving were simultaneously a withdrawal behind the gift. Not, I should note again, the withdrawal of a Giver, but the nonappearance of the mysterious event by virtue of which things are present to us. So it is almost unavoidable that we usually find ourselves fixing our attention on things to the exclusion of their presence. Because presence is elusive by nature, Bugbee sometimes resorts to apophatic metaphors to name it: No-thing. Emptiness. Silence. The Unborn. The Forgotten. The mysterious undifferentiated background from which, as in Chinese scroll paintings, all things emerge together in mutual independence.

Bugbee's favorite positive metaphor for presence is light. Presence is the "light" of intelligibility to which we may awaken only as we are able to "perceive" it from the things it illuminates. This is the light that Bugbee names the "light of eternity":

> Men have sought the light of eternity, and they have often thought to look away from things. Yet is this light something apparent, or is it a light in which things appear? Are not things dense and dark as it is necessary for them to be to take this light? And what is revealed by this light, to what does it supply relevant illumination, if not to things standing forth wonderfully in it?[16]

Eternity is not an attribute of a supreme being dwelling imperishably beyond the realm of generation and decay, but a moment of awakening in which the presence of things dawns on us with a significance that is all-embracing and inexhaustible despite the perishability of things. When on graced occasions we "glimpse" the eternal light in which all things emerge together—when the ultimate mystery of presence instills in us reverence and gratitude—we discover that the world of things in which we move and live and have our being is truly "a holy place."[17] Ironically, the very unknowability of presence has the power to still the restlessness of "Why?" which tries to grasp things intellectually (to discern their causes, their reasons for being) rather than keep itself open to their most intimate touch. In the silence that follows this gentle rebuke to our noetic ambitions, in its constantly turning us toward the things themselves, presence may dawn on us from behind and fill our hearts with joy. To presence uniquely, then, is owed the religious response of reverence, because only as things stand forth in its light does their worthiness of our respect and love come home to us and do we find ourselves worthy of one another's most generous regard.

> Things which inspire us with reverence teach us respect for themselves; but reverence seems to be a matter of accepting their ultimate gift, and not reverence for them. Reverence is a being embraced by a significance that is all-embracive; as a significance found in them uniquely and originally it is the essence of their individuality; but as all-embracive, it sweeps us into ken with them as coparticipants in a universal situation. It both emphasizes and deemphasizes any and all finite beings, infinitely. Every other in which we find a significance which deepens our reception of that other into reverence is experienced as both absolutely other than ourselves and in communion with us; and the counterpart of the otherness of everything other than ourselves, so understood, is our own independence. In reverence is it not clear that our independence can mean neither isolation nor assertion over against other beings? And in reverence, who clings to privilege for himself or any other?[18]

## 5

In certain moments of grace we suddenly *see* our profane world as in truth sacred, but such insights, however profound and redeeming they may be, are not the privilege of a mystical elite. "The themes which seem most adequate to the advent of essential truth," Bugbee makes plain, "are not those of the rare and special experience, discontinuous with daily life, the ineffable transfiguration of the one who is seized (in effect isolating him from the bulk of men, who cannot share his experience), and abandonment of a stake in the everyday world." In another sense, of course, the advent of essential truth *is* an exceptional experience. If to perceive something truly is to be alive to it in its sacredness, clearly many people never have such perceptions, while others may once have had them, in childhood and youth perhaps, but now have them only in memory. A major influence on Bugbee's thinking is Romantic literature, one of whose characteristic themes is regret for lost intimacy with nature and a longing to recover it. Consider Coleridge's "Dejection: An Ode," a prime example of this elegiac mood. The poem describes a crisis in the poet's life when he comes to behold the glories of the world with "a blank eye." "I see, not feel, how beautiful they are," he grieves, and then he offers his memorable lines: "We receive but what we give / and in our lives alone does nature live." It is good to think we shall receive an equal return on our giving, but do we then face the unhappy vision of a nature that "in itself" is dead without us? In this ambiguous picture, if you should happen to run out of things to give, you will find yourself as inert as the world you no longer have the gift to enliven. The giving Coleridge has in mind, of course, is the giving of creative response, the joy we are able to impart to nature through our power to reimagine it. Without this inward giving, continually renewed in active attention, what may come back to us is a nature—to use Bugbee's phrase—in "the image of our own deadness."[19]

Nevertheless, the astonishment that attends moments of awakening—for those still blessed with them—includes the feeling that this is how the world *always* is and that responses such as wonder and reverence are those that most truly answer to its essential nature. What such moments seem to teach is that gratitude is ever the *right* response to things regardless of our *actual* responses. Emerson, another Romantic and a favorite of Bugbee's, captures in a striking image the permanent fittingness of gratitude, which our moments of sudden awakening seem to confirm.

> One might think the atmosphere was made transparent with this design, to give man, in the heavenly bodies, the perpetual presence of the sublime. Seen in the streets of the cities, how great they are! If the stars should appear one night in a thousand years, how would men believe and adore; and preserve for many generations the remembrance of the city of God which had been shown! . . . The stars awaken a certain reverence, because though always present, they are inaccessible; but all natural objects make a kindred impression, when the mind is open to their influence.[20]

Of course, experiences of coming alive to things vary in kind and intensity. Perhaps we might think of our less vivid awakening as adumbrations along an experiential gradient leading up to truly revelatory moments. In principle our humblest perceptions of things may be closer than we think to full-blown appreciations of their sacredness. Beneath the millennial revelation of the stars, there is also, Emerson suggests, a "low degree of the sublime" with the power to renew our capacity to see and to feel.

> What new thoughts are suggested by seeing a face of country quite familiar, in the rapid movements of the rail-road car! Nay, the most wonted objects, (make a very slight change in the point of vision,) please us most. In a camera obscura, the butcher's cart and the figure of one of our own family amuse us. So a portrait of a well-known face gratifies us. Turn the eyes upside down, by looking at the landscape through your legs, and how agreeable is the picture, though you have seen it anytime these twenty years![21]

A child's experiment in seeing, a portrait's revealing angle on a familiar face, a simple change of scenery can acquaint anyone, in a modest way, with what it is like to see with new eyes. It is no strain on the imagination, certainly nothing occult, to appreciate how this general capacity for renewed vision might extend all the way to moments of exhilaration before the gift of things in their presence. Nor is it so difficult to appreciate how the stream of experience might be alive with such moments, only awaiting the proper attunement or receptivity on our part to leap forth into the light. One of my favorite passages in *The Inward Morning* is an allegorical memory illustrating some of Bugbee's most important themes. It is also perhaps the journal's most compelling example of a moment of true perception. Following Bugbee's practice earlier in the journal of titling his autobiographical passages, I shall refer to this one, for obvious reasons, as "Fishing Satori":

> It takes many, many days to learn of what may and may not be in the river. Let us wade right in and keep fishing where we are, with our fingertips touching the trembling line. It is just in the moment of the leap we both feel and see, when the trout is instantly born, entire, from the flowing river, that reality is knowingly defined.
> 
> Now the river is the unborn, and the sudden fish is just the newborn—whole, entire, complete, individual, and universal. The fisherman may learn that each instant is pregnant with the miracle of the new-born fish, and fishing in the river may become a knowing of each fish even before it is born. As he fishes the ever-flowing current, it teaches him of the fish even before it is born, just in so far as this fishing involves "abiding in no-abode," or "unattached mind." If one is steeped in the flow of the

river and sensitized through the trembling line, one anticipates the newborn fish at every moment. The line tautens and with all swiftness, the fish is there, sure enough! And now, in the leaping of this fish, how wonderfully, laughingly clear everything becomes! If eventually one lands it, and kneels beside its silvery form at the water's edge, on the fringe of the gravel bar, if one receives this fish as purely as the river flows, everything is momently given, and the very trees become eloquent where they stand.[22]

## 6

According to Bugbee, experiences such as the one he represents in his "Fishing Satori" have the power to transform our natural fear of death into nothing less than "unqualified affirmation" of our ephemeral condition. "[E]very time I am born [anew]," he writes, "it seems to me that then, if ever, I could be content to die." *Content to die?* This seems a strong claim. I can appreciate how such experiences, if they stayed with us, would be worthy of our most devout attention. But they do not stay, or at least it is not clear *how* they stay. Throughout *The Inward Morning* confident celebrations of the holiness of our place alternate with sometimes dejected admissions that "much of the time I cannot remember that it is true, and I cannot understand what such a saying might mean."[23] Near the end of his journal, in a brief passage that reminds me of Coleridge's blank eye, Bugbee confides:

> [A] flock of wild geese passed over our house—geese such as I have often attended to most cleanly before—and I rushed to the window all-eagerness for them, but with a slightly spoiling expectation. I counted them all before they disappeared in the storm-clouds downwind—there were forty-five. On telling of them and their number I met with a true question: If you counted them, how could you have seen them?[24]

The saving moments come unbidden, if they come at all, and you cannot force them. "Finality establishes the conditions of its own disclosure; we cannot hold them fast and place them at our disposal."[25] I can't resist another passage from Emerson that also captures the thought precisely:

> The shows of day, the dewy morning, the rainbow, mountains, orchards in bloom, stars, moonlight, shadows in still water, and the like, if too

eagerly hunted become shows merely, and mock us with their unreality. Go out of the house to see the moon, and 't is mere tinsel; it will not please as when its light shines upon your necessary journey. The beauty that shimmers in the yellow afternoons of October, who ever could clutch it? Go forth to find it, and it is gone: 't is only a mirage as you look from the windows of diligence.[26]

So it would seem that the relevance of true perception to the hour of our death must turn on *when* one awakens to the sacredness of things. For though it might well be that one feels content to die when the desired experience dawns, that does not mean that it shall dawn when one's life actually moves into the gloaming. I for one should like to know contentment with death *when I die,* but what assurance have I that absolute affirmation will grace my life then? Apparently none. This much is clear, however; Bugbee himself has a sure grasp of the issue: "What in the life of a man can place his life in such a light that he can live his last moments in the most profound affirmation? *Or is such a thing possible?*" But with his characteristic confidence, he forges ahead: "I will not hesitate to say that questions such as these seem to me to set the ultimate philosophical issue in a very clear manner. And the whole drift of my own positive thinking has been imbued with belief in the possibility of such affirmation, with the concern to understand how unconditional affirmation is possible, and with the responsible articulation of that very affirmation."[27]

7

A passage from Kierkegaard comes to mind whenever I reflect on the idea of experiencing eternity in the moment. Although the subject of the passage is the incoherence of otherworldly mysticism as a form of life, a life diametrically at odds with Bugbee's affirmation of *this* world, I nonetheless think that it has relevance to his own emotional ups and downs with respect to absolute affirmation. "It is frightening," Kierkegaard writes,

> to read the mystic's laments over the flat moments. Then when the flat moment is over comes the luminous moment, and thus his life is continually alternating; it certainly has movement, but not development. His life lacks continuity. It is a feeling, namely a longing, that really con-

stitutes the continuity in a mystic's life, whether this longing is directed to the past or to the future. But the very fact that a feeling constitutes the intervening period in this way proves that coherence is lacking.[28]

Ironically, what the mystic most desires—a present luminous with the light of eternity, let us say—becomes dislocated into the dimness of past and future. When the luminous moment lapses, the mystic experiences the present as torn between fetching back to the luminous moments that were and hastening forward to the luminous moments that might be. This split between past and future imparts a sense of unreality to the present, and in doing so it transforms the mystic into an absentee from the only "place" where he might hope to experience the eternal. The criticism of any type of spirituality intent on the repetition of luminous moments (whatever their content) is that it inevitably falls into a pattern of brief insight followed by long yearning. Extended over a lifetime, this revolving pattern results in an underlying sense of absence and loss. For all yearning, whether nostalgically for the past or dreamily for the future, reduces the present to a condition of waiting. In this condition, the very moments that the mystic would have filled with eternity dissolve one after another into the dead time of the wait; and as Thoreau once remarked, you can't kill time without injuring eternity.

The same criticism applies with equal force to a life devoted to moments of sensual enjoyment (which, come to think of it, is also the subtext of Kierkegaard's remarks on mysticism). In his *Reveries of the Solitary Walker,* Rousseau has a passage that suggests comparison with Kierkegaard's:

> In the vicissitudes of a long life, I have noticed that periods of sweet enjoyment and most intense pleasures are, nevertheless, not those whose recollection most attracts and touches me. Those short moments of delirium and passion, however intense they might be, are, even with their intensity, still scattered points along the path of life. They are too rare and too rapid to constitute a state of being; and the happiness for which my heart longs is in no way made up of fleeting instants, but rather a simple and permanent state which has nothing intense in itself but whose duration increases its charm to the point that I finally find supreme felicity in it.[29]

How remarkable it is, reading on, to discover that the "permanent state" of being that Rousseau has in mind is a condition in which his soul is able to "gather its whole being" together

> without needing to recall the past or encroach upon the future; in which time is nothing for it; in which the present lasts forever without, however, making its duration noticed and without any trace of time's passage; without any other sentiment of deprivation or of enjoyment, pleasure or pain, desire or fear, except that of our existence, and having this sentiment alone fill it completely; *as long as this state lasts,* he who finds himself in it can call himself happy.[30]

All Rousseau has done, it would seem, is to transfer his longing for happiness from one set of "scattered points along the path of life" to another. The fact that the "points" of the second set have a different content from those of the first doesn't affect the underlying similarity of the two sets. The remedy Rousseau hits upon, in other words, is the same as the problem he flees: both are equally scattered.

That *is* frightening.

8

The experience of unqualified affirmation suggests a degree of yea-saying most of us rarely if ever attain, and even our approximations to it are infrequent, brief, and easily forgotten. We are ephemeral all the way down, even at that marrow-deep level of understanding that may from time to time reconcile us to our ephemerality. But I don't quote Kierkegaard and Rousseau to "refute" the religious import of Bugbee's periodic insights. In fact, reflecting on those passages brings me to the side of his thinking that is easily overlooked by a too-narrow focus on his high moments of realization. Despite the prominence of Bugbee's celebration of luminous moments, his overall religious attitude, like Kierkegaard's, is finally centered on faith. When we overlook the role of faith in his thinking, we are bound to find his moments of true perception paradoxical and in the long run self-defeating. So we might read:

> Now you begin to understand and now you don't understand—that is what seems ephemeral about our condition. But as understanding comes

upon us and deepens from time to time, strengthening however fleetingly our appreciation of finality, one becomes aware of its relevance to our everyday situation all along. At the same time one becomes aware that much of the time he has been dormant or obtuse with respect to it.[31]

And then we might wonder: if our momentary understanding somehow includes the acceptance that in the next moment we may not understand, does that leave us any better off when the next moment actually comes? If we think of such moments as discontinuous from one another and from the rest of our life, then the answer is obviously no. But Bugbee devotes much of *The Inward Morning* to exploring ways in which his luminous moments are *not* self-enclosed and isolated. His memories of true perception are precisely about maintaining continuity in his life, and while this continuity is certainly not of the sort Kierkegaard has in mind, its aim seems to be much the same: to avoid the fragmentation that results from fixating on high moments of affirmation to the exclusion of their contrary. Bugbee seeks a middle way between what he calls the "untruth of elation and depression."[32] This middle way is the way of faith.

If we place faith in the forefront of Bugbee's concerns, we may get a better angle on the "Fishing Satori." The emphasis of this passage, it now seems, is not so much on the leaping fish (however gladly we may welcome it) as on the fishing itself—keeping one's fingertips on the trembling line. Fishing stands for the life of faith, and the leaping fish stands for those exclamatory experiences—perceptual, mnemonic, or both—that *may* supervene upon that life. Apart from our active commitment to what the river may bestow, we would never cast our lines and the fish would never leap. This does not mean that the fish *must* leap. We can't control their presence, and if we seek for control we shall reduce our lives to continual frustration. Faith, like fishing, has the somewhat oxymoronic character of active waiting—of *keeping* oneself open to whatever may come. Thus wanting a saving experience at the end of one's days not only indicates an unwholesome fixation on something one can't finally possess, but is quite beside the point. The issue is not the availability or durability of such experiences as isolated moments, but rather what they confirm, if and when they do occur, about the "omnirelevant truth"—affirmed and kept in faith—that our world *is* a holy place, that things *are* worthy of love, and that our life together with them *is* affirmable even in our moments of obscurity, and even as we perish. When we are sensitized by faith, reality calls upon us with myriad voices: in works of art, gestures of kindness, the leap of fish, and the remembrance of things past. Faith is not centered on our little eternities alone (however blessed those moments may be) but on the "central strand of meaning capable of bearing the weight of all the disparate moments of our lives."[33]

Remembering may itself be an act of faith.

## 9

If we tie unqualified affirmation too closely to luminous moments, we discover that it is highly qualified after all, not the sort of thing we would wisely spend a lifetime striving for. On the other hand, if we think of unqualified affirmation as the life of faith—where "unqualified" indicates the wholeheartedness of one's commitment over the long term rather than the intensity of transient experiences—then perhaps we may no longer expect hosannas at the end of our days but may come to know what true acceptance is *all* the way down. And the question we must ask is: What in practice does this come down to?

For Bugbee, the life of faith is not continuous illumination but involves its full complement of disappointment and dejection. But the blessing of faith is precisely its ability to win unqualified affirmation despite the variability of moods. Experiences such as Bugbee's "Fishing Satori" bestow insight not in isolation but only within a life actively given to responding to things as intrinsically meaningful and worthy of love. Toward the end of his journal, Bugbee defines faith as "sensitization to intimations of finality in things," a sensitization that deepens from time to time "into the *creative reception* . . . of the ultimate gift of things in their finality." A prime source of such intimations is memory, and Bugbee makes clear that "creative reception" pertains to our recollections no less than to our perceptions. We see *and* remember with the eye of faith.

Bugbee explores a style or technique of reminiscence that forgoes the continuous narrative in favor of a deeper principle of continuity. Each of the memories he records in *The Inward Morning* reveals an instance or aspect of what he refers to as the "essential truth" running like an undercurrent throughout his life. It is this deeper significance or "trend of meaning" that bears the weight of all his moments, good and bad, and imparts a sense of unity to his days. Continually renewing his availability to this abiding significance, even to the day of his death, is the defining task of Bugbee's religious calling and the clarification of his sense of personal destiny. As he expresses it: "The idea of a destiny to be fulfilled suggests that we are followed wherever we go, whatever we do, by a basic significance in terms of which our lives must be construed, and that we act in vain only as we fail to respond consonantly with that significance aligning the otherwise contingent moments of our lives."[34]

By gathering a memory to himself and writing it down, Bugbee delivers himself into the heart of the present. "Fishing Satori" is a striking example of what it may mean to regain the present through the creative recollection of something past. The exhilaration of the leaping and landing of that miraculous fish seems almost of a piece with the leaping to consciousness of the memory itself and of its being landed onto the written page. A past moment of affirmation is brought into the present through lyrical expression, thus lifting the present itself into a moment of comparable affirmation. Bugbee states this connection precisely: "We greet in each remembrance the image of the meaning of this present moment, receiving from it the power of articulateness through which we open out to receive what comprehends us." This clarifies his earlier stipulation of a "strict connection between recall to oneself in one's true mode of being in the present and the depth of recall in which reflection may become concretely continuous with the past." The continuity in Bugbee's life is a constancy of meaning, held in faith and confirmed from time to time in perception and memory, which draws together his otherwise random moments into relationships of mutual illumination. Unlike an autobiography, Bugbee's style of remembrance is an ongoing appropriation of his past, a continual exchange from present to past and past to present in which both terms are enlivened and redeemed. This exchange is the enactment of Bugbee's faith, which keeps him firmly and continuously on his way. "I trust in the remembrance of what I have loved and respected; remembrance in which love and respect are clarified. And I trust such remembrance to guide my reflection in the path of essential truth."[35]

10

Plutarch's remarkable essay "On Contentment" is worth considering here. "Foolish people," Plutarch writes, "overlook and ignore good things even when they are present, because their thoughts are always straining towards the future; intelligent people, on the other hand, use their memories to keep [the good things] vivid for themselves even when they are no longer present." Plutarch admits, however, that the foolish are not entirely without reason for their neglect of the present. After all, the present "is accessible for the minutest fraction of time and then escapes perception." The present—to use my own image—is like the fringe of a summer fog bank that seems to dissolve in the very process of forming; there is no pause in its restless movement to allow us to be fully contemporary with ourselves and with the things about us. But the fool's error, Plutarch goes on to say, is that he hopes to find the remedy to this perpetual vanishing in a future that will be no less vanishing when it becomes present. In his longing for this specious future he ungratefully allows each successive present to slip into oblivion, and this oblivion, Plutarch writes, "prevents life being a unity of past events woven with present ones: it divides yesterday from today, as if they were distinct, and . . . immediately consigns every occurrence to non-existence by never making use of memory." For Plutarch, in other words, life ceases to be an empty vanishing only with the aid of memory, because the retention of the present in memory allows its disappearance to be transformed into something that can be "held" and contemplated. Paradoxically, the only way to be truly in the present, to savor its elusive essence even though it dissolves, is retrospectively. In the moving cloud of the present we cannot find the stable images that lend themselves to steady contemplation and undiluted response. Without the composed images of memory, Plutarch observes, the foolish person is like Oknos in Hades who weaves the rope of his life so absentmindedly that he fails to see that he is paying it out into the mouth of a donkey. When we neglect to keep our experience alive in memory, our life becomes correspondingly incomplete, dreamlike, and empty—a careless feeding of our days into the maw of oblivion. And once the rope of one's life has been swallowed, can one hope to pull it out of the donkey's throat and weave it again?[36]

So the true presence of things might paradoxically *follow* our immediate experience of them. True presence might be characterized by a certain echo effect involving an element of reflection and imagination. Just as sound waves take time to travel from their physical sources before we hear them, perhaps the deeper resonance of present experience takes time to fully impact on our souls, and what hearing is to sound, perhaps imagination and expressive words are to our immediate impressions. An immediacy without temporal distance might be compared (to change the metaphor) to a visual perception without spatial distance: when our face is too close to the thing we would perceive, we see only a blurred image. Perhaps we are always too close to our present impressions really to appreciate them, so that we must give them to ourselves in afterimages whose contours are more distinct. Thoreau, I think, was exploiting this insight when he recommended to poets: "Do not tread on the heels of your experience. Be impressed without making a minute of it. Poetry puts an interval between the impression and the expression—waits till the seed germinates naturally."[37]

II

Let me try again to characterize the relationship between memory and faith in Bugbee's thought. Faith is the active reception of an "omnirelevant" significance whose presence now is often best divined through reflection on certain experiences in which it seems to have been disclosed in the past. What Bugbee receives from such reflections, however, is not so much a summary account of the facts of his life as a prompting to creatively articulate the "essential truth" he believes lives in his memories. This involves an imaginative appropriation of the events of his life so as to derive from them an *image* of the ubiquitous meaning that he believes informs all his experiences whether or not he is immediately aware of it. The element of creativity in Bugbee's appropriation of his past is borne out by his way of sometimes introducing a recollection as though it were a composite rendering of a group of associated experiences. Thus "Fishing Satori" begins: "I recall *mornings,* at the crack of dawn," and "Night Watch" begins: "Of reality given and eternal: certain night *watches* at sea."[38]

## 12

Keeping one's fingers on the trembling line to the present is often the same as keeping one's fingers on the trembling line to the past. Creative recollection of the past is a way of actively nurturing one's capacity to remain open to the present, and this activity is especially relevant in times of obscurity and doubt. Speaking of the alternation between experiences of "exile and homecoming," Bugbee writes:

> It is as if finality filtered through to us in periods of estrangement from it and aroused us to reflection as activity pertinent to our restoration. It is as if we vaguely remembered, and the point of reflection lay in clearing our memory.... Yet the remembering that is essential, that is our homecoming, that is the reflective experience which sets one to thinking firmly in terms of the idea of grace.[39]

In other passages, Bugbee emphasizes the voluntary and active nature of his moments of recollection, as when he speaks of sifting and culling the meaning of things past, or as in the following passage, of earning the meaning of the past, trying to remember, and digging down for the waters of life.[40]

> But reflection, it seems, must earn the gift of the essential meaning of things past. It is as if experience must continue underground for some time before it can emerge as springwater, clear, pure, understood. And reflection is a trying to remember, a digging that is pointless if it be not digging down directly beneath where one stands, so that the waters of his life may re-invade the present moment and define the meaning of both.[41]

Seeing these two passages together, I am struck by Bugbee's use of the phrase "as if." Perhaps he intends to accent both the role of imagination in the writing down of his memories and the role of faith in guiding his imagination. By treating his memories *as if* they have been purified by the passage of time, he actively sifts them with an eye to their essential meaning. Just as a miner panning for gold approaches a stream in the hope that it has already scoured away the bulk of gravel and earth from the treasure he seeks and brought it nearer to hand, so Bugbee approaches the stream of his past in the faith that it has already washed from his memories the inessential and brought their true significance closer to realization. He must only work the stream to expose its hidden wealth to the light of present experience.

But if faith is able to find images of ultimate significance in memory because of the filtration memory undergoes in time, does one ever—or ever enough—realize ultimate significance in the present? Another passage in the same vein ends with a line that certainly raises this question. It begins, "there is more to reality than meets the minds eye," and continues a few lines later:

> [T]his central thought, elusive though it may be, does tend to revive and receive nourishment in those various moments of reflective life when remembrance of things past takes the form of what Proust called involuntary recall. And the meaning of past experience emerges as if having undergone filtration profoundly below the bed over which rush the quick run-off waters of day-to-day. No doubt something of pure springwater is in them, too, *but perhaps not often noticeably so.*[42]

The "more to reality than meets the mind's eye" refers, of course, to the essential truth, the mystery of presence as such, which can bring about a religious awakening but cannot be "pocketed by the mind." It occurs to me, however, that Bugbee might just as well have introduced this passage (in a way perhaps more true to its sense) by observing that there is often more to reality than meets the *physical* eye. The phrase "the quick run-off waters of day-to-day" refers to the fleeting perceptual present, which as Plutarch warns, we must appropriate in memory or lose. I think Bugbee would agree with Plutarch that if we neglect to consciously weave our past experiences with our present ones we shall grow negligent of our very selves, in effect consigning them to oblivion. But Bugbee is saying something more than this. It is not just that we can lose our sense of who we are by ungratefully failing to remember our experiences, but that we all-too-often don't grasp the essential truth of what we experience until long after the fact. We overlook—or are prevented from seeing—the significance of what is happening to us until time intervenes and allows it to come back to us in "purified" double-takes. "I did not realize it at the time," "I did not appreciate it at the time," "Little did I know then," "Little *could* I know then" are common expressions for delayed experience. They mark the curious and often painful discrepancy between things *as we live them* and things *as we remember them.*

## 13

The theme of delayed presence makes frequent appearances throughout *The Inward Morning,* often in contrast to experiences of direct presence. Another example of the latter to set beside "Fishing Satori" is Bugbee's evocation of his peripatetic philosophizing before the war:

> I weighed everything by the measure of the silent presence of things, clarified in the racing clouds, clarified by the cry of hawks, solidified in the presence of rocks, spelled out syllable by syllable by waters of manifold voice, and consolidated in the act of taking steps, each step a meditation steeped in reality. What this all meant, I could not say, kept trying to say, kept trying to harmonize with the suggestions arising from the things I read. But I do remember that this walking in the presence of things came to a definitive stage. It was in the fall of '41, October and November, while late autumn prevailed throughout the northern Canadian Rockies, restoring everything in that vast region to a native wildness. Some part of each day or night, for forty days, flurries of snow were flying. The aspens and larches took on a yellow so vivid, so pure, so trembling in the air, as to fairly cry out that they were as they were, limitlessly. And it was there in attending to this wilderness, with unremitting alertness and attentiveness, yes, even as I slept, that I knew myself to have been instructed for life, though I was at a loss to say what instruction I had received.[43]

Bugbee immediately follows this account of direct presence with one of delayed presence. Shortly after his religious transformation he is drawn into the Pacific war, seemingly as far removed as could be from the instruction of his forty days in the wilderness. During his years at sea the insights of his walking meditations seemed to fall behind him, and it is not clear how present they were even to his memory. Now, some eight years after the war, Bugbee records in his journal a retrospective discovery:

> What I did not realize at all at the time, as it now seems to me, was how philosophy, or perhaps I should say a trend of meaning, continued to take its own course with me. Looking back now, I understand my life at sea as an almost uninterrupted active meditation, continuous, quiet, with the walking I had done throughout earlier years. And so continuous was life at sea with the instruction I had received in those mountains just prior to the war, that the sea absorbed me without a ripple of differ-

ence intervening to make known to me that everything was as it had been before.[44]

The concluding sentence here, with its paradoxical claim that the two experiences were so alike in their power to absorb his attention that he was unable to realize their likeness, tends to detract from the idea Bugbee is trying to develop. That idea, it seems to me, is the contrast between the two temporal modes of experiencing presence, a contrast that makes all the more compelling his later realization of the essential truth they have in common. It seems implausible that Bugbee, at sea in a terrible war, would not have been keenly aware of the disparity between his time in the wilderness, when he *knew* that he was instructed for life, and his time on the mine sweeper, when the grind of shipboard routine so often obscured that elusive knowledge. We have only to repeat one of his more unromantic descriptions of ship life to make us wonder how he could not have felt a longing for his mountains even as he was unconsciously benefiting from the sea's own instruction:

> But what a benefactress is the sea in the exigencies she engenders, time and again stealing your attention back to the task in spite of yourself, cleansing you unawares as you are trapped into concentration on holding a course in a heavy sea-way, straining your eyes in her mists, managing your balance as you go for stores in some cramped hold, as you fight against a wave of nausea in the engine-room stench. Who would choose such things? . . . Nothing delights a sailor more than improvisation on the theme of his miserable fate. Probably nothing could fall more afoul of his innermost ear than to have someone solicit his assent to the life at sea as a matter of choice. What bilge.[45]

If, as Bugbee tells us, his life at sea was "cleansing" him "unawares" and teaching him essentially the same lesson he received in the mountains, nevertheless the operative word is "unawares." Only now, in the very act of creatively recalling the two experiences in his journal, does he see with clarity the true continuity that joins them. After the settling out of a decade, his being in the wilderness and being at sea now show themselves to his memory as having all along shared an underlying truth. That the two experiences *were* largely discontinuous in the living is something Bugbee explicitly states—for example, in the first sentence of the passage I quote in the next paragraph—but his creative style of blending the memory of past experiences with present insight often covers over this fact. It seems to me that this covering over is intentional on Bugbee's part and is somehow key to understanding the healing effect of his style of reminiscence.

The contrast between direct and delayed presence, between essential truth apprehended in the present and the same truth apprehended in hindsight, is drawn with particular vividness in the intriguing double memory—or memory within a memory—which I call "Night Watch." Bugbee nostalgically recalls a time (or rather times) when he and certain of his shipmates found themselves side by side in the dark, contemplating the stars, the stars' reflections in the water, and the phosphorescent waves passing the ship. The silence and darkness, the nearness of the sea and stars, and the motion of the ship enfold Bugbee and his mates in an intimacy that encourages them to open their hearts to one another. Out of this attuning silence, words begin to flow and the men feel encouraged to tell of their nostalgia for better times and places. "The springs of reminiscence flowing upon us, we would find ourselves suddenly living again the long-forgotten, urged to articulate the very quality of what was there and then in relation to our here and now." And so they yearned and dreamed together of times when "surely, reality dwelt and a man *lived,* or someday may live again." For Bugbee, this moment of intimacy, seen in retrospect, was itself a moment of supreme truth, albeit one that he and his shipmates did not completely appreciate as such when they were living it.

> Which one of us who once stood on deck in those far-off watches at sea, reliving them now, perchance, lacks occasion for correcting the impression which we seemed to voice then: that the time in which we really lived belonged to a remote past, or must be deferred until it might revive in some distant future, discontinuous with the life we led there and then? What better hours have we known than those there and then, in which we were flooded with memories in which the essential meaning of things past revived and established us in the present moment, opening us to our present situation, to one another, and to a plenitude of significance transcending the capacity of an endless future to exhaust? Even as we spoke of flowering orchards in Santa Clara Valley, did we not *see* the stars and *hear* the wind and *feel* the sea, partaking in a limitless being which charged our very words with a silence out of which they were spo-

ken and into which we returned from speech? And was the meaning of the past regiven . . . other than the meaning of that present, of our communion in silence, and with the sea? What did we learn in such night watches if not this: that nowhere and no other time might contribute more than more of what was there and then, deepened in ourselves, permeating all things?

Let us remember that in such watches we came to affirm our situation with our very selves, and that our actions testified to the affirmation, when we went about our work with a will, restored and renewed in the harmony of our actual situation.[46]

Despite the completeness of the affirmation that Bugbee at the end of this passage enjoins his shipmates to remember, it is obviously his present nostalgia that is asking and implicitly answering those leading questions. For if he and his shipmates had fully realized the value of their nostalgic communion back then, as the last sentence suggests, there would be no question of their having occasion to correct it now. We can appreciate how their moment of sharing their pasts would have solidified their comradeship and enabled them to go back to their work with renewed vigor, but it also seems likely that only the chance Ishmael in the crew would have endorsed any suggestion then that there were no better hours than the one they had just shared together. The rest might likely have responded, no doubt with affection, "What bilge."

So what are we to make of this ambiguity between things as Bugbee actually experienced them and things as he later remembers them? "Night Watch" is a nostalgic recollection of an earlier moment of nostalgic recollection in which Bugbee's present nostalgia corrects—to use his word—his earlier nostalgia's absence from its present and in doing so manages to correct its own tendency to be absent. Structurally the journal entry presents the two moments of nostalgia as mirror images of one another, and the effect of this mutual mirroring is to dissolve the boundary between past and present. In these passages, it is often unclear where temporally speaking Bugbee stands or to whom he is addressing his remarks, because in fact he is standing in both times at once and addressing both his shipmates of long ago and us, his readers. I think this merging and interpenetration of past and present is deliberate and very much to Bugbee's point. The essential truth—the trend of meaning that defines his sense of personal destiny and permits him to affirm his finitude absolutely—*was* present during those long-ago night watches—*but perhaps not often noticeably so.* Only the unconscious filtration that those earlier experiences underwent over the years enables Bugbee now to see with the second sight of memory that they were informed with absolute significance. It is the sifting of time that enables him to restore to those past experiences their dormant truth. But the ultimate effect of this restoration is to reawaken Bugbee to the present by reflecting back to him the absence inherent in all nostalgia, including that which now draws him away. In the process of creatively articulating and completing those remote experiences, Bugbee undergoes a healing anamnesis that enables him to see the unrealized truth of the past as the living truth of the present, the same truth. Indeed, it enables him to affirm the present as the ultimate if hidden stimulus of his recollections. It is as if the essential truth in the present needs an image in which to see and remedy its own self-absence and it seeks that image in the past. In loosening nostalgia's hold on the past moment of experience by revealing the essential truth that was in it unawares, present memory discovers the same truth in the present and thus delivers itself into it. The act of expressing the memory, of composing it into a stable image, is the very act by which Bugbee recalls himself into the present.

> But the treasure of the remote, of the recalled in tenderness, of the place and the time for which it seems that we long, and all that comes to us now from elsewhere and other times—all this that pervades us with a sense of plenitude and an absolute meaning—where does this treasure lie? Is it not the very meaning of being at sea, here and now? And is not all the yearning and dreaming which seems to place this treasure in the remote, spurred by the mystery of this present moment, which comprehends us, now? Restored to ourselves and in communion with one another, we greet in each remembrance the image of the meaning of this present moment, receiving from it the power of articulateness through which we open out to receive what comprehends us. The remote, then, is the image of infinite meaning received and acknowledged, now.[47]

Note again that Bugbee presents this passage as if it were something he communicated to his shipmates during that nostalgic conversation years ago at sea. But if my reading is correct, what he is actually doing is imaginatively returning to that conversation and completing it in hindsight. He is redeeming a past moment that did not know its own ultimate significance and by articulating that significance back into it he is transforming it into an awareness of omnirelevant significance now. In the act of creatively responding to the very nostalgia that draws him away from the present, he undergoes a sudden unforgetting that leaves him "undeceived of elsewhere and another time to come."[48] What enables this remarkable transformation is at bottom faith. Discussing faith in connection with his interest in Zen, Bugbee remarks late in the journal:

> Faithfulness is possible. And it is faithfulness that makes possible constancy in philosophic reflection, just as in doing anything else which we may come to do understandingly in good time. Zen emphasizes the swift advent of essential truth. . . . Zen [also emphasizes] the all-alongness of that essential truth into which we may suddenly awaken, and it may even bespeak a kind of confirmatory retroactive blending of decisive insight with antecedent presentiment suggesting continuity in the *way* one has come, and imparting a certain wholeness of meaning to one's life.[49]

## 14

Bugbee is exploring a style of thinking that might be called philosophic or metaphysical recollection, a kind of Platonic anamnesis of *this* world of things rather than a transcendent world of Ideas. He is searching in memory for experiential confirmations of the mystery of presence as such. He makes clear, not only in his sample memories, but also in his more discursive meditations on memory that his philosophically guided reminiscences are for the purpose of making explicit a religious significance implicit in all his experiences.

> Our thinking actively partakes of reality as a closed circuit in which we participate with things in so far as we are actually imbued with unconditional concern [faith]. Such thinking is in rapport with our experience of finality in things. As we approximate philosophic contemplation we become continuous in our thinking with that mode of experience of things to which I allude as aesthetic contemplation, or true perception. There is an essential truth about both phases of contemplation, common to

both, as that which sets us free. And it has seemed to me, again and again, that as reflection approximates [philosophic] contemplation . . . , one tends to relive and complete the reception of the gift of things past, initially received in experience approximating true perception. I have also noticed that the passage from philosophic to aesthetic contemplation (to the immediate reception of the gift of things as presences, in their finality) is without a break.[50]

The ultimate focus of Bugbee's philosophical reflection is the mystery of the givenness of things, the "somewhat absolute" that echoes through or "haunts" all his thinking. In its more discursive moments, reflection attempts to elucidate the concept of presence, to draw comparisons with other schools of thought or religious attitudes, and to discern manifestations of presence in art, literature, and music. But the final confirmation of philosophic thinking is in the quick precipitation of discursive insights into concrete perceptual and mnemonic realizations.[51] When philosophic reflection is undertaken in a spirit of being beholden to reality and thus of bearing responsibility for it, it becomes receptive to intimations of essential truth in experiences from the past. At the same time, properly attuned, philosophic reflection tends to evolve into a mode of contemplation in which it is sensitized and opened up to the possibility of coming alive to essential truth in the present. Experiential confirmation of metaphysical truth—of concretely finding oneself feelingly *in* the truth—works in two modes:

> One [mode] is in the gift of involuntary recall, wherein one reflectively taps the vein of the experience of things in their finality, and one is restored anew to the closed circuit of reality obtaining with respect to things past; things past are redeemed in their finality. The other mode of experiential confirmation . . . is our restoration and renewal in the capacity to receive the gift of things present in their finality.[52]

Bugbee remembers the past not so much to recapture it as to complete it, a completion whose ultimate object is to restore him to the reality of the present. The truth of memory is not in how objectively it corresponds to what actually was, but in its ability, through creative response, to impart a sense for the eternal truth that guides all his works and days. He is not concerned with the shifting meanings of the past and future as they play into the ever-changing present, but with the singular experiential truth that is available in all his experiences. And he is interested in using his memory only insofar as it aids in reestablishing him in this "deeper vein of experience."[53]

## 15

What grounds this faith in the ultimate significance of things? How would one defend Bugbee's religious attitude from the charge, for example, that it is only wishful thinking? Such a charge seems especially hard to answer when we recall how completely Bugbee bases his religious attitude on the "closed circuit" of his personal experience. There can be, he says, "no appeal to what we might conceive as demonstrable characteristics of things as warrant for construing love and respect as their due," and therefore "neither things nor the love and respect in terms of which they are realized as finally intelligible can be so understood in abstraction from such experience of them." It would appear that there is no noncircular way to defend the idea, or the direct experience, of things as intrinsically worthy of our love and respect. Toward the end of his journal, Bugbee reiterates the personal and circular nature of his religious attitude when he disagrees with those who "propose an evaluation of our [human] situation in abstraction from the answer always unfinished so long as we live, that answer which each of us alone can understand as it is fashioned in terms of his own response and which cannot be relevantly questioned by him beyond the sphere of his intimacy." In the end, Bugbee's religious attitude seems to come down to exhortation: "Let us reflect, then, [by] drawing on all that has spoken to us with authority in our actual lives. If we have looked upon the mountains time and again, and they have called upon us, and we have responded, let us remember that we have looked upon them with the eye of faith. Let us credit such experience in our reflection as may have prompted us to extend credit to the world."[54]

When it comes to ultimate evaluations, are we each enclosed within the self-confirming circle of our own responses? If so, how can such solitary appreciations keep clear of the subversive thought that they are at bottom subjective and arbitrary? How can one's affirmations in the face of life—much less in the face of death—survive the suspicion of self-deception? What can one say to someone who directly experiences the presence of things as ultimately absurd rather than sacred? I recall in this connection the classic case of Roquentin when he encounters those dreadful chestnut roots under his park bench. It seems to me that his insight into the mute absurdity of things occurs with a visionary force that puts it quite on par with any of Bugbee's own perceptual epiphanies.

> So I was in the park just now. The roots of the chestnut tree were sunk in the ground just under my bench. I couldn't remember it was a root any more. The words had vanished and with them the significance of things, their methods of use, and the feeble points of reference which men have traced on their surface. I was sitting, stooping forward, head bowed, alone in front of this black, knotty mass, entirely beastly, which frightened me. Then I had this vision. . . . [A]ll of a sudden, there it was, clear as day: existence had suddenly unveiled itself. It had lost the harmless look of an abstract category: it was the very paste of things, this root was kneaded into existence. Or rather the root, the park gates, the bench, the sparse grass, all that had vanished: the diversity of things, their individuality, were only an appearance, a veneer. This veneer had melted, leaving soft, monstrous masses, all in disorder—naked, in a frightful, obscene nakedness.[55]

Roquentin is testifying to what amounts to a negative mystical experience, an immediate revelation of the horror of things, which comes over him with what he deems unimpeachable authority. When we pair his experience with Bugbee's exhortation to adhere to "all that has spoken to us with authority in our actual lives," aren't we forced simply to abandon Roquentin to his nihilistic vision and to withdraw all the more resolutely into the closed circle of our contrary vision? If not, what sort of experience-based dialogue or mutual witnessing could there be with a Roquentin? If the authority of one's faith in the meaning of things cannot be based solely on the involuntariness, swiftness, and intensity of singular experiences that reveal them as meaningful—since these same features may also characterize experiences that reveal the absence of worth and meaning—on what, then, is it based? When we ask these questions in the context of "our" objectivistic worldview, for which reality is at bottom only externally related objects devoid of intrinsic meaning, who is to say that Roquentin's vision is not a confirmation at the level of direct experience of what our best scientific theories have to tell us about reality?

A phrase from Thoreau runs through Bugbee's journal almost like a refrain. "Let us not suppose a case, but take the case that is." But there are cases presented to us with such haunting realism that they seem more than just suppositions in the idle sense Thoreau's line seems to suggest. Sartre's art enables us to see what Roquentin sees, and once having seen it, even if only indirectly, have we not in a sense lost our innocence? Has Roquentin's case not at some level become our own case as well?

16

Here is a suggestive passage on roots to set beside Rouqentin's. It comes from a letter by van Gogh to his brother Theo:

> To forget it [my gathering troubles] I lie down in the sand by an old tree trunk and make a drawing of it—in a linen blouse, smoking a pipe and looking at the deep blue sky, or at the moss or the grass. That quiets me. . . . [I]n the black gnarled and knotty roots, I wanted to express something of the struggle for life; or rather because I tried to be faithful to nature as I saw it before me without philosophizing about it; involuntarily . . . something of that great struggle is shown.[56]

Comparing Roquentin's experience with van Gogh's might we generalize as follows? What the roots *are*—what we "involuntarily" and "without philosophy" see them *as*—depends on many things, not the least of which is *why* we go to them in the first place and *how* we attend to them. If we go to them to seek quiet and to forget our troubles and attend to them with a sketch pad on our lap, how differently they may appear than if we drop down beside them in a fit of dejection and passively stare at them till our eyes sting. To put the matter this way, however, suggests an ontological relativism that, I feel sure, Bugbee would want to deny—even if he too at times speaks like a relativist: "there are all manner of relative givens, and they are relative to the modes of receptivity in which the given may be received." Such a remark seems not so far from the nowadays fashionable view that there is no one way the world really is; there are as many worlds as there are ways of inhabiting "it." But however differently people differently disposed may experience the world, Bugbee believes to the marrow of his bones that there *is* a way the world really is and that that way is sacred. Moreover, he is as sure as he is reluctant to insist that creative love is the normative mode of response for disclosing how the world really is. "[A]nything definite becomes definitively given as its presence comes home to us; but the presence of things does not come home to us except as presence is completed from within ourselves. Love is such a matter of completion of presence from within ourselves."[57]

I think Bugbee would not hesitate to say that van Gogh's mode of response is much more in keeping with what it means to complete presence (reality) than Roquentin's too-ready surrender to his perceptual crises. Plurality of experiences of the real does not lead Bugbee to conclude that reality in the conclusive sense is also plural. Yet the only ground he has to stand on in pursuing this faith is inward experience that he cannot fail to acknowledge as authoritative. The "within" of which he speaks so often in *The Inward Morning* includes the inwardness of memories that do not play him false.

> The reflective understanding of reality, then, has seemed to me helped by the incursion into the present moment of remembered situations from which one gains his bearings and his stance as a human being. Thus the recollective understanding of one's actual experience is intimately connected with the reflective understanding of reality. And it may be that the vein in which one undertakes the responsibilities of reflection also determines the depth from which the filtered meaning of past experience can come home to one, here and now. There is a believing with all one's heart, in no wise contrary to carefulness of thinking, upon which alone it would seem possible to understand reality as grounding our belief. Above all else, then, I trust in the remembrance of what I have loved and respected; remembrance in which love and respect are clarified. And I trust in such remembrance to guide my reflections in the path of essential truth.[58]

What alternative is there to entrusting ourselves to whatever in our experience speaks to us as worthy of our trust? Bugbee answers elliptically: "Consider the tumbleweed." Thoreau put the issue in the form of a commandment: "Discipline yourself to yield to love; suffer yourself to be attracted."[59] So again we come full circle.

## 17

I detect that I am trying to make an issue of Bugbee's themes, turning them into debate topics that I can chase around in circles and perhaps come away from feeling a bit more philosophically trim. Is life worth living or not? Are the things of this world real or appearances? Shall we ever find the measure of our endlessly disputed tastes, our ever-multiplying perspectives? But the spirit of debate is not the governing spirit of Bugbee's style of philosophy. While Bugbee can entertain an argument with obvious sophistication, and be entertained by it as well, in the end he seems to be telling us—in a tone bordering on tenderness—to "get off it" and consider concretely all that actually holds us to the world. The people we love and admire, the places we call home, the work we feel it worthwhile to do, the visions of landscape that gladden our hearts, the works of art and thought that give us strength and understanding—these provide the primary themes for philosophic reflection. Only as we examine our *lives* have we any hope of discovering what makes them worth living, and everything depends on the faithfulness with which we undertake this self-examination.

This recommendation to consider our lives and discipline ourselves to what we deem best in them may sound egocentric and dangerous, as though it were enjoining us to go on believing what we believe "deep down" anyway and disregard everything else. Coming from an unreflective soul, the faith declaration "Here I stand; I can do no other," may signify little more than a mock-heroic way of stopping one's ears. But this observation must be balanced with another. The pose of philosophic neutrality, with its equally mock-heroic conception of reason as the final arbiter of value, can be just as egocentric and dangerous. If I truly detach myself from my commitments and from an objective distance inquire into the "foundations" of commitment as such, am I bolstering my commitments or toying with the possibility of betraying them? Does the question "Are any of my commitments objectively grounded?" come down to the question "Is there any 'real' reason I should hold myself to any of my commitments?" For Bugbee, the prospect of betrayal far outweighs any arguments he may encounter about the nonobjective character of value. Our ethically defined lives precede ethics as a reflective discipline, and ethics itself becomes little more than arid blowing when uprooted from the soil of respect and love. My commitment to abstract inquiry into the ground or groundlessness of value has scant claim when measured against the specific values that govern my life. When my friend calls me in an emergency, I drop the skeptical sockdolager I am working on and rush to his aid, and anyone would consider me weirdly out of touch with reality if I were so enamored with my argument that I felt no obligation to respond. An intellectual reservation in a moment of pressing need does not attract response at the same level of intellectual "interest." What it attracts is censure. In such a moment we do not humor our skeptic with counterarguments but demand to know, "What is *wrong* with you?"

Experience does from time to time impose upon us the need to reevaluate our commitments, but this requirement bears in upon us against a background of more encompassing commitments, as the very sense of *having* to reevaluate indicates. No rational person ignores her commitments simply because philosophers have yet to refute the thesis that the ethical per se is noncognitive; nor is it a mark of her intellectual responsibility, much less moral responsibility, to keep herself open to the possibility that that thesis might yet be proven true.

## 18

Is it plausible that we might have a better understanding of what it means to be committed by setting ourselves apart from actual situations in which we experience moral necessity? Is it plausible that the reality of value is something to be proven by translating ourselves wholly into a world of facts and then trying to *reason* values back into it? Let us consider how trivial such an exercise becomes next to the demands of our actual lives. Is this not as much proof as any *reasonable* person should need as to the cognitive nature of morality? Morality *must* be a development of affect. What sort of *claim* upon us could a moral claim have if it were not *deeply felt*?

To Bugbee's way of thinking, the relative importance of philosophic doubt when compared with the absolute importance of the presence of things is on the same ethical level with the relative importance of philosophic doubt when compared with the absolute importance of human beings. Consider his extended reflections on Kant:

> By "leaving things be" I do not mean inaction; I mean respecting things, being still in the presence of things, letting them speak. Existing is absolute. Things are of infinite importance in existing. But as Kant says, existing is not a character of things; it is their givenness. And since the givenness of things is what I take to be the foundation of respect for *them*, I cannot see that emphasis on things of a certain character, as opposed to things lacking this character, affords an ultimate purchase for interpreting the possibility of respect. . . . I have been unable to follow that tradition of thinking personality to be a necessary character of anything deserving respect. And I cannot see why religious encounter should be limited to the circumstance of encounter with persons. This is not to say, however, that anything can take the place of persons as capable of testifying in the manner of respect. And it may be well to follow Kant here: in making central for the idea of the dignity of man man's capacity to bear witness in respect. But isn't this a capacity to find and to act upon a meaning of things which is final? And if so, must one follow Kant in thinking of respect in a way that excludes the possibility of respect for things? I cannot follow such a way of thinking. It seems to me to ignore the finality of the existing. And if *denial* of the finality of the existing is pressed, this denial may well turn into an insistent refusal that bespeaks nothing but the impoverishment of experience, a severance from reality manifest as things. What is needed to substantiate affirmation of respect for things as a genuine possibility of experience? What more is needed than experience in which this possibility is clearly fulfilled as genuine, authentic? But the interpretation of such experience, that indeed is a matter for reflection.[60]

With respect to our reverence for the presence of things and our respect for the things themselves, we are deeply implicated ethically. Our very uniqueness and dignity in the natural world is defined by our capacity and responsibility to bear witness to the final significance in which nature stands revealed to us. And this implies that in our failures to respond to reality and to affirm it with our whole heart we ultimately slight ourselves. How can we have esteem in our own eyes if we fail to discern worth in that universal dimension in which we find ourselves standing forth with all things?

## 19

What qualifies a given mode of response as more original or fundamental—more "true to reality"—than another? For Bugbee, the answer lies ultimately in the realm of personal experience, in an immediate sense for things that devolves upon him with absolute authority and upon which he is prepared to stake his all. The question is whether this is philosophically a "responsible" position for him to take. The basis of this conviction is neither objective nor subjective. Arguments and evidence are relevant, of course, but they are never decisive, and preferences and volitions are also involved, but they are not whimsical projections upon a neutral background of fact. "Philosophic responsiveness," Bugbee writes, is "the assumption of responsibility to reality in its plenitude."[61] Ontology, understood as reflection on our most intimate acquaintance with reality, is ethical from the start; it must assume—in both senses of the word—responsibility for things in order to complete their reality by bringing them to full realization. Things lay claim to our love and respect and reveal themselves as worthy of such responses only in our active involvement with them as things eliciting love and respect. When confronted with arguments that things in themselves have no such objective worthiness, Bugbee's response is not to bolster his conviction to the contrary with counterarguments, but to remind himself, often through memory, of the ethical bond that already unites him with things. His counterresponse consists of a continuous sensitization to the reality and worth of things relying on as many perspectives—personal recollection, philosophy, painting, literature, music—as he can bring to bear. He is less worried that his appreciations of the intrinsic worthiness of things might be contradicted than that, in crediting those contradictions, he might forsake what he knows in his bones to be a sacred trust, a trust on which his own dignity as a human being depends. His ethical involvement with things ultimately overrides any possible theoretical involvement with them, or any experiential involvement that arises from shunning the ethical bond that calls upon his ongoing creative affirmation. In other words, there are two senses of what it means to be arbitrary, one intellectual, the other ethical. Bugbee clearly implies that where our most fundamental valuations are concerned—whether, for example, we rejoice with things or find them inane—there is a measure of commitment to reality that it would be ethically arbitrary to challenge and that it is only within this commitment that the intellectual arbitrariness of the challenge becomes most clear.

20

Can one propose a "conversion of attitude" without the arrogance of proselytizing?[62] How would one go about converting a Roquentin, for example? For the question of whether reality is meaningful or not—to those who feel impelled to ask it—is not likely to be helped much by argument. I can only suggest a possible approach:

I acknowledge and accept responsibility for the quality of my perceptions because I assume that reality is not "out there" merely to be stumbled upon, but is there to be completed by me because my very self participates in it. Reality makes no sense, not even a negative sense, without response of some kind. Does it not seem arbitrary to suppose that the discovery of reality lies in the direction of my imaginatively or theoretically absenting myself from it, of being disengaged and passive with respect to it? You, my friend, seem to take reality as whatever reveals itself to your blank stare. You sit on your bench and your eyes fall on those roots; that is all you have to give them. So it doesn't surprise me that your dead scrutiny receives in return a frightful ugliness that seems to spread out and envelope everything in your vicinity. But is it not true that your dark reverie is also a response for which you are finally responsible? That is how I view the matter. Whether you acknowledge it or not, it *may* be the denouement of your whole way of life, the cumulative effect of certain habits of perception and comportment that together have put in motion the hidden trend of meaninglessness that has been leading you along unawares. If that is so, any denial of responsibility for that vision is bad faith, is it not? You turn a blank eye to things and then declare that they are intrinsically unable to warm the heart of any undeceived man or woman. I experience reality as a call from things that bids me to complete them with whatever love and respect I am able creatively to turn toward them. And I feel bound by this bidding, beholden to it. Somehow on certain occasions—and I should be happy to tell you about them— things seem to beckon my participation, as if they needed me to bring them to completion. Those are the experiences of things that I credit, which I lay down as my norm and guide in this question of reality and its meaning. In my better hours things seem as glad for me as I am for them, and in my worse hours I search in memory to receive again the blessing I believe is in them. In itself, most abstractly or nakedly considered, anything I encounter just *is* its making itself available for response, and I have no final criterion as to how I should respond other than whatever in my experience I may be able to call upon as trustworthy in what it discloses. Can I on the strength of such experiences as I might relate refute your experiences to the contrary? No. I can only ask you to witness to those experiences in which you yourself implicitly place your trust. And what are they? Your own descriptions testify that you are appalled by what shows itself. So I must ask you, how does it occur to you to place your trust so completely in what appalls you? Why would you be *intent* on remaining passive to such experiences? Is not passivity itself the very mode of response most likely to beckon forth the absurd?

21

By intrinsic worth of things, Bugbee does not mean their value apart from any possible presence they might have to him, but precisely the value they reveal to him when he is receptive to their presence in particular ways: say, with an attitude of wonder and gratitude rather than anxiety and aversion. What makes this mode of reception normative and not merely subjective? Again, we seem stuck with a choice: whether we view normative in an epistemological sense or in an ethical sense, where the distinction between knowing and valuing is assumed. Bugbee's argument is that there is no such clear-cut distinction between facts and values, knowing and responsibility; or rather that when we assume such a distinction we will never find the argumentative route back to affirmation of the world. What unites Bugbee to things in the vital circle of reality is his loving attention rooted in his faith in the "all-alongness" and "omnirelevance" of essential truth, even when he finds himself counting geese. As for the more abstract and skeptical question of what makes one response to things more apt for disclosing reality than another, perhaps the only answer is a Zen-like counterquestion on the order of: "Would you stare at your roots or would you draw them?" In the final analysis perhaps the question of ontological truth is always a question ad hominem—though the one to whom the question is ultimately posed is oneself. "Each day's thinking seems to be at the mercy of the man one is," as Bugbee expresses it. "For a man in his entirety is the pivot on which realization of essential truth turns."[63]

## Notes

1. Henry Bugbee, *The Inward Morning: A Philosophical Exploration in Journal Form* (1958; reprint, with a new introduction by Edward F. Mooney, Athens: University of Georgia Press, 1999), 160–61, 164.
2. Ibid., 136, 131.
3. Ibid., 130, 158.
4. Ibid., 39, 129.
5. Ibid., 96–97, 156, 176.
6. Ibid., 129–30, 164.
7. The phrase "milieu of presence" and the characterization of experience as transpiring from our epidermis outward rather than from our epidermis inward are borrowed from Frederick A. Olafson, *What Is a Human Being? A Heideggerian View* (Cambridge: Cambridge University Press, 1995), 246–47. Olafson's Heideggerian interpretation of presence—"the profound anomaly that is at the root of all our knowledge, and of our lives as well" (253)—has greatly enhanced my appreciation of Henry Bugbee's thought. While Olafson himself does not identify the anomaly of presence with religious mystery and the sacred, he does seem to recognize the compelling way in which its strangeness and resistance to explanation might draw one in that direction.
8. Bugbee, 97, 71, 164.
9. Ibid., 203.
10. Ibid., 164.
11. Ibid., 209.
12. Ibid., 161–62, Bugbee's emphasis.

13. Ibid., 76, 209.
14. Ibid., 162–63.
15. Ibid., 170, 102, 162, 220.
16. Ibid., 162.
17. Ibid., 152, 169, 165.
18. Ibid., 219.
19. Ibid., 197, 146; Samuel Taylor Coleridge, "Dejection: An Ode," in *The Oxford Authors: Samuel Taylor Coleridge,* ed. H. J. Jackson (Oxford and New York: Oxford University Press, 1985), 113–17.
20. Ralph Waldo Emerson, "Nature," in *Ralph Waldo Emerson: Essays and Lectures* (New York: Library of America, 1983), 9.
21. Ibid., 34.
22. Bugbee, 86–87.
23. Ibid., 129, 165–66.
24. Ibid., 227.
25. Ibid., 131.
26. Emerson, 16.
27. Bugbee, 74, my emphasis.
28. Soren Kierkegaard, *Either/Or,* vol. 2, ed. and trans. Howard V. Hong and Edna H. Hong (Princeton, New Jersey: Princeton University Press, 1987), 242.
29. Jean-Jacques Rousseau, *The Reveries of the Solitary Walker,* trans. Charles E. Butterworth (New York: Harper Colophon Books, 1982), 68.
30. Ibid., 68–69, my emphasis.
31. Bugbee, 131.
32. Ibid., 231.
33. Ibid., 221.
34. Ibid., 220, my emphasis, 140, 145.
35. Ibid., 174, 56, 106.
36. Plutarch, *Essays,* trans. Robin Waterfield (New York: Penguin Books, 1992), 229.
37. Henry David Thoreau, *H. D. Thoreau: A Writer's Journal,* ed. Laurence Stapleton (New York: Dover Publications, 1960), 54.
38. Ibid., 86, 176, my emphasis.
39. Ibid., 132.
40. Ibid., 178.
41. Ibid., 140.
42. Ibid., 105, my emphasis.
43. Ibid., 139–41.
44. Ibid., 140.
45. Ibid., 182.

46. Ibid., 178, Bugbee's emphasis.
47. Ibid., 178.
48. Ibid., 177.
49. Ibid., 201–2.
50. Ibid., 174.
51. Ibid., 131, 170.
52. Ibid., 174–75.
53. Ibid., 144.
54. Ibid., 167–68, 129, 224, 116.
55. Jean-Paul Sartre, *Nausea,* trans. Lloyd Alexander (New York: New Directions, 1964), 126–27.
56. Vincent van Gogh, *Dear Theo: The Autobiography of Vincent van Gogh,* ed. Irving Stone (New York: Signet, 1969), 117.
57. Ibid., 70, 76.
58. Ibid., 105–6.
59. Ibid., 133; Thoreau, 83.
60. Ibid., 155–56, Bugbee's emphasis.
61. Ibid., 169.
62. Ibid., 99.
63. Ibid., 197, 108, 154.

# 2

# Wilderness and Experience

"Wilderness" may evoke raw, dramatic features of an inhospitable locale. But in Thoreau or Bugbee, it takes on more subtle connotations related to our modes of experiencing a place—any place that comes unbound, blessed, or clothed in the sublime, that stills our will to mastery and calls on wonder and respect. George Huntston Williams contrasts wilderness, desert, and wasteland in the context of biblical views of paradise and exile, and then places *The Inward Morning*'s wilderness against the background of the North American vision of untrammeled space awaiting settlers facing west. This vision of wilderness as possibility cannot be simply optimistic: suffering and disaster can wait around the bend. In any case an easy faith in the restorative powers of the wild diminishes as the Earth increasingly succumbs to ecological and cultural destruction.

Technologies of domination lay waste to wilderness and strip down our very concept of enlivening experience. Andrew Feenberg offers a typology to make this point. Experience is not just sense-data nor merely raw material, information to be exploited in legal, academic, or entrepreneurial projects. It can mean the flow of lived-experience; wilderness can sensitize our receptivity to the sweep of daily experience, or to the sweep of extraordinary experience as it overtakes us in moments of wonder or insight. At yet another level, experience designates a growth toward wisdom and maturity in the ways of a craft or a way of life. And at the deepest level it can point toward a primal reality from which subject and object differentially emerge. Linking Bugbee's idea of "experiential philosophy" to awakening our sensibilities, joining thought to lived experience and action, and evoking the basic conditions that ground a world, Feenberg characterizes *The Inward Morning* as "the only truly original work of existentialist philosophy written by an American." He also draws a parallel to Suzuki's Zen Buddhism, which Bugbee knew well. Suzuki drew on the Japanese philosopher Nishida's view that in moments of "essential truth" perceiver and perceived are taken up in a primordial "prior unity."

David Strong pursues the contrasts between a technologically truncated view of experience and richer views by contrasting tools that alienate us from the world and from each other, with tools that bring us closer to the grace of things. Finding things wild and uncanny is to find them before they get corralled and branded, allowing us access to forgotten springs of significance, sources that can keep us vital. Things have their recuperative luminosity as do minds attuned to inward wild.

# Wilderness as Wasteland and Paradise

GEORGE HUNTSTON WILLIAMS

In the Palestinian world the Hebrew equivalents of *desert* and *wilderness* denoted roughly the same terrain. In Europe, outside the relatively dry Iberian Peninsula, the terms have become over the centuries differentiated. On the geophysical level *desert* denotes dry, sandy terrain; *wilderness* and its equivalents in other European languages suggest the wilderness of the dark forest, the dismal swamp, and the mountain fastness.

In the long evolution of the biblical terms and their translation and transformation in the course of European history, the term *desert* has now largely lost all but its geographic sense, and the term *garden* has come to be used only in its horticultural sense. In contrast, the biblical term *paradise*, which originally could have the horticultural sense of a *royal park,* as well as its primordial meaning in Genesis, has now become exclusively religio-mythical or poetic in its application.

In between, it is the word *wilderness* that has retained both its purely geophysical and its potently religious meanings. Indeed, the one word in its theological sense has drawn into itself the power of the associated designations and still suggests all the mystery and ambiguity of its Hebraic antecedents. It is a word that can be intoned or invoked. Its incantational potency is felt.

To be sure, like every metaphor, that of the wilderness can become merely a rhetorical gesture. But even in a muted or mutilated version one can detect something of the sweep of a great tradition into modern times.

A glance at the permutations of the wilderness motif in contemporary American philosophy, literature, and art reveals the persistence and the power of the ancient ambiguities. *The Inward Morning* of Henry G. Bugbee Jr., for example, brings the reader at once into contact with current reflections on the meaning of the wilderness.

Bugbee acknowledges his indebtedness to and kinship with John M. Anderson, whose *The Individual and the New World* summarizes well one aspect of the American commitment, when he writes:

> Americans often thought of their conquering of the wilderness in terms of the development of a garden for mankind; and they have continuously seen the frontier experiment in the terms of an ideal human community. . . . In such institutions, Americans have seen themselves as marching across the wilderness and with more or less clarity have conceived of themselves as representatives of mankind's ultimate place in the universe.[1]

But while Bugbee has the literal wilderness of America in mind and more specifically the swamps and woods explored as a boy and notably the ocean during his three years of service at sea in World War II, he has gone much farther than Anderson in transmuting the term *wilderness*. And although he never appeals directly to scriptural or Christian tradition, except for frequent citation of Eckhart, it is his redefinition of the ambiguity of our metaphor that best fits into our survey as a representative and concluding modern document.

His philosophical exploration in the form of a journal is sympathetically introduced by Gabriel Marcel, who recognizes from his vantage point at the Institut de France what a young American philosopher, greatly indebted to him, means when he writes: "Here is what I miss most in the thought of Marcel—the wilderness theme."[2] And an American Catholic interpreter of the philosophic journal, sympathetically reviewing Bugbee's effort to "flush" philosophical meaning out of his concept of the wilderness, points out that the theme, however philosophically and artistically elaborated, remains indeed as authentically American as the greeting, "Howdy, stranger," which likewise emerged out of the American frontier experience.[3]

The wilderness for Bugbee is at once the world without and within perceived no longer as wasteland but as reality beheld contemplatively as "our true home";[4] as "the world of every day," experienced in faith.

Here the ambiguity is the metaphor of the desert terminologically eliminated by making *wasteland* the equivalent of *desert* in the primitive, negative sense while *wilderness* has come to bear the combined meaning of wilderness in the protective sense and also paradise. Yet even here the two terms are related as two phrases in the redemptive vision of the world; for to experience it first as wasteland is a prerequisite for enjoying it as "wilderness." Speaking of Jean Paul Sartre, Bugbee writes:

> He has laid bare the wasteland in which we find ourselves in so far as we lack good faith—faith, that is. And this can also be a step upon the threshold that opens out into the wilderness and is the reality of faith. It is to this theme of reality as a wilderness that I want to move.
>
> This, so far as I can tell, is the theme which unifies my own life. It enfolds and simplifies, comprehends and completes. Whenever I awaken, I awaken to it. It carries with it the gift of life. And it lives in the authenticity of every authentic gift, every true blessing confirms it deeper; it is always with me when I come to myself. Through it I find my vocation, for the wilderness is reality experienced as call and explained in responding to it absolutely.[5]

Bugbee's frequent citation of Eckhart and specifically of his "still desert" *(wueste)*[6] and the frequent illusion to early American exponents of the idea of the wilderness, like Henry Thoreau and Herman Melville, make especially significant, within the context of the present survey, Bugbee's extraordinary definition of philosophy itself as "learning to leave things be: restoration in the wilderness here and now." By this he means not inaction but "being still in the presence of things, letting them speak."[7] Thus he can speak of his boyhood experience of "the gladness of being in the swamp" as "the immanence of the wilderness there,"[8] of a wartime "Christmas in the wilderness of the sea,"[9] of the world as "a holy place, a universe of things ['existing in their own right'], a wilderness."[10] Here it is through the aesthetic discipline of solitude in the wilderness rather than through the ethical discipline of the wilderness that paradisic understanding is restored: "Things exist in their own right; it is a lesson that escapes us except as they hold us in awe. Except we stand on the threshold of the wilderness, knowingly, how can our position be true, how can essential truth be enacted in our hearts?"[11]

Bugbee's description of the wilderness is both a testimony and a helpful analysis. The wilderness must first be experienced as wasteland to be known as paradise. Moreover, in the fullness of human history, precisely the literal designation of the word is acquiring an unexpected religious significance.

Man, according to the biblical myth, was primordially set in a garden at harmony with the multitudes of God's other creatures. Even after the Fall, man in the cataclysm of divine wrath was charged with the care not only of the domestic beasts of immediate utility to him but also of all creatures, "of clean animals, and of animals that are not clean, and of birds, and of everything that creeps on the ground" in order "to keep their kind alive upon the face of all the earth." Truly the stewardship of Adam for all creatures in the Park of the Great King and the redemptive assignment laid upon Noah before the Deluge is literally in man's keeping today.

Ours is the age of the bulldozer as much as it is the age of the atomic bomb. For good or ill, we need no longer conform to the contours of the earth. The only wilderness that will be left is what we determine shall remain untouched and that other wilderness in the heart of man that only God can touch.

For the first time in the long history of the redemptive meaning of the wilderness, it is in our age that the forest, the jungle, the plain, the unencumbered shore, the desert, the mountain fastness, each within its myriad denizens fashioned by the hand of the Creator in their natural haunts, are becoming, surely more than he now knows, necessary for the completeness of man himself, the only creature fashioned in the image and likeness of God. Man would be less than man without his fellow creatures in all their variety and divine immediacy. Man needs now some companion in the garden bigger and freer than himself.[12] Without prejudice to the ecclesiastical meanings of the wilderness traced in the foregoing essay, we know with St. Paul that the whole creation has been in travail together with us until now. Only amidst the circumambient wilderness of tundra with its musk oxen, of the sea with its whales, the mountain fastness with its condor and its puma, the jungle with its tiger, the woods with its warblers and crows, the veldt or prairie with its gnu and its bison, can man tend the garden in which through discipline and the grace of the arts and the sciences and his faith he maintains his hold upon that life that God created and called good.

Unless some believers in every generation can, through that poverty by which we divest ourselves of all lordliness, join St. Francis in his canticle addressed to the sun and to the bears as brethren, to the snow and to the swallows as sisters, then in the present stage of mankind's awesome capacity for enforcing lordship over nature—whether in ruthless urbanization of the countryside, or in exploitation of natural resources heedless of generations to come, or in any careless experimentation in the realm of life, disease, and death—we shall presently find that we can no longer address even one another as brother and sister and that a utilitarian view of nature will have blasted our human nature. We shall find that the garden of culture, like the garden that is the Church, will wither or bewilder when it is by artifice fenced off from the ground of our creatureliness.

Wherever we live and work, we must have in our being or refresh within us the awareness of a real wilderness, which now we are called upon not only to contemplate periodically as did the desert Fathers but also to conserve for ourselves and our posterity as well as in the interest the myriad creaturely forms themselves.

Ultimately of course this outer wilderness, both as savage and as benign, as the mystics knew, is also within. It is our true creaturely estate, and gives substance to the hope that the image within us mirroring That which can alone assure us from beyond is indeed glimpsed and recognized only in the serenity of the primeval and the primordial solitude, which are one.

## Notes

This essay is taken from the author's *Wilderness and Paradise in Christian Thought* (New York: Harper & Row, 1962), with permission. See also the author's "Christian Attitudes toward Nature," *Christian Scholar's Review* 2, nos. 1–2 (1971): 3–35, 1012–26.

1. John M. Anderson, *The Individual and the New World* (State College, Pa.: Bald Eagle Press, 1955), preface.

2. Ibid., 164.

3. Walter S. Ong, S.J., "Personalism and the Wilderness," *Kenyon Review* 21 (1959), 297–304.

4. Henry Bugbee, *The Inward Morning: A Philosophical Exploration in Journal Form* (1958; reprint, with a new introduction by Edward F. Mooney, Athens: University of Georgia Press, 1999), 76.

5. Ibid., 128.

6. Ibid., 75, where Bugbee refers to Ernst Cassirer, *Language and Myth* (New York, 1946).

7. Ibid., 155, where besides referring to Oriental literature, he again cites Eckhart.

8. Ibid., 43.

9. Ibid., 71–72.

10. Ibid., 165.

11. Ibid., 164.

12. This, with special reference to the threatened elephants of Africa, is the theme of Romain Gary, *Les Racimes du Ciel* (Paris: Editions Gallimard, 1958).

# Zen Existentialism
## Bugbee's Japanese Influence

ANDREW FEENBERG

In 1958 Henry Bugbee published the only truly original work of existentialist philosophy written by an American. Titled *The Inward Morning,* Bugbee's book is a philosophical diary in the spirit of Gabriel Marcel. Like Marcel's *Metaphysical Journal,* Bugbee's diary follows the detours of his thought as he confronts the central issues of his philosophical life. And like Marcel, Bugbee is guided by a deep religious intuition, which he expresses in philosophical terms. But instead of Marcel's Christianity, it is the Zen Buddhism of D. T. Suzuki that illuminates Bugbee's path.[1]

In the early 1950s, when Bugbee was writing his journal, Suzuki was practically the only Japanese essayist or philosopher known in the West, so it is not surprising that it would be his work through which Bugbee gained access to Japanese thought. But the connection was more intimate. While Bugbee was a junior faculty member at Harvard, Suzuki made his first lecture tour in the United States, and while Suzuki was speaking at Harvard, it was Bugbee's task to ferry him from talks to dinners to rooming quarters. Later, when Suzuki was lecturing on Long Island, Bugbee would make the drive down from Cambridge on a regular basis to hear Suzuki's talks and pursue further conversations with him. The concept of experience Suzuki brought to Harvard and to Bugbee's attentive ears arose in Japan in the work of the great Japanese philosopher Kitaro Nishida (1870–1945), a lifetime friend and associate of Suzuki's.

Nishida's theory of "pure experience" (*junsui keiken*), presented in *An Inquiry into the Good,* marked the beginning of original philosophy in Japan. Like many of his contemporaries in the West, Nishida attempted to conceive immediate experience as an ontological absolute. It was this approach that enabled Suzuki to develop his modern reinterpretation of Zen and that was communicated to Bugbee through Suzuki's work.[2]

Nishida's theory of pure experience was derived from William James. In Nishida's version of radical empiricism, subject and object are not foundational categories but arise from reflection within an original unity. Prereflective consciousness comes to exemplify experience by contrast with thought. This concept of experience had a great influence on Suzuki, who popularized the identification of enlightened consciousness with a kind of immediacy prior to all reflection. Suzuki's influence, in turn, is explicitly present in Nishida's later theory of Japanese culture where he writes that "No-mind (*mushin*) can be considered the axis of the Oriental spirit (Suzuki Daisetz)."[3] Both Nishida and Suzuki considered Zen enlightenment as the mode of experience characteristic of Japan and as Japan's unique contribution to world culture.

Suzuki's writings were remarkable in the Buddhist tradition for clearly distinguishing between the potentially universal Zen experience and the historically specific doctrinal content of the Buddhist religion. As Kirita writes, "Suzuki was the first Zen Buddhist deliberately to distinguish between Zen experience and Zen thought." Having made this distinction, Suzuki went on to admit that the Zen experience could be articulated in a variety of different systems of thought, including Western philosophy.[4] Nishida's early philosophy of experience was in fact an attempt to provide a conceptual bridge between Western thought and Buddhist enlightenment—an association close to Bugbee's interest.

There were also strands in Bugbee's concept of experience from Thoreau, Emerson, and Dewey, and from W. E. Hocking, a senior Harvard professor who had been one of Husserl's first American students. Husserl, as is well known, registered his disappointment with both British empiricism and neo-Kantian rationalism in a phrase that stands for the spirit of a whole epoch in twentieth-century thought:

philosophy, he affirmed, must go "back to the things themselves," precisely the ambition of Bugbee's own approach.

These strands were further joined to ideas drawn from the work of Gabriel Marcel (himself, of course, influenced by Husserl's and Heidegger's phenomenology), resulting in a unique style of thought that Bugbee would come to call "experiential philosophy."

Following Gabriel Marcel most explicitly, and implicitly drawing on Suzuki, Thoreau, and others, Bugbee proposes an alternative interpretation of experience to that of the dominant empiricist philosophy of his time. As he puts it, "experience is not a subject-matter susceptible to objective representation and deliberate control." Instead, it is our "undergoing, our involvement in the world."[5] The fundamental relation to reality is active participation in a world to which we belong, rather than contemplation or technical manipulation. We exist primordially in community with others and with things rather than through knowledge and control of objects.

These ideas too lead us back to Suzuki, but before going further into these intriguing cross-cultural comparisons, it will help to distinguish four aspects of the often undifferentiated concept of experience. Isolating these will enable us to better define Henry Bugbee's concept of an experiential philosophy, a philosophy that "returns to things" in their resounding presence.

1. Experience as epistemological foundation: the empiricist idea of experience as the basis of knowledge versus dogma. This view is familiar in the West, where it is associated with the rise of science. Its detailed texture has been the center of much controversy in epistemology, a familiar controversy that we can well bypass here. What is significant for our argument is the link between this idea of experience and the promise of modernity to free human beings from slavery to dogma and unmastered nature. That promise had obvious appeal in Japan, where Suzuki struggled to make Buddhism compatible with the larger modernizing trends engulfing his society. Nishida went still further and argued that modernity would be incomplete without the contribution of Asian culture as philosophically articulated in his own system and represented historically by the Japanese nation.[6]

We will see that Bugbee too is sensitive to the demands of modernity, although unlike these Japanese thinkers he has no need to show that American culture is capable of meeting them. He starts out from the problem of how to appropriate modernity in a meaningful spirit. Like Nishida and Suzuki he rejects the positivistic and materialist worldview associated with scientific-technological modernity without rejecting modernity itself. "Not science, but scientism as the arrogation to science of philosophical ultimacy, is the anti-philosophy so troublingly insinuated into present-day thought."[7] Thus Bugbee is not haunted by nostalgia for the premodern past, nor does he dismiss democratic culture as merely conformist or utilitarian. He takes quite a different and deeply democratic line based on the idea of respect for others and for things, developed through concepts such as receptiveness, communion, vocation, and creativity.

2. Experience as life, *Erlebnis*: immediacy versus reflection. The empiricist concept of experience is not as concrete as it seems. What is counted as experience in this sense is only the shared and, indeed, the measurable content of perception, that is, data. Left out of account is the specifically "subjective" dimension of consciousness. Thus by contrast with the empiricist idea of experience, there has always been a romantic conception of experience as life, as *Erlebnis*. Not sensation as an object of thought but feeling comes to exemplify experience. These two concepts might be contrasted as experience known versus experience experienced. William James was the first to conceptualize this latter approach to experience as the "stream of consciousness." This idea of experience also became influential in Japanese thought as modernization increasingly alienated the individuals from themselves and their world. Bugbee's many stories of immediate contact with reality, say at the sight of a leaping fish or at the moment he looks into the eyes of a man just saved from drowning are examples of this sort of prereflective, immediate encounters with reality that he relates to Zen enlightenment.

3. Experience as *Bildung*: the progressive construction of personality or collective historical experience versus the cycles of nonhuman nature. Both the first and second concepts of experience have in common a momentary, disconnected character. The dialectical concept of experience as *Bildung* introduces temporality and connection. Here the contemplative viewpoint is left behind. As a practice engaging all

the faculties of the subject, experience is a process the subject undergoes rather than a sensation or datum it receives. Experience results neither in knowledge nor feeling but in the construction of the subject itself.

We find this idea of experience reflected in Bugbee's work in his confession that reviewing, meditatively and in journal form, his early experiences, forms part of a reassessment of his life and an essential element in his ongoing maturation as a reflective thinker immersed in the particular calling that is his own. We also find this concept implicit as he works through various texts from the Western and Eastern traditions. Clearly coming to grips with texts is more than a matter of interpretation, but contributes rather to the reader's depth of experience, depth, we might say, of soul. Or to use a different image, it is part of a person's finding a voice that is uniquely his or her own. As we will see, Bugbee extends this idea democratically to include every form of creative engagement with experience, not just that of the scholar.

4. Experience as ontological foundation: the phenomenological-existentialist idea of experience as the unsurpassable horizon of being, versus objectivity understood as a detached "view from nowhere." This fourth definition of experience is the most important for the interpretation of Bugbee, but also the most difficult and controversial. I want to approach his version of it indirectly through the thought of Nishida and Marcel, for whom it is a central theme.

By a remarkable coincidence, both Nishida and Marcel developed this theme as a response to neo-Kantianism during the period around World War I and left the record of their struggle with that doctrine in dense and exploratory works that read more or less like intellectual diaries. These are Nishida's *Intuition and Reflection in Self-Consciousness* (1913–17), and Marcel's *Metaphysical Journal* (1914–23), which inspired Bugbee's own philosophical diary.[8]

Marcel claims that "the central theme" of this early work is "the impossibility of thinking of being as object." He argued there that all objectivity presupposes a nonobjectifiable basis in what he calls an "absolute presence." This presence is accessible only from the standpoint of a philosophy that refuses "to treat all reality as being in the third person in relation to the kind of community that I form with myself."

But paradoxically, enlarging that community to recover concrete experience requires a detour through concepts so abstract they can hardly be described. Marcel writes that "we are not even left with the resource of saying that the universe is present to me myself because that would involve reintroducing a duality, a distinction between subject and object within what by very principle can involve no such distinction. It is doubtless by an evocation of the pure act of feeling [*sentir*] understood as an interior resonance that we will be best assisted . . . 'mentally to imitate' this presence which 'subtends' the 'integrality' of our experience."[9] Abandoning the attempt directly to articulate the ground of experience, Marcel went on to develop his method of "secondary reflection" for exploring the concrete texture of our lives from within.

Although Nishida's philosophical approach at this time was quite different from Marcel's, and led to a new form of systematic philosophy rather than existentialism, something similar emerged from his reflections on the limits of neo-Kantianism. Nishida sought an ultimate subjectivity that could not become an object because all objects appeared before it. We can infer the existence of this founding subjectivity from the fact that the first-person position of thought is ultimately unsurpassable and yet constitutive of objectivity: "If knower and known are represented as separate realities . . . the individual thus objectified cannot be the real subject, for as the constructive unifying activity of consciousness, this cannot be made an object of reflection."[10] Beyond the subject-object split lies an act that posits them and that is not itself a possible object.

It is out of this background that Nishida later developed his theory of "place" (*basho*), which aims to restore the philosophical significance of the world in its concreteness as against all cognitive mediations. His concept of the place of nothingness (*mu no basho*) refers to the ultimate locus of experience, the nonobjectifiable background against which it appears. This concept resonates with Bugbee's notion of being as "standing forth" from nothingness, the silence that supports sound. And both Nishida and Bugbee appear to have much in common with the Heideggerian idea of truth appearing, not so much to a subject, but "in the light," or "in the clearing," truth (or reality) "showing up" in the radiant contours of the place. As Nishida put it, this is the "daytime" perspective "in which truth is things just as they are, as opposed to the colorless and soundless perspective of night found in the natural sciences."[11]

Bugbee's concept of an experiential philosophy can now be sketched against the background of our fourfold differentiation of the concept of experience, and our discussion of its relevance to the thought of Marcel, Nishida, and Suzuki. Bugbee's "experiential philosophy" is a version of the fourth, foundational, concept of experience discussed above. But Bugbee, like Suzuki, develops his thought in terms of the second concept of prereflective experience. What he finds precious in the Zen tradition, as Suzuki explains it, is the notion of immediate unity of acting subject and world. This Bugbee calls "immersion" or "absorption." He finds in it a kind of preestablished harmony of the individual as actor and the world of humans and things in which action takes place, a harmony revealed in the moment of decision. The real, he thus affirms, is eminently given only to the person capable of attending to it absolutely and engaging with its intrinsic finality. At several important junctures, Bugbee relates this insight to Suzuki's concepts of "no-mind" and "nothingness."[12]

Bugbee's emphasis on action contains an implicit protest against the alienated reflectivity exemplified by objectivism, scientism, and the worship of technique in the modern world, unfortunate tendencies that he finds in his own pragmatic tradition. In his paradoxical attempt to reflectively overcome this alienation, Bugbee demands that philosophy become "a distillate experience of our condition as active beings."[13] The idea of immersion appears as a privileged existential experience, comparable to anxiety in Heidegger, for example, which reveals a deeper ontological unity underlying the opposition of subject and object. Bugbee relates this notion to pragmatic instrumentalism. While he does not identify pragmatism with American culture so thoroughly as Nishida identifies Zen with Japanese culture, the parallel is obvious. Pragmatism at least attempted to articulate the American national experience of the privilege of action over abstract thought. And like Nishida appropriating Zen through Western philosophy for an alternative modernity, Bugbee wants to appropriate pragmatism's discovery of the centrality of action through Zen.

But is Zen adequate to the task? The problem is Suzuki's emphasis on immediacy, which belongs to the second concept of experience sketched above. There is a certain tension between this concept, spontaneous lived experience, and the fourth concept of experience as the foundation of the subject-object split. In the Western context (2), immediate experience is a protest against the reification of bourgeois culture and daily life and it harbors a strong subjectivistic tinge, while (4) the transpersonal ontological basis of "reality" strives to get beyond the opposition of subjectivism and objectivism altogether in response to philosophical difficulties in nineteenth-century neo-Kantianism and naturalism. In this context, we must take care to separate conceptually in Bugbee's narrative those flashing momentary experiences when "reality strikes," as in a kind epiphany or enlightenment, from the more reflective, "after-the-fact" proposals of a deep ground from which subject and object have not yet separated and to which we might, in some sense, have theoretical access.

There is some historical connection between these two ways of understanding experience (2 and 4), but there are major conceptual differences, as well. Lived experience as a momentary realization is an elusive ideal of unsullied immediacy that stands opposed to the excess of modern reflectiveness and calculation. But experience as ontological foundation is the always already present ground even of reflection itself. Russell called this latter nonpsychological version of pure experience a "neutral monism." As such, it is a theory about the commonality of being underlying the distinction between subject and object—not a description of an event in the mind suspending that distinction.

In the end, it seems to me, Bugbee cannot quite accept the opposition between experience and reflection implied in Suzuki's view. "I cannot follow Zen, however, in the tendency to regard reflection merely as a kind of preparation through disillusionment for the non-reflective advent of essential truth."[14] He hopes to find a saving accommodation to modernity, with its emphasis on personal identity and agency, rather than a spiritual alternative to it. Thus increasingly as his diary proceeds he emphasizes the possibility of a reflective mode of active involvement, which he identifies with the concept of vocation. An old synonym for this word is "calling," the response to the call of a craft or trade. Here we are in the realm of *Bildung,* the self-creation of the subject through activity in the world of meaning. Bugbee finds in the generalized interplay of such call and response another way of signifying the "standing forth" of persons and things against the ground of "nothingness."

In one of the last entries (October 23), Bugbee argues for a corresponding reconstruction of the concept of agency in terms of the vocational relation of creator and created. Although we take it for granted that the agent is in charge of its activities, Bugbee argues that the locus of control is blurred as soon as an element of creativity enters in. "Is it not more accurate to say that we participate in creation than that we create? Is not creation as it touches us in what we do an interlocking of the resources with which we act, an interlocking of them with that which firms and claims them as a province assimilated to incarnation? To participate in creation is to be relieved of undue emphasis or accent placed upon ourselves."[15]

On these grounds Bugbee dismisses an account of creativity in terms of production. The productionist model of action breaks the subtler links between agent and object that are involved in true creation. But Bugbee goes on to argue that the rejection of productionism is not a rejection of production proper. To the extent that productive activity has elements of creativity, "[t]he stress on the agent as ultimate is lifted, and agency must now be conceived as meta-problematic, meta-technical, meta-artifactual, even though it may also be conceived as involving the solution of problems, technique, and artifacture."[16]

Curiously, at the very moment when Bugbee distinguishes his approach from Suzuki's, he comes closer than ever to Nishida, whose writings of course he could not know. Nishida too felt the inadequacy of a merely inward response to modernity. Like Bugbee, he attempted instead to separate the modern orientation toward action in the world from what he considered Western subjectivism and voluntarism. And like Bugbee, he found a solution in creation, through which the split between subject and object is transcended. "It is not in affirming the self that we become creators but in thinking and acting by becoming the thing. Our true self is an intrinsically perfect expression of the world."[17]

Perhaps it is time to follow the path that leads through creativity "to the things themselves." Perhaps here we can find a modern value that points beyond the crisis of Western culture toward a reconciliation of human beings with each other and with nature.

## Notes

Portions of this chapter will be included in *Philosophy East and West* 49:1 (1999): 28–44.

I thank Edward F. Mooney for his contribution to this chapter.

1. Henry Bugbee, *The Inward Morning: A Philosophical Exploration in Journal Form* (1958; reprint, with a new introduction by Edward F. Mooney, Athens: University of Georgia Press, 1999); Gabriel Marcel, *Metaphysical Journal* (Chicago: Henry Regnery 1952).

2. Kitaro Nishida, *An Inquiry into the Good*, trans. Masao Abe and Christopher Ives (New Haven: Yale University Press, 1990). For a more detailed presentation of the author's views on Nishida, see Andrew Feenberg, *Alternative Modernity: The Technical Turn in Philosophy and Social Theory* (Los Angeles: University of California Press, 1995), chap. 8, and Andrew Feenberg and Yoko Arisaka, "Experiential Ontology: The Origins of the Nishida Philosophy in the Doctrine of Pure Experience," *International Philosophical Quarterly* 30, no. 2 (1990).

The priority of Nishida's theory of experience is claimed by Robert Scharf, "The Zen of Japanese Nationalism," in *History of Religions*, vol. 33, no. 1 (1993). Certainly there was much mutual influence in the relation of Nishida to Suzuki. Cf. Thomas Kirschner, "Modernity and Rinzai Zen: Doctrinal Change or Continuity?" *Zen Buddhism Today*, no. 13 (1996) for a critique of Sharf.

3. William James, *Essays in Radical Empiricism and A Pluralistic Universe* (New York: Longman's, Green), 1943; Kitaro Nishida, *La Culture Japonaise en Question* (Paris: Publications Orientalistes de France, 1991), 72.

4. Kiyohide Kirita, "D. T. Suzuki on Society and the State," in *Rude Awakenings*, ed. J. Heisig and J. Maraldo (Honolulu: University of Hawaii Press, 1994), 67.

Daisetz Suzuki, *The Zen Doctrine of No-Mind* (New York: Samuel Weiser, 1973), 45. See also Suzuki, *Zen in Japanese Culture* (Princeton: Princeton University Press, 1959).

5. Bugbee, 58, 41.

6. For a thorough discussion of Nishida's nationalism, see Yoko Arisaka, "The Nishida Enigma," *Monumenta Nipponica* 51, no. 1 (1996).

7. Bugbee, 169.

8. Kitaro Nishida, *Intuition and Reflection in Self-Consciousness,* trans. V. Viglielmo, T. Yoshinori, J. O'Leary (Albany: State University of New York Press, 1987), and Marcel, *Metaphysical Journal.*

9. Marcel, *Metaphysical Journal,* viii, 264, 331.

10. Nishida, *Intuition and Reflection in Self-Consciousness,* 70. See also Nishida, "The Problem of Japanese Culture," in *Sources of the Japanese Tradition,* vol. 2, ed. and trans. W. T. de Bary (New York: Columbia University Press, 1958).

11. Nishida, *An Inquiry into the Good,* xxxiii.

12. Bugbee, 86–87.

13. Ibid., 201.

14. Ibid.

15. Ibid., 222.

16. Ibid., 223.

17. Nishida, *La Culture Japonaise en Question,* 102–3.

# The Inward Wild

DAVID STRONG

Reading *The Inward Morning,* like entering a grove of redwood trees, makes one want to say: Here is something great. Here is something understood by someone as well as it can be understood. It is the kind of work that Heidegger in "Poetically Man Dwells" calls an "authentic gauging of the dimension of dwelling."[1] I approach this work with gratitude, thankful for its disclosure of reality.

I hear Bugbee describe his work as

> truly peripatetic, engendered not merely while walking, but through walking that was essentially a meditation of the place. And the balance in which I weighed the ideas I was studying was always that established in the experience of walking in the place. I weighed everything by the measure of the silent presence of things, clarified in the racing clouds, clarified by the cry of hawks, solidified in the presence of rocks, spelled syllable by syllable by waters of manifold voice.[2]

Thus the redwoods themselves instruct us and awaken us. True, "one may be struck clean . . . by the massive presence of rock" or tree. Just so, "there are things that we may read, such as we have from Kant or Spinoza . . . which may call upon and summon him to reawakening. He remembers, and is himself again, moving cleanly on his way. Some measure of simplicity again informs the steps he takes; he becomes content to be himself, and finds fragrance in the air . . . things invite him to adequate himself to their infinity."[3]

And so I would add to the texts of Spinoza and Kant *The Inward Morning* itself because, often enough, as I study this text, I find I am struck clean by it.

## 1. Basic Mind

Let me begin with the idea of the inward wild. Whatever else I may mean by this wild, I do not mean Freud's discovery of the unconscious, characterized as containing uncontrollable forces, wild things or wild times. Nor do I think the inward wild should be associated with the chaos of a wild party. What I mean by the inward wild comes closer to especially harmonious times.

As we can see from its title, *The Inward Morning* is mostly about a dawn that occurs from within. It concerns the basic attitude and standpoint from which we act in our situation and from which we approach things, an attitude to which we are recalled by certain texts and by the things of the natural world itself. It is this standpoint that trues our perception, trues our actions, trues our words and our reflections. I'll call this basic frame of mind the inward wild. How does this inward wild come to be established in us? It seems neither innate nor something one can count on with just any human being. It comes to be created or generated in us through our "involvement" with things, and may fail to arise through absence of involvement with things.

There would be no discussion of being recalled to a basic attitude if it were not possible to stray from it and so to stray from ourselves. Henry Bugbee calls this the ephemerality of our condition. Even in the course of one day or an hour, we may be, at one moment, firmly within this basic standpoint, and the next moment, we may be left like stranded sea creatures on the beach, gasping for the element within which we can swim. False detachment can "dislocate" us from our more basic mind and standpoint. By contrasting "good days" with "bad days" we can understand the notion, central to *The Inward Morning*, that things and events need to be completed from within, from our "inward wild."

On "bad" days—days when we are not in touch with ourselves, when our lives seem to be detached from both our actual circumstances and our basic mind—we can find ourselves anxious to manipulate and to possess, and to squash any challenges to our stance, insistent and imperious in our actions, argumentative or grasping in our thinking. Discontent with myself as myself, I seek to aggrandize myself and to support that aggrandizement before myself and others, and seek to defend "my idol," as Gabriel Marcel puts it, against all threats and all time. This is the attitude from which we approach our situation as ripe for manipulation and control. "We take everything that may be said of our condition as instruction on how to go about dealing with it, alert to cues for success."[4]

We forget about our finitude. What is another adventure to the young Odysseus? He has all the time in the world. What is another hour before the television? We live as though we will live forever and that these things will always be there for us; and us, for them. We fantasize about what we do not have, thinking that we have many lives and that there is always another place, another day, another time, another person, another life, another planet. We forget real place and our utter containment in this place. We see but we do not see, hear but do not hear, feel but do not feel. We touch but are not touched, and think but do not think. We are strangers to the intimacy of this place.

"Good" days are not necessarily days of elation. They are times where we welcome and are welcomed into the presence of things, whether these be the presence of things past, as in involuntary recall and what Bugbee calls "philosophic contemplation" of them, or whether these be the presence of things present, as in true perception of them or what Bugbee calls "aesthetic contemplation." On these "good" days, we are content to be who we are and we are moved by the mystery of each and all things.

In many ways *The Inward Morning* is fundamentally about appreciation, and our failure to appreciate: This moment, this place, these people, these things, that event, or that contribution. We need to remember to appreciate existence, things as existing, and ourselves as bound up in a sacrament of coexistence with them. As we become thankful, warm, welcoming, and thirsty, so we become appreciators of existence and accommodate the gift of the world in our experience of things. "That ours is a holy place has ever seemed to me true when I have been most awake, and I take it as a mark of awakening whenever it dawns upon me again as true. But much of the time I cannot remember that it is true, and I cannot understand what such a saying might mean, if it were it occur to me to dwell on it at all."[5] We stray from the experience of this "holy place" and may never come back to it. And even if we are sensitized to the fluctuations of the ephemerality of our condition, at times, it can seem as though there is no relief from this estranged condition. We stand in need of an awakening, of an inward morning.

What is the emplaced thinking of aesthetic contemplation? How to think about weighing things in their importance? To be able to step back, not as an observer, to firmer ground. From the cliff tops of the Pryor Mountains one looks out over the distant Bighorn canyon and basin of Montana and Wyoming and sees the more than human, the before human, and the after human. No houses, farm fields, roads, or signs of humans are visible. The sun is desert bright, and the air, unblemished by smoke or moisture, is clear enough to see the details of mountains and benches more than a hundred miles away. In this distance, everything seems still. Everything seems still—and stilled. Here is what does not change, what lasts forever, what cannot play us false. The emergence of stilled things, the things that stay still in our lives, the things that stay with us, have blessed us, bless us, and continue to bless us. Every great play ends with a view, as it were, from the mountains.

"Might not the sound of a stream of running water, too, call a man to his senses and out of the intricacies of a 'wisdom'? . . . I think of the instruction of walking on a beach; a long walk on a stormy day." In the presence of rock and wave we are restored to the sense of reality as wilderness. We remember and live again a life that is continuous with the inward wild. Bugbee recalls the resounding peals of a bell that seemed to echo through him, cleansing him of all that was unsteady, stilling what was unsettled, silencing what was mere noise, dissolving what was discord, resolving what was tangled, firming what before could not be decided.[6] In the presence of the bell is the presence of bedrock, the presence of essential truth.

## 2. Ecstasis

Of his doctoral dissertation, Bugbee writes, "But it seems to me that I left man out of account, and in so doing, falling short of a philosophy of action, I entirely failed to connect the meaning of existence which I was trying to bespeak with the experience of acting, of commitment, of standing forth as a man, as one who is made to stand forth (I use the term 'ecstasis' for this being made to stand forth)." And hence, from beginning to end, from the first story about swamping to the last story about Taxco, Mexico, we see the importance of ecstasis. Things, existents stand forth. But they do not stand forth except as we ourselves stand forth with them, both independently and in union with them. "At its heart existence and decision interlock. One is himself the leaping trout." In ecstasis, "the importance of things becomes unmistakably clear."[7] The sketches about swamping and Taxco define ecstasis.

In "Swamping," it is perhaps early March: chilly and windy but there is no snow or skating. The days are gray and rainy. It seems a senseless place and time of year, and swamping seems a senseless activity. Yet, we find "there was something about the water in the swamps that made it impossible to stay out." It couldn't be otherwise. Perhaps the shivering cold was not particularly pleasant, "but there was no mistake about the gladness of being in the swamp or the immanence of the wilderness there." Through immersion in this senselessness, we discover that what seems like austerity is really wealth: This is a kind of American Zen enlightenment or satori story. What seems ridiculous makes ultimate sense. We are awakened to the delight of existence, not through the all-too-tame experience of the indoor gym, but through the experience of the depth of things. The boys are animated by the waters to discover the paradoxical depths to real things—the wilderness of things. They come forth enlightened by immersing themselves, even as the reality of the swamps comes forth. This illuminative event of co-emergence of togetherness and distinctness is ecstasis.[8]

"Swamping" is the first story in *The Inward Morning*. The last story is about Taxco, Mexico. The first discloses love of nature; the last, love of city; both disclose love of place. Taxco is filled with noise: chaotic bells, fireworks, barking dogs, squealing pigs, braying donkeys, loud speakers blaring. "What made it all supportable, I came to ask myself?" Bugbee awakens to hear the single note of a high-pitched bell in the middle of the night. "Then I knew how I had come to love the place, and understood the bells in full peal: The alembic through which even Taxco's noise is supervened upon and assimilated to sound. Even fireworks seemed natural there." One enters these places bodily, listeningly, seeingly, and patiently. One completes this presence from within, rather a completion that must be evoked by the places themselves and not a matter of will.[9]

Ecstasis, necessity, and evocation are worked out together in *The Inward Morning*. We come forth as we discover what we must do and how we must respond. The claims of necessity here can be those we feel when confronted by the exigencies of nature, swimming for shore or refueling a small ship from a tanker amidst a storm on the open sea. Or more gently, these claims can be felt as the way things evoke determination in us. In "Swamping," "it seemed as if there were no way of not getting into the swamp." Nature seizes us in attractive and unattractive ways.

### 3. Immersion

Bugbee is concerned to show that illumination requires immersion, but another kind of immersion takes place here as well. As the boys become immersed in the swamp, the swamp becomes immersed in them. It moves inward. The wild moves inward. What is the significance of this inward movement?

Within the Zen tradition, D. T. Suzuki writes, "When you see a flower . . . not only must you see it but the flower must see you also. . . . When this seeing is mutual there is real seeing." Here an identification takes place between the seer and the seen as the internal dialogue of self-consciousness disappears. Suzuki comes closest to *The Inward Morning* when he comments on a Haiku poem. He points out that the poet was entranced by a morning glory utterly forgetting herself and her mission to get water. "She was, in fact, carried away by it; she was the flower and the flower was she." The morning glory, entwined with the handle, seized her water bucket away, as it were, and she had to go to neighbors for water. Such an event seems close, indeed, to the theme of necessity and ecstasis.[10]

*The Inward Morning* emphasizes more our bodily existence and our bones than our consciousness. It focuses more on immersion than perception, as in Zen, so that in *The Inward Morning* it is more a matter of coimmersion than a matter of identification of seer and seen. As we step into the wilderness, it steps into us; as we walk into wilderness, it walks into us; as we climb the mountain, it climbs into us.

Often the wild immerses itself in us, moves inward, in a kind of lyrical moment: The one faint bell tossed off in the night, the one leaf upon the water, John Schultz muttering, "you was rowing," the song on Christmas day, the wheelhouse in the storm, the minesweeper and the tanker alongside one another, the man crawling ashore, the bird's song, and of course, the leaping trout. These "individuals," perceived distinctly, flare with meaning and uniqueness. They collect and reflect, gather and radiate. In these lyrical moments, the wild draws near in love and respect. "Then I knew I had come to love the place." Writing of a steelhead trout, "If one eventually lands it, and kneels beside its silvery form at the water's edge, on the fringe of the gravel bar, if one receives this fish as purely as the river flows, everything is momently given, and the very trees become eloquent where they stand."[11]

The wild moves inward and, it seems to me, slips into our bones, resides there, and we become bone bright by virtue of it. The geese passing overhead call out to these inward geese; commotion in the outward wild sets into motion the creatures of the inward. Our human life is stretched out between these two wilds, and so too is the agreeableness or disagreeableness, music or noise, of our hours, days, and lives. As these things and events invade us from without, they are formative of our basic frame of mind, which I spoke of as the inward wild. As they get into us, they give us what we come to know in our bones. Thus, involuntary recall, "the incursion into the present moment of remembered situations," may provide us with our "bearings and stance as a human being."[12] Such recall can present a firm challenge to mere speculative thought and to a life lived otherwise, to thought and to life dislocated from the inward wild.

## 4. Saying

What we before called illuminative events can now be thought of as embracing events. The things and places embrace us as they become immersed in us. In contrast to the estrangement we feel from things on "bad" days, we here experience an intimacy with things and places. How do we give these lyrical moments a say? On the one hand, we give them a say when we listen to what these evoked memories are trying to tell us. They may fly up as a protest in us. On the other hand, we give these events a say when we present them in stories that remain true to the force of the informing experience. The real challenge is to find a language that does not merely describe the properties of things and reduce them to objects nor merely account for our feelings and reduce the event to a psychological account, but steps beyond objective and subjective and evokes a sense of the embracing event itself.

We cannot write with adequate force about embracing events without using a kind of anthropomorphic language. Things are warm, sensual, intimate; they draw near, into friendly relations with us, embrace us. So we need languages that personalize our relations with things. Maybe it should be called not an anthropomorphic language—that's too vague and too easily misunderstood—but more specifically, a philomorphic language. *Philo* means friend or lover as Plato points out. With a language of friendship, we speak of this intimacy with the wild. On the other hand, since this is a coimmersion and correlational coexistence, it works in the opposite direction as well. We can describe the particularly intimate moments with other people in terms drawn from our encounters with the natural world, its places and things.

Such philomorphic language differs from the objective language of science because that detached language is not evocative of embracing events. We may, to varying degrees, learn from it to understand and appreciate nature apart from the human presence, but one senses that hearing finality in the song of a Swainson's Thrush at dusk is also a part of the natural world and, in some sense, a fact of experience. Things as presences are not things as objects in their altogether otherness, as if discoverable in the absence of our full and fully engaged (evoked) human capacities for realizing reality. The price we pay for limiting ourselves to a scientific account is thus impoverishment.

However, it differs, too, from the much-criticized anthropocentrism and anthropomorphic languages of theology and industry. For instance, in the 1950s the Army Corp of Engineers ran an advertisement to win support for damming the Snake River. The ad ran, "The Snake Wants to Work!" Here, with this petty homocentric stance, things speak to us in a way that challenges us to bring them under control and utilize them. In this mode they are not respected as independent but are eyed only as mere means and subordinated to our ends.

In *The Inward Morning*'s account of ecstasis, humans and natural things coemerge in both union (the sense of intimacy) and independence. To find things as independent in this sense is to find final meaning in them as presences. We do not need to look beyond things to find sufficient meaning in them to still our concern. Things themselves, realized in embracing events, answer what is otherwise endless questioning in the middle of the night. *The Inward Morning* is significantly informative about our world. It is not a traditional philosophical work in being concerned about the preconditions of the truth of the world, leaving the informative truth of the world to science. Nor does it inform us about the world the way science does. *The Inward Morning* reaches the world in the way the world reaches us in our involvement with it. It lights up both the inward and outward wild.

The philomorphic language of *The Inward Morning* does not inform us by presenting an idealized world. It is, in a Zen manner of speaking, a finger pointing at the moon, for the finger could be mistaken for the moon if one failed to see it as pointing and simply stared at it. Nevertheless, the finger as a pointing finger can be orienting. The moon to which *The Inward Morning* points is the unknown and unknowable reality as wilderness. It points to unforeseeable gifts of things discovered in their depths: the wilderness of things, a wilderness that we can get into and that, simultaneously, can get at us and sink into us.

It also leaves us yearning, for we cannot substitute the stories for the wilderness nor the reflections for the experience. But these reflections can help show us our waking moments, such as we see with the young man who nearly drowns in the Trinity River, and alert and open us to such moments.[13] Unlike that same man who seems to set aside his bewildering experience, the journal helps us to make something of these events, let them have a say, for our lives and our thinking, and finally our culture.

## 5. In Light of Wilder Measures

*The Inward Morning* profoundly challenges traditional and contemporary philosophy, and by implication it challenges our culture. The special character of these challenges can be discerned by turning to Heidegger's essay "Poetically Man Dwells." Heidegger there distinguishes between poetic dwelling and unpoetic dwelling, finding that the age of technology is altogether unpoetic in its dwelling. For all its "curious excess of frantic measuring and calculating" it is unable to take the measure of the full dimension of human existence. Our time is full of merit, to be sure. Never before have humans achieved so much building on Earth as they have since the Industrial Revolution. We earn our rewards on the basis of our ambition, strength, skill, and knowledge. "Merits due to this building, however, can never fill out the nature of dwelling. On the contrary, they even deny dwelling its own nature when they are pursued and acquired purely for their own sake. For in that case these merits, precisely by their abundance, would everywhere constrain dwelling within the bounds of this kind of building."[14] As long as human existence is confined to such a realm, it remains unpoetic. Analogously, it would be as though we lived our entire existence in terms of a game without realizing the larger setting within which the game appears as a game and our activity appears as play. In a game, we know when we are winning or losing; what it means to be a success; what the rules and boundaries are; who our opponents are; what it takes in terms of endurance, skill, and expertise to win; and what prizes and acclaim to expect. But to think that that is all there is to life is shallow and superficial. We have done so much building that we fail to go outdoors and divest ourselves of our too-limited conception of existence. The merit-game has become totalized.

In contrast Heidegger maintains that basic human dwelling is poetic. "For dwelling can be unpoetic only because it is in essence poetic. For a man to be blind, he must remain a being by nature endowed with sight. A piece of wood can never go blind."[15] Because we do not look out of the confines of this unpoetic realm, we may conclude that this realm is inclusive of all there is; and hence we are blind to our condition and to what lies beyond it as the broader setting of human existence. Were life confined to this blindness, it would be unpoetic indeed. But Heidegger writes that there is something more and something other to be seen than this meritorious unpoetic life. Authentic poetry opens our eyes to it and to the dawning awareness in us that we were blind before. Poetic dwelling comes to pass when our eyes are opened by poetry in this way to the full dimension of mortal dwelling. It provides us with the measure by which we see what is what. Such a measure and insight would then provide a basis for challenges to ways of doing philosophy and living our lives, which remain out of touch with and uninformed by this sense of being—this is a point upon which *The Inward Morning* is especially keen.

*The Inward Morning* is self-contained in a way that Heidegger's essay is not. Whereas Heidegger relies on Hölderlin for poetry, *The Inward Morning* often relies on its own poetic prose sketches. The philosophical reflections (what Heidegger calls thinking) are grounded upon and enveloped by these sketches. If they are authentic poetry, in Heidegger's sense, we ought to have our eyes opened by them to measures that span the dimension of poetic dwelling.

Remeasuring our measures is the explicit theme of the sketch "Rowing." Conventionally considered, we measure something when we take a known and lay it alongside an unknown. If rowing is a skill, there is a clear measure of when you have it and when you don't. There is a clear standard of achievement, a ladder, between team members and between teams. Coaches could make the young men feel these measures. But like poetic dwelling, "rowing turned out to be something else again, something more and something other than anyone pointed to or made prominent."[16]

Bugbee is awakened to this unnoticed dimension of rowing by John Schultz, one of the rowing coaches. He learns, within the wilderness of things, that winning and losing and even being in the race may not matter as much as the initial all-too-tame standards would suggest. "You was there," Schultz tells him parabolically. Schultz gets him to see that the demands of rowing, even in practice, are what must be engaged first and foremost. "It was as if rowing had a ground-bass meaning for him . . . and seemed to demand relevance from the oarsman in each and every stroke." There were young men, one gathers, who hardened themselves against this coach and his teachings, but in Heidegger's terms, "kindness" stays with Bugbee's heart toward John Schultz. And so, on rare occasions, "those six miles would round out into an incorruptible song, and you would be realizing its finality as you flew under the bridge and came up abeam of the float." At such moments, Bugbee, I believe, could answer affirmatively Hölderlin's question in Heidegger's essay: "May, if life is sheer toil, a man lift up his eyes and say: so I wish it to be? Yes."[17] At such moments, too, the idea that one "merits this success" is given the lie as one finds oneself overtaken by powers beyond what one could will.

One carries away from these events other measures by which to define and judge rowing or any other human activity. In light of an awakened understanding of the full dimension of human existence built up through the various sketches, a firm challenge is made to other philosophies. For example, although Bugbee does not address his philosophy, John Rawls has made the concept of a "life plan" fundamental for his social and political theory, and I too find this concept helpful. Yet there are limitations to it that need to be acknowledged as well, for without that recognition, we will overlook the full dimension, especially the dialogical character, of human existence. Too much emphasis on planning can make us deaf to listening. In the sketch "Building a Dam" for instance, the adults are the ones with plans for their lives, plans that make the boys' quiet determination look silly. The boys never really had a plan—what began in idle play became work in earnest without losing its inspirational and spontaneous character. Yet the boys do build a dam with a pool as in a cupped hand beneath the flaming maple, and receive an affirmation of their building: the beauty that sings out when one flaming leaf touches the pool. The boys innocently built a thing that makes them at home in the world and allows them to dwell.[18] The sketch (a poetic "building") and the later reflections think through the relationship between building and dwelling—this sketch may be seen as a kind of microcosm of human existence lived well. If the notion of a life plan isn't going to be lopsided, it must acknowledge the way these plans are derived from a deeper and more alive basis where the world and its things appeal to us and challenge us, as in this story. If we are not to detach ourselves from this call of the world, as is easy to do, then we need to listen continuously to the ways the world and things call us, drawing our nourishment from this dialogue. Otherwise we may approach life without sufficient feeling and in a merely cerebral way, as with the adults in the story, deaf and dead to any other, more poetic way of dwelling. As we think, build, and dwell with *The Inward Morning*, we become sensitized to what we ourselves and others are blind and deaf to much of the time, and we weigh the shortcomings of these ideas in light of these wilder measures.

More generally, Bugbee writes of the three sketches from his youth that they have helped "clarify for me the possibility of commitment in depth which cannot be interpreted in terms of goal-oriented endeavor, nor in terms of acquisition or achievement, nor in terms of the fulfillment of explicit moral standard, nor in terms of the realization or satisfaction of the ego."[19] A philosophy that takes such terms to be fundamental is blind to the full span of the dimension of human dwelling. Such a constricted philosophy is analogous to the young men in their first year of rowing. They are insensitive to how human life hangs together more fundamentally by something more and something other. Without insight into the full dimension, into poetic dwelling or into a sense of reality (as the full text discloses it) the condition for the possibility is missing for much of what such a philosophy claims. So it is from this dimension-informed standpoint that Bugbee critiques aspects of Plato, Aristotle, the Stoics, Descartes, Spinoza, Hume, Kant, Kierkegaard, Mill, James, Dewey, Sartre, Russell, C. I. Lewis, Walter Stace, Niebuhr, and Arthur Miller as well as Zen, mysticism, science, and a host of others. In one way or another they remain deaf to poetic dwelling and take their bearings from unpoetic dwelling. The disclosure of how things evoke determination in us, the theme of necessity, underlies, for instance, his critiques of necessity, certainty, and resoluteness in Sartre, Dewey, the Stoics, and Kant, none of whom have accommodated this sense, except in suppressed ways, into their philosophy.

In general, for Bugbee, when philosophy becomes too speculative it is liable to stray far from the deliverances of experiences that guide its more profound searches and findings.[20] Now we need to turn to a critique of the technological society. Perhaps just as *The Inward*

*Morning* critiques shortcomings of other philosophers in terms of insights derived from enlightening intimacies with things, we can critique technology's shortcomings in this light too. Just as the neophyte rowers have no idea, really, of what rowing is, so too, our technological society madly pursues its products with little reflective understanding of the deeper and more real good of the felt intimacies it excludes. How can wilder measures help us to civilize technology?

## 6. Staying Powers

Technology culture does call for a kind of involvement and immersion, but it is not *The Inward Morning*'s. We are all aware of the ladder. Its measures are clear: how to play the game, what it means to win at it and gain the attention and praise of the world. The ambitious among us spend much of their time and energy at it. Yet as we continue to maximize and universalize technology in the same old ways, we undo our intimacies with each other, the things surrounding us and nature. We are good at the game but have we lost our sense of reality?[21]

One of the tasks of *The Inward Morning* is that of living a life, daily and cumulatively, that is continuous with the inward wild. Its basic task of thinking explores both the fluctuations of the ephemerality of our condition and the sense of reality disclosed to us from our immersion with things. Being intimately involved with things, not "going at" them in an imperious manner, is described as a life of "destiny" in contrast to a life of "fate." From this standpoint, we should be concerned about the quality of the activities, as individuals and a society, that fill our daily life and lifetime. Most of these consumptive activities simply leave us no room for the kind of coexistence we see honored again and again in pages of the journal. The free time we have created with technological devices is filled with those same devices, and this consumption has crowded out most other activities. From the light-switch and thermostat to the keyboard to the remote control, technological life puts us in the driver's seat of control. If we do not ourselves bulldoze, we wield immense power with our fingertips. Our technological practices cannot but call forth an outlook where everything else is made to serve me and my purposes. Rather than a mutuality of being, the accumulation of these activities points to a petty homocentrism in an extreme.

Just as there is little room in our lives and society for activities of coexistence, it might seem that there is no place, no role any longer for the journal's wisdom and philomorphic language. Ironically, the kind of materialism that technology sponsors does not, as materialism would seem to suggest, emphasize the this-here-now character of the human condition in contrast to an elsewhere, another time to come, or as some traditional religions have it, a better life in another life. In other words, the ideals of technology can be seen as life-denying rather than life-affirming, especially when viewed in relation to Earth and nature. We are hardly living a style of life that is in balance with the Earth's supply of resources or its capacity to absorb our pollution; our technological society is unsustainable, especially if we expect from it a measure of social justice. But we don't live between life-affirming rims in other significant ways as well. The virtual realities that are exchanged for natural reality do not point toward a heaven or afterlife but a virtual nature. We would rather live on a different, virtual planet than on Earth. We want life "on our terms," not according to nature's rhythms of night and day, its winters and its summers, its wet days and sunny days, or the humble entertainment it offers in its "off" seasons. When we do exercise, many choose to do so indoors, preferring controlled environments, even if such a space station, as it were, is located in a subdivision of de facto wilderness. Without the insulation provided by these space stations, space suits, and vehicles, we do not like the kind of demands that nature in the raw makes upon us. When given a say in what we do, we make sure that nature says what we want it to, making certain that any other kind of say that it may have is listened to and controlled by our technological devices. We may profess a love of nature and the Earth but we live otherwise: most of nature bothers us. Our actions, the culture we have built and are building, bespeak that the Earth is too much for us. We are the animals that use our brains to escape not only its hardships and miseries but, even more so, every possible burden nature may send our way, having evolved to the point where we don't seem to be able to tolerate much of nature's "hassles." Rather than meeting nature's demands, we demand, demanding that life on Earth be cushy and that we not be moved from our cushions. We are the hypersensitive and lazy creatures with the big brains.

Are we basically this caricatured, overevolved animal or do we have a mostly unexercised capacity for transcendence? The insights of *The Inward Morning* encourage us to hope for the second, untried possibility. Rather than building a technological society that is at some remove from the Earth and that removes us from each other and from things, we could develop a technological society that has closer, friendlier ties to the Earth and connects us to each other. We can learn to live between the rims by discovering what lies hidden in the wilderness of things: the "staying powers" of things and places. Without the recovery and discovery of these staying powers, no other discussion of sustainable practices and cultures will be of much consequence, or it will be at most a conversation between ecologists and engineers about how to keep the spaceship hovering.

To develop this idea of staying powers, we first need to understand the special nature of this transcendence. Transcendence is *The Inward Morning*'s alternative to disengaged observing in science and the disengaged reasoning of much of modern philosophy. "The thing that does not *touch us,* the merely 'looked at,' the mere object, cannot be manifest reality basically understood. In the ancient Hebrew sense of the word—that with which there is not the intimacy of touch is not truly '*known.*' No intimacy: no revelation. No revelation: no true *givenness* of reality."[22] Objectification here is the attitude that one hopes to be recalled from by the inward wild, hoping for this more profound involvement and intimacy with things. Yet, and here we are stepping outside *The Inward Morning,* what needs to be transcended is not only objectification but devicification, if you will. The special dualism our time needs to transcend is a material dualism. Generally technological development has followed a separation pattern, resulting from the split between means and end that occurs with devices, as Albert Borgmann has argued.[23] Devices have severed our relationships, our intimacies and involvement, with each other, things, and nature. We are surrounded by familiar surfaces resting on unfamiliar depths from Formica to the control panels in our automobiles. It shows up in virtual reality as the division between the experience of virtual reality and the larger context once we turn off the machine.[24] Stamped into every aspect of our lives, this material dualism in fact prevents intimacy and involvement. If objectification is the attitude that one hopes to be recalled from by the inward wild, devicification is the character of the reality of our built environment that needs to be changed before one can hope for this kind of intimacy with things.

It is impossible to transcend most of this material dualism by understanding and fixing the unfamiliar machinery of the devices, although this may be promising in some cases. Nor can we will a world without modern technology, without devices, both because of the genuine advantages of many of these devices and because it is unnecessary for transcending this material dualism. Devices have their place within civilized technology. The problem is their universal presence in our world. When they are everywhere and used all the time, they become like weeds that choke out the native things. So there is yet another way to transcend the division of devices: limit their use to make room for the coexistent activities they threaten to obliterate. For that to happen we would need to have a good reason, a wilder measure, for thinking it is better not to use these devices simply because they are available.

If we understand this to be a material dualism, due to the very material structure of devices, then unlike the transcendence of more traditional dualisms that typically make transcendence an act of consciousness and attitude, this transcendence of material dualism will turn upon material arrangements, requiring arrangements that bespeak continuity rather than division.[25] For instance, opening the window of his straw-thatched house in Japan each morning when he wakes, D. T. Suzuki draws back the entire wall of the house so that the house continues into the garden. Unlike a house in London or America, there are no walls, no divisions between the house, its occupant, and the garden.

> So by opening Japanese windows, the house continues into the garden. And I can look at the trees quite easily, not as I look from the English window—that is a kind of peeping out into the garden. I just see the trees growing from the ground. And when I look at those trees growing right from the ground, I seem to feel something mysterious which comes from the trees and from the mother earth herself. And I seem to be living with them, and they in me and with me. I do not know whether this communion could be called spiritual or not. I have no time to call it anything, I am just satisfied. Then there is the little pond, a little lower down the garden. I hear the fish occasionally leaping out of the pond as though they were altogether too happy, and could not stay contented swimming

in the pond. Are they? I do not know, but I somehow feel they are very happy indeed. Just as we dance when we are filled with joy, so the fish are surely dancing. Do they also get something from the element in which they live and have their being? What is this something, after all, which seems to be so stirred in my own self, as I listen to the dancing of the fish in the pond? Then this is the time for the lotuses to bloom. The pond is filled with them, and my imagination travels far out to the other end of the globe.[26]

Here is something akin to Heidegger's nearing of the farness. "In thinging, [the thing] stays earth and sky, divinity and mortals."[27] To stay for him means that the near remains continuous with the far. In old wine, the local spring, rock, earth, seasons, and year stayed, continued so the nearness of its taste can resonate with the far. For things to near a world they must be continuous with the world; for things to reach us they must reach a world and bear a hidden wilderness in themselves. No one would want to deny that mind and attitude are important in this transcendence, for we have the testimony again and again in *The Inward Morning* that trees, fish, and flowers can at times mean nothing to us, but the experienced intimacy with these things on our good days has everything to do with being immersed in a world in which things have a chance to reach us. They cannot reach us if we are walled in, either literally or with our technologies.

In sum, things must have a reach and we must be within their reach. In *The Inward Morning* we find the author immersed in wholesome and full physical settings and transcending separations within these settings, whether building a dam, rowing, at sea on a ship, in the stream, or simply walking city streets. It just wouldn't do if these stories were about rowing on machines, surfing on artificially produced waves, snow skiing indoors, fishing in a stocked pond, walking in the indoor mall, or damming a stream on a computer screen. It certainly cannot be done on a ship if a sailor's job becomes so simplified by technology that it is obsolete and eliminated. Thus devicification, too, needs to be transcended, and transcended through continuity. That means finding activities akin to those in *The Inward Morning* to immerse ourselves in. These activities involve an entire person with an entire world of nature and culture and of people in the flesh. They are simple yet holy activities. (Etymologically, holy is related to whole.)

It is not enough merely to place ourselves in these activities; we are then only at the beginning of the path that *The Inward Morning* can guide us along. Of immersion in routine on the ship, Bugbee writes, "the round of definite tasks becomes something from which you can hardly withhold yourself; staying with them you discover staying power. . . . [Y]our routine becomes transfigured into a true life at sea. An utterly silent blessing of finality teaches you the necessity of the task at hand, dwelling at the very heart of ordinary work."[28] These, of course, are the good days, when, even in spite of ourselves, the sea steals our attention back to the task at hand, since it is not entirely at our push-button command. Immersing ourselves in these holy activities, opening ourselves to their staying powers, staying with them even on our bad days, and making something of these discovered staying powers by allowing them a say in our lives, speech, and thought—these are things I take home from *The Inward Morning*. And these are the lessons our culture most needs to learn if we are to civilize technology and incorporate the wilderness of things into our lives in the form of the inward wild and so a culture of transcendence.

The challenge for us is the creation of a culture that does not absolutize technology, seeing the products of technology as final goods, therefore universalizing this approach and maximizing its goods. Technology goes wild when this happens. Civilizing technology will mean to relativize it, making it relatively good only when it is beneficial to the more important intimacy with things and each other that it can otherwise easily discourage and destroy. I do not ride my bike across town. It is too dangerous. Paths I used to run now greet me with signs, shouts, and guard dogs. Skiing in town is safe only when the cars are stuck. The air is full of sulfur dioxide. My childhood haunts were replaced by subdivisions, an interstate exchange, a McDonald's, a shopping center, gas stations, and a large, unsustainable sawmill. Trails I have hiked have been obliterated by logging and road-building. We are losing de facto wilderness daily. Once peaceful lakes and streams now roar with hell-raising speed boats. Technology has radically transformed the natural and built replacement environments. We have but a weak understanding of what the cumulative effects of this physical rearrangement have upon the Earth's environment, and we have an even weaker understanding of what this physical rearrangement cumulatively means for us humans.

What role do physical things play in the decisive issues of who we become and the quality of lives we lead? Without the presence of real physical things, of rock as it were, and a setting that allows and encourages these things, the better part of ourselves, such as we see exercised in *The Inward Morning,* may just lie unawakened. An inward wild requires an outward wild. Our all-too-soothing comfortable lives leave us with an inward slumber. Yet a few things have got to stay the way they were and have been, like the nearby wilderness area and national park. Imagine wealth at the expense of affluence. Imagine an individual life that no longer pursues a high and rising standard of living, but in place of that activity, shoulders the responsibility of world citizenship and cultivates more intimacy with a few real things and real places, and with friends, family, and community. Imagine communities where it is not just the merchants for a pre-Christmas sale who close down the main street. Imagine what we as a people could do if we found that the creation and protection of public goods (metaphorical wilderness areas like parks, paths, open spaces, concerts, celebrations) is a more enjoyable and satisfying, a deeper and more reliable good than the fickle glamour of the rich and famous. All this could happen—the cultivation of intimacy, of holy activities, of the inward wild—even more reliably so in a setting of technology. But it is not going to happen unless we begin to see that the choices we face are more and other than pulling a different knob on the vending machine. *The Inward Morning* does not contain a well-formulated critique of technology. More innocently and less self-consciously, its pages shine with this more profound alternative, which is not quite out of sight, and shows us why it matters that we choose it. "I weighed everything by the measure of the silent presence of things."

## Notes

1. Martin Heidegger, *Poetry, Language, Thought,* trans. Albert Hofstadter (New York: Harper and Row, 1975), 227.

2. Henry Bugbee, *The Inward Morning: A Philosophical Exploration in Journal Form* (1958; reprint, with a new introduction by Edward F. Mooney, Athens: University of Georgia Press, 1999), 139.

3. Ibid., 155.
4. Ibid., 89–90, 121.
5. Ibid., 165.
6. Ibid., 226, 229–30.
7. Ibid., 141, 130, 106.
8. Ibid., 42–43.
9. Ibid., 230–31.
10. Daisetz Teitaro Suzuki, *The Awakening of Zen,* ed. Christmas Humphreys (Boston: Shambhala, 1987), 23, 75.
11. Bugbee, 87.
12. Ibid., 105.
13. Ibid., 171–72.
14. Heidegger, 228, 217.
15. Ibid., 228.
16. Bugbee, 47.
17. Ibid., 51; Heidegger, 220.
18. Bugbee, 44–45.
19. Ibid., 53.
20. As I have shown elsewhere, *The Inward Morning* not only critiques those theoretical ideas but also, time and again, recovers the experiential basis for philosophical terms, so Socrates, Spinoza, and Kant acquire experiential interpretations from *The Inward Morning.* See my *Crazy Mountains: Learning to Weigh Technology* (Albany: SUNY Press, 1995), 172–73.
21. See ibid., 12, 99–101.
22. Bugbee, 130.
23. Albert Borgmann, *Technology and the Character of Contemporary Life: A Philosophical Inquiry* (Chicago: University of Chicago Press, 1984).
24. See Borgmann, *Crossing the Postmodern Divide* (Chicago: University of Chicago Press, 1992), 87–97.
25. See ibid., 96–147, for an extended discussion of the importance of continuity.
26. Suzuki, 108.
27. Heidegger, 177.
28. Bugbee, 181–82.

# 3

# *Finality, Responsibility, and Communion*

Albert Borgmann asks if a necessity or finality can exist for persons as a universal point of aspiration without a God or a Platonic Good to guarantee its ultimate coherence or existence. What can be the source of the felt-necessity of response, say, to the suffering of another? Without at all discounting human susceptibility to hatred, destructiveness, or nihilism, Bugbee affirms a point beyond hopelessness, a place where sense and affirmation can reside. Borgmann pursues the possibility that universality and existential bindingness can converge along the lines suggested in *The Inward Morning*. Perhaps we are akin to explorers moving up a complex watershed from a delta to a mountain source. At first we find ourselves spread out across diverse terrain: the options for advance are mazelike, baffling, and make conflict over goals and tactics inescapable. We face fragmentation, isolation, and a bewildering plurality of paths. Yet we may know in our bones that as we arrive, the source will yield the singleness and relative simplicity whose promise had set us on our path.

Autonomy as freedom from others and license to act as we will, with minimum constraint, has been a powerful engine of liberation struggles. But it has also fostered the malaise of lonely atomic individuals, where persons are sealed off from communion with others and with things, or take things only as objects of consumption. But worthy, life-enhancing action does not flow only from the unfettered choices of autonomous centers of desire, interest, and will. Henry Bugbee reminds us of moments of responsiveness where the call or need of others or of a setting defines what we are and what we must do. At least initially, the sort of moral and spiritual necessity that Alasdair MacIntyre discusses in the foreword runs counter to the force of autonomy as *the* master ethical ideal. Heeding what is necessary, what calls on us with finality, is a mark of responsible action: we respond to needs perceived and keep still enough to see them. Finally, ethical response, however rooted in the particular, is not narrowly insular but can speak to a potentially omnirelevant truth available to all.

Bugbee affirms the values of compassion, respect, and responsibility, without rooting them in an all-encompassing autonomy. Taking his lead, Gordon Brittan suggests that autonomy can be self-deceptive, and he explores the rootedness of responsibility in something other than brute choice. Michael Palmer continues in a similar vein, seeking deeper understanding of our responsibility and of the promise of communion in the light of Bugbee's accounts of situated compassion and respect.

# Bugbee on Philosophy and Modernity

ALBERT BORGMANN

"What I have called finality," Henry Bugbee says in the preface to *The Inward Morning,* "proves to be the unifying theme of the work." And on the next page he adds, following Spinoza: "The true good is discovery of the union between oneself and all beings. Thus the meaning of the final word is universal." In the reflections on finality that follow, universality more often than not is linked to finality.[1]

Philosophy owes the notion of finality to Aristotle. Finality is the Latin equivalent of teleology—the center of Aristotle's thought. The concept of universality can be traced to Plato via its underlying adjective *universal*. In early medieval philosophy, the universals were the dim reflections of the Platonic ideas. Aristotelian finality and Platonic universality served the same philosophical task—to constitute binding ethical norms in a time of religious and political crisis. Similarly, the medieval controversy over the universals was a struggle about whether the world had a pervasive and intelligible coherence or not, a question the nominalists denied while the realists affirmed the universals as the bonds of cohesion that were ultimately anchored in the mind of God.

Although finality and universality, suitably interpreted, can be discovered at the very beginning of philosophy, the words never became technical philosophical terms the way "teleology" and "idea" did. But their referents certainly remained issues that have occupied and troubled the history of modern and contemporary philosophy. At the same time "finality" and "universality" are common vocables in today's literate discourse. Thus they are well-suited to linking philosophical reflection to contemporary life—the task and accomplishment that distinguish *The Inward Morning*.

As for their destiny in the course of modern philosophy, we find finality and universality characteristically joined at the very start. Descartes and Bacon saw themselves at the threshold of a new era where the supreme good would come to pass through the liberation of humanity from the confinements and burdens of the past, a liberation that would be achieved through the principled procedures of science and technology. There was a call for a burst of finality, an energetic and confident mobilization of human enterprise toward the goal of a free and prosperous life for all. The signature of the new epoch was precisely this linkage of finality and universality. Science and technology would make the good life available to all. While for Aristotle the truly good life was the privilege of the leisured and intelligent few, powerful technological machinery would provide leisure for everyone, and surely everyone would be able "to enjoy the fruits of agriculture and all the wealth of the earth without labor."[2]

Modern finality and universality are ironically linked to the Platonic notions. In both instances, the universal is the promise of the final, of the good life for all. For Plato, the universal is the realm of the ideal ethical norms that in principle are accessible as guides for the good life to everyone, though in the *Republic* Plato demurs on whether this is feasible. In the modern age, the universal detaches itself from the final and declines from norm to instrument, from end to means. Yet the means are thought to be so powerful and benign that the end could be expected to follow easily. Given universally and boundlessly efficient means, who could possibly be embarrassed or confused about the ends of happiness?

One who thought that such embarrassments and confusions are inevitable and morally debilitating was Kant. Finality being unavailable as an ethical norm, Kant made universality the mark of moral authority. To act in a way that is possible and sensible for everybody is to act well. Such action will rarely and at best incidentally secure happiness. What it does guarantee is moral dignity. This sort of eudaemonistically defiant and ethically heroic position is where Kant leaves things in the *Foundations of the Metaphysics of Morals*. But in the first and second *Critiques* that precede and follow the *Foundations,* Kant is unwilling to deny happiness in order to make room for duty. He thinks of moral dignity as the worthiness of being happy, and such worthiness, he reasons, implies the legitimacy of believing in an afterlife where God rewards the immortal soul according to its deserts.

Kant is the first philosopher to show clearly how facile and dubious is the common linkage of finality and universality in the modern period. We may think of Hegel's philosophy as a determined and gigantic effort to recover and present the profound synthesis of finality and universality and of Marx's thought as the endeavor to delineate this synthesis in the social and economic conditions of his day and of the imminent future. Yet the final word of modern philosophy was Nietzsche's. He scorned the teleological hopes and universal pretensions of his age and opposed genealogy to universality and eternal recurrence to finality.

Contemporary philosophy forged a new and distinctive structure of finality and universality. It rejected both the Kantian exclusion and the Hegelian apotheosis of finality and specified the vaguely optimistic finality of Descartes and Bacon as a matter of individual choice. Universality becomes the character of the political and economic structures that are to undergird and guarantee individual finality. In this utilitarianism and Rawlsian liberalism are agreed. As regards finality, Mill and Rawls are unanimous. When it comes to universality, Rawls defends a stricter and inclusive version. The universal structures of government and the economy must be more than generally benign and productive; they must guarantee every last person's liberties and basic welfare. Significantly, Mill and Rawls not only agree on the individual determination of finality but also share grave concerns about the aggregate moral and cultural quality of the individual choices, and both in their ways seek assurances that the outcome will be acceptable, Mill by way of a cultural elite, Rawls by way of an Aristotelian model of self-realization.[3]

When Bugbee wrote about finality and universality, he contended not only with a tangled philosophical tradition but also with a troubled contemporary setting. It is both a strength and a limitation of this still astounding and enduringly illuminating book that it takes its diagnosis from philosophy and its therapy from life. The enormous significance of this enterprise comes into first relief when we consider the condition of philosophy and culture nearly half a century ago when Bugbee wrote his journal.

The early fifties represent the apogee of the American century. Having emerged victorious from the Great Depression and the Second World War, the United States was without equal economically, politically, and culturally. With all its glory, it yet possessed the vigor and promise of youth. It had just begun to install a window on the world and a route to everywhere for everyone—television and the interstate highway system. When Nietzsche considered Germany under similarly victorious and promising conditions, he was moved to set down his *Unfashionable Observations* (1873–76) and to warn of the moral and cultural hollowness that was concealed by the veneer of power and prosperity.[4]

One will look in vain for anything like a moral or cultural critique of U.S. society in *The Inward Morning*. What exercised Bugbee in part and prompted him to reflect and to write was the state not of mainstream culture but of mainstream philosophy. The proponents of the latter, with the notable exception of Quine, had little regard for his work, and Bugbee had grave doubts about theirs. The genius of Bugbee had led him to teach at Harvard. But the spirit of Harvard's philosophy would not grant him an enduring place. This dissonance was one of the spurs in the movement of *The Inward Morning*:

> For five years I have been writing in an exploratory way, gradually forced to recognize that this was the case and I must accept it, along with its professional consequences. My task has been to learn to write in a vein compatible with what I can honestly say in the act of trying to discover what I must say. It has been a precarious business. I have found myself thinking quite differently from the majority of men who are setting the style and the standard of philosophy worth doing. Only when lost in my own work, and especially in communication with those students who have shared the venture with me, have I been able to transcend the uneasiness and the defensiveness incurred in diverging from the main trends of thought in current academic philosophy among English-speaking circles. It has already become apparent that the thought which

I am concerned to define is not easy to produce on demand. Often I do not know what I am trying to say.[5]

On occasion dissonance rises to criticism of the dominant form of philosophy much in the spirit of Nietzsche's critique of dominant late nineteenth-century culture in Germany:

> The demand for proof can always take the form of an insistence on abstraction. It can conceal the dislocation of explicit mind from immanent reality, whence alone what we attend to can come under an evaluative perspective in which *de jure* force may obtain. This *whence* is not a direction we can turn attention upon. We cannot rub each other's noses in immanent reality by argument. Adversary attitudes entail argument which can be resolved only by conversion of attitude. An argumentative attitude, as we know, is as inflexible and unrealistic as can be.
>
> The kind of "objectivity" of mind which distresses me philosophically is that kind of abstractedness of mind from immanent reality which entails the reduction of what is explicitly attended to, to an exclusively *de facto* status.
>
> This is a matter in which I am surely groping my way.[6]

Later and still more emphatically:

> What could be more comfortable intellectually than to yield over our experience of the world without remainder to what can be demonstrated as true about it, and to take from the very mouths of the spokesmen for religious experience not only the denial that there is positive purchase for religious experience in the world, but even an added confirmation for the naturalistic thesis about our experience of the world? A nice clean solution—like rendering to Caesar the things that are Caesar's. The philosopher can then continue to be a good hard-headed, tough-minded character, who needn't be ashamed of himself in any intellectual company, and at the same time "find a place for" religious experience where our experience of nature supposedly leaves off.
>
> I cannot help saying just what I feel about this: The clarity is false clarity, the tough-mindedness and hard-headedness conceal a refusal (which no proof can dislodge) to accommodate reflectively the gift of the world in the experience of things. And the genuine religious mystery—which is none other than that of the existence of things, of ourselves and all finites—is likely to be substituted for by mystification.

There may be as many truths as you please; but a philosophy that is thus twofold seems to me unlikely to be on the right track in either of its disparate moments.

I know I am unclear. But I want neither false clarity nor mystification.[7]

Bugbee's dissatisfaction is with what we have come to call analytic philosophy, which at the time was, much like U.S. culture, in its most self-confident and vigorous phase. We have since learned to realize, taught largely by Richard Rorty, that at the very time, when U.S. philosophy seemed most certain of its task and status, it also had begun to sequester itself from the conversation of humanity and to slide into cultural irrelevance. One might hence conclude that Bugbee was poorly served in making professional philosophy the scandal that moved him to think and write.

Whether Bugbee realized it or not, however, he had grasped contemporary philosophy at the very level where it was one with the aspirations of the common culture. Analytic philosophy was to become culturally irrelevant because it was too close to rather than too distant from the spirit of the time. It was all too timely in attempting to effect at the most radical level possible the liberating and enriching transformation of the human condition that was the goal of modern science and technology. But analytic philosophy succeeded in surpassing the scientific and technological efforts in naïveté and arrogance only, and those latter traits made it finally irrelevant.[8]

How this deeply held philosophical attitude issued in overt research programs and in day-to-day work is a separate question. It is in any case not the question that concerned Bugbee.[9] What he noticed clearly is the characteristic way in which both the "philosophy worth doing" and the culture worth emulating took up with reality. In both instances there is an attitude of control that paradoxically loses what it sets out to capture. Yet neither philosophy nor culture is brought face-to-face with its failure. Rather there is a semblance of success and solidity and a feeling of comfort and assurance.

At least in the culture at large there is to some extent more than mere semblance, and some of the tough-mindedness and hard-headedness is well rewarded. Consider water. We have learned to control its sources, secure its channels, and provide its utility to everyone. Dysentery, thirst, and laborious hauling are things of the past. We look at this accomplishment with a real sense of comfort and security. Still something has been lost. The water that flows from a faucet is no longer the water that has flowed together from many streams so that one may "be steeped in the river, constantly alive to it in its ever-unfolding." It is not the water that has gathered in a pool "alive with these glancing, diving, finning fish." Nor is it the water that rises from the sea as "a flying shroud of spray" or assaults you on the deck of a ship as "a madness of waves from which one water-laden gust has drenched you before you have even secured the door."[10]

Not that everyone had such vigorous encounters with water when it was drawn from creeks, springs, and wells, and it is now both impossible and undesirable to exchange the utility for the poetry of water. The momentum of contemporary culture becomes truly questionable, however, when it moves in on the commanding presence of water with an insistent tough-mindedness, when it needlessly regulates rivers, dams up the course of the diving and leaping fish, and procures sea adventures in theme parks. It is then that we try "to produce on demand" what can only appear on its own terms, that we "conceal the dislocation" of explicit excitement from the immanent reality that we yet draw upon, and that we refuse "the gift of the world in the experience of things."[11]

Mainstream philosophy has failed both more and less than the culture at large. Unlike the latter, it has failed to make good even in part its purportedly clarifying and liberating project of radical reconstruction. While all agree that drinking water in this country is largely safe and plentiful and we all know what it would take to make it more so, there is in standard philosophy no agreement whatever on what knowledge, truth, and meaning are. But neither has philosophy actively mechanized, commodified, or despoiled the things we hold sacred. It has, however, discounted them and left them to mystification.

It is against this background that Bugbee raises the issues of finality and universality, urging the first against standard philosophy and wresting the second from it. Since philosophy shared with the general culture an obtuse if optimistic sense of ends or final goods, one might expect Bugbee simply to remind his colleagues of how grave and difficult a problem finality is. Bugbee is in fact aware of this problem: "Human happiness, or well-being, is thought of as if it required no careful reflective interpretation; as if anyone, any old time, were adequately informed with respect to its meaning." From this diagnosis one might infer that what ails us is the lack of a clear conception of ends. Critics of technological culture in fact often put it this way—our means have outrun our ends, they say, or, equivalently, we need to get clear about our values. Bugbee realizes, to the contrary, that there is something deeply amiss when we try to guide human action by way of values or ends, specified "in terms of an objective extrinsic to action."[12]

Bugbee finds this grave mistake in both pragmatism and utilitarianism, and he elucidates it as follows: "Both philosophies suffer a misfortune of teleological ethics. When they think of the necessity of action as requiring explication in relation to the realization of finality, they think of the necessary action as necessary in relation to a subsequent realization of finality. This forces them into the reduction of practical intelligence into the aspect of technical intelligence." He restates the point toward the end of that day's entry: "Finality construed as a consequence justifying what we do renders no action necessary, and carries practical intelligence no further than its aspect as technical and prudential."[13] Once again, Bugbee's critique of contemporary thought reaches down to the depth where philosophy and culture hang together. Detaching ends from means is a characteristic procedure of contemporary culture and implies the very suppression of the moral (the "practical," as Kant and Bugbee put it) and the loss of commanding force in action (the loss of necessity as Bugbee has it) that we see in the "misfortune of teleological ethics." Once the availability of clean water is specified as "an objective extrinsic to action," the way we act becomes a matter of "technical intelligence" that tells us whether to get water from the surface or from wells and, if from the surface, whether to make it safe by protecting a watershed or by chlorinating the water. But here too the real misfortune occurs when we isolate ends, not in the realm of utility but in the higher reaches of the culture. Real moral damage is done when we reduce the sacred force of water to recreation or entertainment and supply the latter by whatever technical means are most efficient—speed boats, luxury liners, or Disneyland.

Real finality comes to Bugbee gradually and slowly. It surfaces in the early sketches of "Swamping," "Building a Dam," and "Rowing." Each ends with a word that shows where finality emerges. In the first sketch it does so in the concluding "immanence of the wilderness there," in the second in the likewise concluding notion of the instance: "How instant the touch of each leaf upon the live water. But one leaf in an instant touch upon the water is enough." Toward the end of "Rowing," finally, the notion emerges explicitly: "There were occasions, however, when those six miles would round out into an incorruptible song, and you would be realizing its finality as you flew under the bridge and came up abeam of the float." Finality is a matter neither of goals nor of choice. Rather "finality is ever the *spring* of necessary action."[14] Finality, in keeping with one of its common meanings, is as much decisiveness as it is teleology. Bugbee speaks of the density and darkness of things to bring out their unsurpassable and inexhaustible authority.[15] Especially in the account of life at sea, the inescapability of things is brought home to the reader. It is this great thing, the sea, that "attends you unremittingly, outlasting your reservations and protestations, until, perhaps in your hundredth or thousandth watch, it has taught you that enduring is truer than withholding."[16]

In giving voice to the authority and depth of things, Bugbee clearly set his philosophy off against analytic philosophy from Ayer to Rawls. In fact he replies precisely and in detail to Ayer's account of the relation of religion, philosophy, and science. And the doubt he expresses as to the wisdom of assuming that the conception of the good must be left to the individual "as if anyone, any old time, were adequately informed with respect to its meaning," implies a central objection to Rawls's theory of justice. Similar replies could be drawn from *The Inward Morning* to most of the standard analytic positions.[17]

As for continental philosophy, Bugbee's reflections had remarkably clarifying and stimulating force. Consider this passage for example: "Even the rationale of coherent thinking seems to involve 'something' which is indispensable to the *de jure* force of a system of coherent propositions which cannot be reduced to a mode of relationship between the propositions explicitly maintained. It is as if there must be a background, necessarily implicit, from which whatever becomes explicit for us can derive intelligibility and *de jure* force."[18] This could well stand as the motto for much of Hubert Dreyfus's influential work.

It is one of those remarks that not only connects closely with Bugbee's notion of finality but also is so profoundly directed against standard philosophy that the critical application to contemporary culture can be made consistently and fruitfully. Many of us have taken up the instruction and task that Bugbee has left us, replying to mainstream philosophy while at the same trying to make room for the finality of things in contemporary culture.

There is one bequest of Bugbee's, however, closely connected to finality, that few if any of us have been able or willing to take on. When it comes to the finality of things, most of us have entered pleas that are premised on some sort of pluralism. But Bugbee is very clear on the universal force of finality and in an engagingly uncomplicated way.

One might at first think that universality is just a synonym for necessity and the latter is necessity for me, here and now, and the universe in question is my life or my world and nothing more. In fact what impresses Bugbee most in the universality of Kant's moral law is its unconditionally commanding force.[19] But Bugbee immediately goes on to note that truly compelling authority is inseparable from individuality. Several passages in *The Inward Morning* suggest finality can be resolved into individuality and universality, the former indicating the unique presence of a thing, the latter referring to the force of the thing that informs the will of a person and moves him or her to act well, a force Bugbee often calls necessity.[20]

All these reminders are in line with the suggestion that Bugbee's universality has a restricted meaning that is compatible with cultural pluralism. An alternative route to compatibilism is to think of universality and necessity as generic features of finality, shared by a plurality of final things or occasions. There is a passage in *The Inward Morning* that invites just such an interpretation: "We live in a universe which is universal by virtue of the omnirelevance of simplicity and necessity. Anything we understand in its simplicity and necessity we therefore understand in its universality." But right away Bugbee rejects the notion of the necessary "as an instance of a class," and concludes with disarming straightforwardness: "The necessary is individual, and whatever is appreciated as necessary is appreciated as individual, unique. It is in this way that I seem to connect the thoughts of universality and of individuality, respectively."[21]

Is it postmodern *tristesse* that has taught us to give up on universal relevance? Or are we unduly impressed by the noisy talk of diversity and multiculturalism? Omnirelevance is clearly what Bugbee means by universality. He uses the word repeatedly as a synonym of the latter.[22] But how is one to argue for the universal relevance of "the moment of the leap we both feel and see, when the trout is instantly born, entire, from the flowing river," or of the struggle with the steering wheel in a storm-tossed night at sea when "gradually you are drawn into it in the only way it can be done, working with the wind and the waves and the ship"?[23] For, to repeat, it is not what these moments have in common that is universal, rather each moment as unique and individual is universal.

What conceals the incompatibility of finality and universality in *The Inward Morning* is, apart from Bugbee's untroubled confidence, the narrative cast of the book. Within the scope of one person's life (or one people's destiny, for that matter), finality may well come to pass in a sequence of final events, each universal in an unfolding and historically sensible way. The reader may be all too ready to smooth the conflict and where such a resolution becomes difficult, will draw for help on the powerfully implicit contemporary understanding that takes universality to be generic or instrumental and finality to be individual or optional.

Given that Bugbee clearly rejects these solutions, how can we possibly demonstrate the compatibility and, more, the coincidence of finality and universality? Bugbee, to begin with, replies that finality is not an object of "conclusive knowledge" or "absolute knowledge."[24] In a more general but utterly pertinent vein he has earlier said:

> What I wish to suggest now, however, is the possibility that a philosophical interest in knowing, in action, and in reality might be served by thinking of these as matters we wish to understand, as matters about which our position is less akin to that of knowers and more akin to that of testifiers, witnesses. We must learn to bear witness to meanings that dawn on us with respect to them, and this may be quite different from advancing propositions which we can claim to demonstrate.[25]

Perhaps the lesson that many of us who have learned finality from Bugbee have evaded is that in authentic testimony to finality, universality arises inevitably. Rather than daring to be a "participant in the infinite importance of things" we settle for "a would-be appropriation of such importance." If something truly dawns on me as final, it is all that matters to me and through me to everyone. But of course if finality has failed to dawn on the many and has appeared only to me or to us precious few, the burden of testimony seems unreasonable. Bugbee adverts to just this onus: "It seems to me that our thinking is informed with finality just to the point of the depth of our reflective appreciation of our communion with one another. And though it might be a tougher thought to think through, I am impelled to add that our communion with one another must be fathomed within communion with finite being."[26]

But is shifting the burden to "finite being" possible? Can it bear up under such a demand in a world that is intellectually pluralist and culturally obdurate? Bugbee realizes that finite being can warrant our testimony only in the "sacramental act, and the sacredness of all things." Sixteen days later, he resumes the theme of transcendence that rises from the notions of sacrament and the sacred. "Things which inspire us with reverence teach us respect for themselves," he says and continues "but reverence seems to be a matter of accepting their ultimate gift, and not reverence for them." Some lines later, he seeks to shed more light on the matter by way of considering "an ambiguity in 'ultimate concern' which might be cleared up a little," and finally offers this: "It might be put this way: Religious interest in things includes respect for them and transcends it in so far as it involves receiving the ultimate gift of things with reverence." Yet Bugbee's own ambiguity remains unresolved. "The ultimate gift of things"—are the things givers or givens, and if the latter, who is the giver? One is reminded of Heidegger's last great essay that revolves on "Es gibt," yet never names the giver.[27]

Only God can save us in our predicament. Bugbee was unable and unwilling to give this simple answer, the one that resolves the apparent conflict of finality and universality.[28] The suddenness of this avowal must be moderated with the reminder that there is a conciliatory way of thinking about pluralism and conviction. We tend to think of the diversity of convictions either as a cloud of balloons that floats above the sturdy common structures or as a bunch of pit bulls confined to an arena. In the former case pluralism is immaterial, in the latter it is intolerable. It cannot be either.

Instead we may think of pluralism as a watershed. All of us much of the time are the lower riparians who inhabit the banks of our culture's one great river. Yet all of us are descended from the headwaters, and some of us return to them for orientation and renewal. As you move up, you seek companionship, and at first, inevitably, all who are willing to move go in the same direction. But when you reach the first fork, some will go left and some right. At the lower forks where deeply polluted channels empty into the river you will try to persuade everyone to stay away from the tributaries and with the main stem of the river. But as you and your companions ascend higher, trying to persuade everyone that you know the path to the one great clear spring becomes more difficult and perhaps less important.

We can think of each fork as an ambiguity to be resolved and of the move upstream as the progressive resolution of ambiguities, the initial ones being fairly coarse, the final ones rather fine. The enterprise entire is the effort to renew the culture. When all of us will finally get to see the leaping trout and renewal will come to redemption, God only knows.

## Notes

1. Henry Bugbee, *The Inward Morning: A Philosophical Exploration in Journal Form* (1958; reprint, with a new introduction by Edward F. Mooney, Athens: University of Georgia Press, 1999), 10, 11.

2. René Descartes, *Discourse on Method,* trans. Laurence J. Lafleur (Indianapolis: Bobbs-Merrill, 1956), 40.

3. John Stuart Mill, *On Liberty,* ed. Currin V. Shields (Indianapolis: Bobbs-Merrill, 1956), 77–90; John Rawls, *A Theory of Justice* (Cambridge: Harvard University Press, 1971), 424–33.

4. Friedrich Nietzsche, "Unzeitgemässe Betrachtungen," in vol. 1 of *Werke,* ed. Karl Schlechta (Munich: Carl Hanser, 1966), 137–49.

5. Bugbee, 79.

6. Ibid., 99.

7. Ibid., 160–61.
8. A detailed argument to this effect can be found in my "Does Philosophy Matter?" *Technology in Society* 17 (1995): 295–309.
9. But see note 17 below.
10. Bugbee, 82, 86, 180, 183.
11. Ibid., 79, 99, 160.
12. Ibid., 212–13, 211.
13. Ibid., 207, 208.
14. Ibid., 43, 45, 51, 207.
15. Ibid., 161–62.
16. Ibid., 183.
17. Ayer's proposal is found in Alfred Jules Ayer, *Language, Truth, and Logic*, 2d ed. (New York: Dover, 1946), 117–19 and Bugbee's reply in *The Inward Morning*, 160–61; Bugbee, 213.
18. Ibid., 98–99.
19. Ibid., 61, 153–54.
20. Ibid., 87, 104, 132–33, 152, 161, 166, 181, 227.
21. Ibid., 104. See also 218.
22. Ibid., 52, 104, 113, 132, 209, 219.
23. Ibid., 86, 184.
24. Ibid., 134.
25. Ibid., 96.
26. Ibid., 219, 208–9.
27. Ibid., 209, 219; Martin Heidegger, "Zeit und Sein," *Zur Sache des Denkens* (Tübingen: Niemeyer, 1969), 1–25.
28. For his reasons, see *The Inward Morning*, 214–16.

# Autonomy and Authenticity

GORDON G. BRITTAN JR.

I

I met Henry Bugbee for the first time in the 1970s at a public hearing in Livingston, Montana, on the creation of an Absaroka–Beartooth wilderness area. He impressed me at once, not simply by the gravity of his reflections, soon after published in the classic essay "Wilderness in America," but by their idiosyncratic eloquence and perspective. While everyone else at the hearing talked in a utilitarian vein about the beneficial or harmful consequences attendant on the creation of a new wilderness area, Bugbee spoke of how, in fact, our lived relationship with wilderness both transcends and undermines a narrowly human point of view and with it the whole notion of "beneficial consequences." Wilderness makes certain demands on *us*.

Not that these "demands" are easy to discern, in wilderness or out. Since that first meeting, I have tried with real difficulty to enlarge the compass of my own thought and action by listening for the ways in which they might be addressed to me. Inevitably this led to a closer consideration of Bugbee's *Inward Morning*. His reflections on the story of Oedipus caught my attention at the outset. The story provided common ground on which I felt I could meet him. In particular, I tried to make sense of his reading in it "a connection between responsibility lived as autonomy, however well-intentioned, and destiny which comes to assume the visage of fate. It is in a seeming assumption of responsibility which is really a distortion of responsibility that destiny is converted from a significance which we may fulfill with our very lives into a fatal discrepancy between what we intend and the way things turn out."[1] What follows is my attempt to grasp the differences between two types of responsibility suggested here, one lived as autonomy, the other (for want of a better word) as authenticity.

## 2

Let me begin in this way. The concept of the self has a forensic character. By this I mean that the first question to ask is not, What is the self? (a hopeless question in any case) but rather, To what *purposes* is the concept of the self to be put; what sort of *work* do we expect it to do? I suggest that these purposes are not so much metaphysical as *moral*. Any adequate concept of the self should help clarify the grounds of our moral agency—avoiding pain, discharging duties, pursuing ideals— the self as acting freely and ultimately responsible for its actions. How is selfhood, what it means to be you and to be me, to be construed in the context of free action and ultimate responsibility in which we humans primordially find ourselves? This is the eventual question.

## 3

The answer I have always found most attractive is Kant's, in large part because it seems to provide firm foundations for the liberal democratic way of thinking to which I am committed. According to Kant, the moral self should best be understood as self-governing, or in his somewhat technical sense of the term *autonomous*. But Bugbee criticizes this self-governing or autonomous view of the self; it is (in my words, not his) asocial, unnatural, and self-deceptive. Coming in 1954, at the height of the Cold War, and surrounded by a national rhetoric of personal liberty and a national practice of conformity, this criticism was so fundamental that few could have grasped its import. It reveals the need, he thinks, to replace autonomy with a concept of the self as authentic however radical the implications.

Thus this essay has three parts. First, I sketch the autonomous view of the self: what it involves, how it is used, the importance it has for our own democratic way of thinking. Next, I set out Bugbee's three-level criticism of the concept of autonomy and of the "autonomous" way of life. Finally, I discuss Bugbee's own "authentic" alternative, what it might mean, how it is to be embodied, and why it is in certain ways profoundly democratic. In order to give some sense of the range of his thought, I have necessarily had to sacrifice much of the richness.

An additional misgiving accompanies the enterprise. My own way of proceeding is very different from Bugbee's, less obviously engaged, less concrete, less engaging. As should already be clear, I am someone who works in what Bugbee and Marcel call the "spirit of abstraction" common to most philosophers. By this abstracting spirit Bugbee "understand[s] an attitude in which elements of insensitivity, indifference, and sometimes of repudiation figure so as to cut our thought off from the life of the spirit."[2] I won't argue the point; for me to work in a different spirit on this occasion would itself be inauthentic. I also work in what Bugbee calls the "assertive" mode, drawing inferences, providing counter-examples, dogmatic throughout. My defense is that in its remoteness, abstraction allows us to gain some view of the whole, to sort things out, and to put them in place. I think, indeed, that this abstract way of proceeding, however far it is from Henry's, eventually makes contact with my own lived experience. I can only hope that it will do so with yours.

## 4

Now to the concept of autonomy. The central idea is simple and familiar. We are autonomous to the extent that we are self-governing, where "self-governing" means subject to rules of our own choosing. We are free insofar as we choose the rules, in contrast to other animals whose behavior is governed solely by natural laws over which they do not have any control. We are responsible insofar as these rules are our rules, self-chosen and self-applied. It is in virtue of the fact that we are autonomous, moreover, that we have moral worth and a unique kind of dignity. Kant amplifies this concept of autonomy in two ways that need to be mentioned here. First, we can choose any rules to govern our behavior, just so long as these rules can be applied to all cases and to everyone. The moral life does not allow for exceptions. Second, we are free to pursue our own destinies, our paths to and conceptions of our own self-fulfillment, just so long as these destinies are consonant with those chosen by other people. Autonomy requires that each person respect another's desires.

These amplifications suggest the following picture. Each of us enjoys a private sphere of action, free from outside interference to the point where we begin to interfere in the spheres of other people. Where these spheres intersect, there our public life begins. This public life is governed by rules, for the most part proscribing certain kinds of behavior, that we have collectively chosen, ideally as free and rational beings. But this picture is just that associated with our democratic way of thinking, however arcane Kant's vocabulary and the distinctions it is used to draw might be. Democracy *is* rational self-government. It is "self-government" insofar as we individually form and pursue our own conceptions of happiness and collectively adopt certain rules to govern our public behavior. It is "rational" insofar as our behavior does not result, as in the case of other animals, from antecedent needs, but from a consideration of what reason requires from us in the way of consistency, mutual respect, and disinterestedness. Members of a democratic society are thus, in Kant's memorable words, "legislating members in a possible kingdom of ends."

5

The concept of autonomy has particular bite in institutional settings and is, concomitantly, closely tied to the notion of individual rights. These rights define the private sphere, the boundaries of which cannot be transgressed by a collective authority under any circumstances. The individual is autonomous vis-à-vis the attempt by something or someone else to coerce or otherwise control her.

Perhaps because my parents are very old, perhaps because a good friend of mine is interested in the subject, perhaps because my own bones are beginning to creak, I have become interested in nursing home life. Recent legislation—the 1987 Omnibus Budget Reconciliation Act and the Patient Self-Determination Act of 1991—attempts to expand the autonomy of the institutionalized elderly. This legislation is motivated in part by psychological considerations. The dependence associated with institutions often leads to depression, illness, even premature death. But it is also motivated by a conceptual connection between autonomy and what it means to be a human being. To the extent that the elderly are deprived of their ability to make fundamental choices about the way in which they are to live, and in the process are deprived of at least some of their rights, to that extent they are dehumanized. As one study puts it, those who are on the receiving end of care often feel that "their control over the ordinary decisions of their lives, their autonomy, their dignity, even their sense of self, is lost in the routines, policies, and constraints of nursing home life."[3]

6

There is, of course, a great deal more to say about the concept of autonomy. But perhaps enough has already been said both to remind you of its power to move us and to provide a context for Bugbee's criticism of it. The criticism takes place on three levels.

On the first level, autonomy is asocial. It assumes, and makes room for, a great diversity in conceptions of happiness, no one of them particularly informed by a conception of communal life. Indeed, on the dominant Kantian conception of autonomy, what drives us to form social organizations in the first place is mutual fear and not the recognition that our individual needs, both animal and human, can best be met in a collective fashion. Kant does say that the happiness of others is an end that is at the same time a duty, but this is at best a very "thin" and abstract conception of communal life. In particular, it refuses to admit that the social roles we play or the ways in which we are recognized by others bear in the slightest on the character of our identities or the evaluation of our actions. Autonomy marks a rather sharp division between "private" and "public" spheres of activity. It is rooted in a contrast between the individual, who formulates, asserts, and defends her rights, and a society that constantly threatens them. It is embodied, in fact, in a market economy that allows for individual choice while at the same time requiring individual competition. This point is sometimes made, and is by Bugbee, in underlining the "atomistic" character of a society composed of autonomous selves.

On a second level, autonomy is unnatural. Self-determination is purchased at the price of its separation from things, indeed from every constraint that the world of our experience might impose. In the apt words of Lewis Beck, Kant dares "to weigh nature in the scales of reason and to declare that she is wanting and does not contain the destiny of man. The practical—what man ought to be and how he ought to transform his existence—in this conception takes precedence over what nature is and what she demands of man as part of her order. Nature produced man, but brought him to the stage where he can finally assert his independence of her."[4]

This independence can be brought out in two different ways. We have already noted that Kant's characterization of autonomy depends on a sharp distinction between the rules to which we submit our behavior and the laws on the basis of which all natural phenomena can be predicted. But it also depends on a distinction between the way the world is, fact, and the way it ought to be, value, the latter having its source not in nature but in human reason. "The ultimate destiny of the human race," Kant concludes, "is the greatest moral perfection, provided that it is achieved through human freedom," that is to say, as a result of our naturally unconstrained choices.[5]

Unfortunately, I can do little more here than list Bugbee's criticisms of the ways in which autonomy separates the self from nature. These criticisms go to the heart of his case for wilderness. To begin with, autonomy leads to a purely instrumental conception of things and to their eventual misunderstanding and misuse. In saying famously that people are to be treated as ends, and not means, Kant draws an explicit distinction with things (i.e., every nonhuman thing), which are to be treated as means and which, even in the case of other animals, are as a result not to be recognized or respected in their own right. In this way, autonomy leads to a kind of arrogance.

Moreover, autonomy does not provide a true ground for action, for on Kant's account we can give no other reason for choosing to behave in a particular way (insofar as our choice is autonomous) than the mere fact that it is our duty, that it conforms to a rule that we, guided in part by reason, chose to follow. But choice by itself does not confer value on the end chosen, nor does the mere exercise of freedom validate or ground that exercise. If our action is to be grounded, it must be by way of something other than the fact that we are autonomous agents, that is, it must be by way of something other than ourselves.

What this something other than ourselves, "nature" in the largest sense of the word, is must await the account of authenticity to be given shortly. Finally, the concept of autonomy is unnatural insofar as it separates us from our own human nature, insofar as it separates us from our own happiness-seeking human nature, disjoining, in Bugbee's words, "the well-being of the individual . . . from his capacity to meet the demands of universality in action."[6]

On a third level, autonomy is self-deceptive. This is the point on which to meditate, the source of much of what is truly original and noteworthy in Bugbee, although at this juncture I am more conscious than ever of the possibility of misconstruing his thought. We need to proceed much more carefully and cautiously than before.

In fact, autonomy is self-deceptive in a twofold sense. On the one hand, it is self-deceptive insofar as the autonomous individual, the moral agent, is indistinguishable as such from any other individual. According to Kant, reason requires that you are to "act only on that maxim through which you can at the same time will that it should become a universal law." He calls this requirement the Categorical Imperative. Only actions whose descriptions generalize are permitted, that is, only actions whose descriptions would apply to all cases and to everyone. As noted earlier, there can be no exceptions. The underlying idea seems to involve a contrast between policies that it would be rational for some people (but not others) to adopt with policies that it would be rational for all people to adopt.[7] That is, only some people would have good reasons for adopting policies of the first sort. But a policy is moral only if everyone were to have a good reason for adopting it. Kant enlists two considerations in support of this claim. In the first place, if there is such a thing as morality, it must be objective. If morality is subjective or relative, then Protagoras is right, there really is no such thing as morality. But if some people and not others have good reasons for adopting a policy, then it must be in some sense "subjective." Whether or not it is a rational policy varies from individual to individual. Therefore, if there is such a thing as morality, then it must be rational for everyone to do it. Objectivity entails universality. In the second place, according to a common intuition, I am responsible only for those actions that are in my control. Actions that are brought about by reasons that are good for some, but not others, invariably have to do with personal desires and what Kant calls "inclinations." But desires and inclinations are not, again according to Kant, under our control; they come and go of their own accord, as when I am suddenly seized with the otherwise inexplicable desire to see an old Annette Funicello film. Therefore, I am responsible only for those actions whose descriptions or "maxims" generalize. Responsibility entails universality.

The argument here is not particularly easy to follow, but its implications, and its persuasiveness, are clear. Morality requires that every individual be treated in exactly the same way, as an end in him or herself. There cannot be any exceptions in the moral life, not for oneself, one's friends, or one's family. In this same sense, autonomy requires anonymity, the suppression of any individual characteristic that, since it is entirely contingent and hence merely "subjective," is completely irrelevant to the moral evaluation of our actions. On Kant's ethical position, each of us is everyman. Or as we might also say, morality requires that we make no distinction between persons.

But from Bugbee's perspective this will not do. If a good reason for a truly autonomous action is such that everyone would have it, then no one can be held profoundly responsible for any of his actions. Or to put it in a more Kantian way, if truly autonomous actions are those done for the sake of duty and not as the result of inclinations or desires that are both subjective and out of control, then the appropriate justification of my actions—"I was only doing my duty"—would at the same time seem to absolve me of any particular responsibility for them. Furthermore, insofar as autonomy entails the anonymity of moral agents, it undermines the possibility of grounding our actions in any aspect of the concrete situation in which we find ourselves, as for example when I cannot bring myself to tell the whole truth about another person just because he is my father. The autonomous self, self-contained and complete, as such cut off from the human and natural relationships that at least in part supply the context and motive of our behavior, must deny its own individuality and uniqueness. It is in this sense self-deceptive.

Bugbee's criticism of autonomy has a much deeper basis than this, however. It is that, anonymity aside, autonomy lays the basis of avoiding responsibility for all our actions, whether moral or not, and hence drains the concept of the self of its significance. By the same token, the "freedom" it makes available is merely transitory and illusory. Since the point is at the center of *The Inward Morning,* I want to spell it out as clearly as I can.

The idea this time is that there is a crucial difference between those descriptions we typically give of our actions, what we intend to do, and those descriptions of our actions that are to be given of them, all things considered. Recall that for Kant we are permitted to do anything so long as the description of what we intend to do generalizes, that is to say, just so long as the "maxim" or policy it involves can be universally applied. Thus suicide is prohibited, since there would be a kind of paradox involved if everyone were to do it, while sex (in its more or less normal forms) is allowed. Presumably the description of our action, at least so far as Kant is concerned, is the one we would give of it at the moment. It would state our intention, what we are at any moment trying to do. Moral evaluation of our actions and the ascription of responsibility for them are with respect to such intention. But according to Bugbee, this account provides no more than "a seeming assumption of responsibility."[8]

The difficulty is that the descriptions we provide of our own actions, the statements of intention with which we accompany them, are rarely the descriptions that should be given of them, all things considered. As Bugbee puts it in the wonderfully oracular way that invariably prompts us to further reflection, "It is in a seeming assumption of responsibility which is really a distortion of responsibility that destiny is converted from a significance which we may fulfill with our very lives into a fatal discrepancy between what we intend and the way things turn out."[9] Bugbee does not believe there must be a discrepancy between what we intend and the way things turn out. Indeed, as we shall see, he thinks it is possible to reconcile the two and thus consciously to fulfill our individual destinies. But he is sure that the pride and sense of self associated with autonomy often blind us to the real meaning of our actions. But then if we typically do not know what we are doing, we act in ignorance, and therefore cannot be held responsible.

Let me tell you a brief story that I hope makes part of the point, although in certain respects it might be misleading. In the middle 1960s, when I began teaching, the movement against the war in Vietnam reached its height, and our campus had its share of protest, centered around a daily noon rally in front of the library. In ways that might now seem hard to believe, the antiwar movement was a very "big tent," and anyone who wanted to protest anything was provided with the opportunity. On one occasion, a campus leader by the name of "Sweet Ernie" Smith harangued us on the subject of some parking tickets he had received. For all I know, he was a drug dealer; the license plate on the front of his powder-blue Cadillac read "Sweet E." In any case, Smith's harangue took the form of denouncing, in colorful but clearly indecent language, the young woman who wrote out the tickets. The vice-president for finance, happening to hear this from his office window, called the police and they arrested "Sweet Ernie" on a public obscenity charge. Well, a number of us rose to his defense, taking our stand on free speech and the First Amendment to the Constitution. If anyone had asked us what we were doing, what our intention was, we would have responded "defending free speech," an action that passes every Kantian test of rationality with flying colors and is itself a principal ingredient in the defense of autonomy. But as I came to discover, we were kidding ourselves. For what we didn't realize at the time was that Smith's harangue, so rich and colorful as it seemed to us, was slanderous in the extreme against women generally. Not realizing it at the time, not trying to defend the culturally sanctioned abuse of women, we were not to be held responsible for it. But in Bugbee's way of looking at things, we were responsible for it. This is what we did, whatever our intentions might have been.

It is important to note two things about this story. One is that its point doesn't turn on considerations of "political correctness" or the fact that standards of social acceptability change from one generation to the next. Whether it was or is socially acceptable, we did, in fact, defend someone who was slandering women. And Bugbee would add that we should be held responsible for what we did, as long as we weren't forced or coerced into doing it. The other thing about the story is that, with a larger perspective and greater insight, we could have understood what we were doing and acted, if not differently then with greater self-awareness. I'm not suggesting that free speech be curtailed any more than it is already; the point is simply that what we say, or even think, we are doing often turns out, upon reflection, not to be the case. In which case, what we intend to do, at the moment, simply sideslips the question of our ultimate responsibility.

So there you have it. The concept of the autonomous self, freely and independently choosing this course of action or that, captain of its soul and master of its fate is, on Bugbee's reading of it, asocial, unnatural, and self-deceptive. It cannot serve the purposes to which it has been put.

7

The alternative, so far as I can make it out, is the concept of an authentic self that acts with respect to the relevant description, or real meaning, of its actions, all things considered, and in the process assumes genuine responsibility. If our "destiny" has to do with the real meaning of our actions, all things considered (including the ends to which they lead eventually), then the authentic self acts with respect to its destiny. But there is more to it than this. What more there is can best be indicated by way of Bugbee's compelling narrative of life at sea on a minesweeper during World War II.

> Perhaps you are dead, dead tired, dead asleep in your bunk. A hand shakes you and a voice calls you once again to go on watch. The ship is reeling through the night. Wrenched from oblivion, you sit upright, clutching the chain by which your bunk is hung, staring into darkness, swallowed up in the crazed enormity you have been summoned to endure. Sick, sickened and dreadfully alone, you stagger onto the main deck, into the openness, into a darkness, a madness of waves from which one water-laden gust has drenched you before you have even secured the door. If you endure your way to the bridge, you'll never make it; a smash against the bulkhead jolts you out of endurance into fighting your way along. By rushes and hand-holds you reach the pilot house. How is it the ship isn't pounded to pieces? You turn toward the man at the wheel and the ship tilts upward, hanging in the air. She pitches forward, throwing you ahead; you grab the man before you and hold on against the shuddering shock at the bottom of the fall. "Don't grab me, take the wheel," he yells. "Course is two-three-five. Steering engine is out; it's on manual." "Two three five," the words come thickly from your tongue.

Manual. With the first attempt to move the wheel you have the full weight of the ship's departure from course, backed by the thrust of wind and sea, translated from the rudders to your arms and shoulders and back. You begin desperately, you fight back. But gradually you are drawn into it in the only way it can be done, working with the wind and the waves and the ship....

Maybe the next time you go to steer that watch, you go to steer. Not to fight, nor to endure, but to hold a course in a difficult sea.[10]

In his foreword to this book, Alasdair MacIntyre talks about Bugbee's "I must." Here it stands revealed. At sea, in these conditions, it is not a matter of determining on the basis of some rule what "I ought" to be doing, conditioning my commitment to each of the men on board. To invoke the Categorical Imperative at this point would be to distance myself from them and from the events in which we are all involved, to abdicate responsibility at the very moment when I seem to assume it. Or to put it the other way around, it is only when my actions express an unconditional commitment on my part that I accept genuine responsibility for them.

The notion of an "unconditional commitment" has at least four dimensions, although to separate them in this way is already to undermine the "I must" of lived experience. First, what I do is not my "duty," or anything like the usual understanding of the word. It is not trivially "moral," to the extent that it is even possible to distinguish between the moral and the nonmoral, between actuality and necessity in situations of this kind. Second, what I do can be generalized, if at all, only upon reflection, abstracting from the details of the situation and undermining the necessity of my action, the "I must" with which they were originally intended. This is not what every rational being would have good reason to do in a similar situation, if in fact there are "similar situations." Third, what I do, staggering on to the main deck, fighting my way to the bridge, are not means to some end, perhaps righting course, in terms of which they are to be explained and justified. Each has its own unconditioned character, its own "finality." Fourth, there is in fact no "I" here at all (note its complete absence in the narrative), no sharp distinction between the subject of experience and its objects, between the self and the other. (And in casting my discussion throughout in terms of a concept of a self or subject I have, as Hubert

Dreyfus pointed out to me, distorted the character of Bugbee's thought; the "I" or self emerges only in distanced reflection, and for this reason among others cannot possibly be "authentic.")

All this and more is in the narrative. But I want to return to the theme of acting with respect to the relevant description or real meaning of one's actions on which I have been dwelling. For it seems to me that it is this theme that is at stake in Bugbee's comments on Oedipus with which we began, the idea that his tragedy lies in a "fatal discrepancy between what we intend and the way things turn out." From this point of view, I think, the sea narrative is to be read roughly as follows. We are continually in the midst of situations we did not choose and over which we have little control. Fighting and enduring, typical responses of individuals who want to demonstrate and preserve their autonomy, are not sensitive to the demands these situations make on us; they mistake the deeper meanings of our actions. In this particular situation, a deeper meaning of our action, what we are really doing as against what we happen to think we are doing at the moment, is to hold a course in a difficult sea. To come to realize this and act accordingly is what it means to live authentically. It is a matter, Bugbee says, of fulfilling rather than charting a destiny.

Perhaps somewhat in the dreaded "spirit of abstraction," this account of authenticity needs to be enlarged in two different directions. In one, emphasis must be placed on the temporary and inconclusive nature of determining the adequate description or real meaning of our actions, all things considered. Not all things can be considered. Hence we may get it wrong, or subsequently revise it. The authentic self knows that it has no knowledge of what it is really doing but acts on faith, affirming in its action a particular meaning that may, upon reflection, prove to have been mistaken. Realizing the ever-present possibility that what we intend to do turns out not to be the case, the authentic self is, Socratically, tentative and open to doubt. Any other course is simply self-deceptive, blind to our condition.

I have been reading August Hecksher's fine biography of Woodrow Wilson, the man who transformed "self-determination" from a watchword of American democracy to the basis of her foreign policy.[11] It is a kind of case study of the autonomous self. In pressing in a deliberate and goal-directed way for a League of Nations, first at the Paris Peace

Conference and then in a relentless speaking tour across the United States, Wilson shut himself off from all doubts and uncertainty, trying to force events, and could not see, still less understand, the tragedy that was unfolding around him, a fatal discrepancy between what he intended and the way things turned out. As a result, although his actions were voluntary in the sense that they were not coerced, he was not aware of what he was, in fact, doing, was not aware of the meaning of his actions, and hence he was not really able to take responsibility for them. In this respect, he might be contrasted with Lincoln who as president was always trying to grasp the larger significance of the Civil War and act accordingly.

In another direction, emphasis must be placed on the more-than-subjective, and completely nonarbitrary, character of the deeper meanings of our actions, all things considered. Again in a necessarily summary way, I want to make three points. The first is that on Bugbee's view we discover meaning, we do not, as Sartre and the Existentialists suggest, impose it. Surely he is right about this. In reflecting on episodes in my own life, I sometimes come to realize what they meant, really, in contrast to what, at the time, I thought they meant, sitting next to my wife in a university classroom thirty-four years ago, for instance. That we can distinguish between appearance and reality here is indicated by the fact that we are often forced to revise our account of what we did or are doing, to admit that our original assessment was mistaken. Perhaps some of you will be inspired by this essay to ask that copies of *The Inward Morning* be removed from your local library. If so, that will be, I think, part of the meaning of your reading, completely independent of what I intended, still less of what I might be likely to report to members of my family.

The second point is that there is no way we can set out, methodically, to discover meaning. Paradoxically, as my colleague Marvin Shaw likes to say, the attempt to do so defeats the purpose. Meaning, according to Bugbee, comes unbidden, although we must be ready to receive it, in clarifying moments, which admittedly are never self-authenticating. We all know what these moments are like. Suddenly, if only temporarily, everything seems to come into focus and we can make out the larger significance, provide the fuller and more adequate descriptions, of the events comprising our lives. For Bugbee these moments seem to come standing watch at night during war, or looking for trout rising on the river, or hiking in a wilderness area.

The third point is that the meanings discovered have largely to do with our relation to things, the demands they make on us, the ways in which they address us. One way to appreciate what Bugbee is getting at here is to relocate oneself imaginatively in a world dominated by the gods, or natural forces over which we have no control, or a chain of being in which we humans occupy some intermediate link. In such a world we have to face up to what the gods demand of us, or reorient ourselves with respect to the forces, or undertake the duties that our station imposes. The gods have died and we now control, at least to some extent, the forces. The idea of a chain of being has long since been given up. As a result, we tend to downplay or ignore the fact that our lives are caught up in larger schemes of things, and that it is in terms of these schemes, if we could only make them out, that our lives have the meanings they do. One part of Bugbee's case for wilderness rests on the fact that within our culture it represents a last vestige of the sacred and untamed, and reminds us that our destiny is given and not our own to refashion. Another part of his case has to do with the fact that wilderness provides us with a withdrawn standpoint from which to reflect on the instrumental and autonomous character of our everyday relation to the world.

The philosopher Charles Taylor recently gave some lectures over the CBC that have been republished under the title *The Ethics of Authenticity*. Although no mention is made of Bugbee, there are echoes of him all through the book. But in two fundamental respects they differ, and about both Bugbee is correct. In talking about authenticity, Taylor writes:

> This is the powerful moral ideal that has come down to us. It accords crucial moral importance to a kind of contact with myself, with my own inner nature, which it sees as in danger of being lost, partly through the pressures of outward conformity, but also because in taking an instrumental stance to myself, I may have lost the capacity to listen to this inner voice. And then it greatly increases the importance of this self-contact by introducing the principle of originality: each of our voices has some-

thing of its own to say. Not only should I not fit any life to the demands of external conformity; I can't even find the model to live by outside myself. I can only find it within.[12]

Bugbee is all for originality. And his firm belief that "each of our voices has something of its own to say" was one reason for his great success as a teacher. But he does not think that there is an "inner voice," still less that by listening to or for it you can discover who you are or what you ought to do. Our lives for him are too much caught up in the world; we have to be attentive to it if we are to have any chance at grasping our elusive destiny. Authenticity in the Taylor vein, too much akin to autonomy in its insistence on a distinction between me and what threatens my sphere of action, is once again self-deceptive. Genuine authenticity involves transcending any separation between ourselves and things, understanding that the "inner voice" may be talking nonsense, denying that I can ever have anything approaching knowledge of myself, and hence that such "knowledge" can ever provide the motive of my actions.

I said at the outset that the concept of the self is forensic, and that any adequate concept had to provide coherent accounts of freedom and responsibility. Briefly, the authentic self is free not insofar as it makes choices, pursues goals, is self-creating over the course of time, but to the extent that it does not know how things will turn out, hence cannot be captive to such knowledge. It might be misleading to say so, but the authentic self is free to the extent that it gropes in the dark, with only occasional flashes of light to aid it, admitting, as Oedipus did not, that we are for the most part blind. It is responsible insofar as our commitments are individual, unconditional, and made with respect to a more or less adequate, enlarged, and enlightened description of them, one that will not soon turn out to be mistaken and so absolve us of any complicity in what we do.

## 8

What, then, are we to make of all this. Suppose we agree to lead "authentic" lives as Bugbee characterizes them: how should we live, in what sort of life does the authentically "good life" consist? I don't think these are easy questions to answer, among other things because autonomy is still a goal and not yet an achievement for so many people. The battle for individual human dignity and social justice has not yet been won, and too many people are leading dependent lives or worse.

Well, we can't always take the wide and long view. It was immensely relieving to read Henry admitting this. "What a painful discrepancy between the spirit in which I reflect, on some days, and that in which I go about doing other things. . . . The world as I take it reflectively and the world as I muddle through it then seem excruciatingly worlds apart."[13] And we can't always be open and tentative; decisions have to be made and actions taken. "Authenticity" seems to leave so many questions open. That Bugbee in his own thought and life has filled several of them helps, but it doesn't resolve them for the rest of us. Watching trout rise, or hiking through the wilderness, even standing watch at war do not seem ipso facto "authentic." Indeed, there are no types of activities that are ipso facto "authentic." It is not so much the lives we lead as the way we lead our lives. "Authenticity" defines a style, a manner—as my friend Albert Borgmann likes to say, a way of taking up with reality.

What does this way of taking up with reality involve? For one thing, it involves an attempt to orient one's life in response to what really matters and not with respect to what is commonly agreed to really matter, not even with respect to what one thinks really matters. It is very difficult to determine this, and it is our lot as human beings that for the most part we can do this only after the fact. For another thing, it admits that we might always be wrong, and while assuming complete responsibility for our own actions it is great-hearted and generous toward those of others. The "authentic" life is in this sense humble, a reflection of the fact that we are not sources and centers of significance but mere aspects of a larger whole. Since all of us are in basically the same situation, we share a profound equality and only a truly cosmopolitan outlook is adequate to it. Recognition of these facts brings not happiness, as it is usually understood, but a kind of inner contentment or peace of mind, in contrast to the restless attempts at self-fulfillment typical of the autonomous self.

Perhaps you recognize this ethic, and the conception of the good life that accompanies it. On my understanding of Bugbee, it is very much akin to the ethic of the ancient Stoics, although he has little patience for their ideal of the enduring sage. In fact, the philosophers who haunt his imagination are the Stoics and Spinoza. Spinoza thought we should try, if only intermittently, to view our experience *sub specie aeternitatis,* from the point of view of eternity, as God would see it. Viewing it in this way would bring us to understand that there are genuine limitations on what we usually think of as our "freedom," but it would make easier an acceptance of our condition as well. As he likes to say, there is necessity in our lives. Refusing to believe this is what characterizes the autonomous self and, ultimately, desperation and self-deception.

Let me try to relate this to the nursing home lives mentioned somewhere near the beginning. We understand pretty well what autonomy means in this context: not becoming totally dependent, making at least some decisions, dressing oneself, walking under one's own power, having a private sphere in which to move, even if it involves no more than a room, the color of the walls, the choice of furniture, a telephone. We understand pretty well how it can be achieved: restricting the ways in which institutional personnel can guide, interfere, and control, encouraging attempts at mobility and expression. "Authenticity" is more difficult to determine. But I think it would involve an attempt to grasp the meaning of one's life, near its end, in a way that transcended one's room and furniture, and the nursing home itself, to one's family, friends, and career, both successes and failures, to the ways in which one has lived during the "American Century" (our collective destiny, as it now seems to me), and finally to one's place in an evolving, embracing natural landscape. This is reality, as it is and not as it is imagined. Making contact with it occasionally should bring, I've already suggested, a kind of acceptance. Such acceptance is to be distinguished from resignation, for central to it is an "I must."

Indeed, the fact that it is to be distinguished from resignation, which is acceptance based not on understanding but on lack of control, leads us finally to see a role for an "authentic" life in a democratic society centered on self-determination and autonomy. For "authenticity," in its being true to the way things are and not "to oneself" (the idea makes little sense), provides us both with a way to take final and ultimate responsibility for the way we lead our lives and with a standpoint from which we can reflect on and criticize these lives and those of others, apart from the conventional wisdom of our times. Surely the genuine taking of responsibility and the possibility of criticism define a democracy. When I first read these remarks as a Bugbee Lecture in 1993, several people complained that I had not made clear the idea of authenticity or done justice to the complexity of Henry's thought. I readily admit the latter. But let me try one last time to clarify the idea of authenticity. The idea is not difficult. What is difficult is applying it in detail to one's life.

We are moral agents only to the extent that we are responsible for our actions. We are fully responsible only to the extent that our actions are undertaken in an authentic vein. On my understanding of it, "authenticity" has to do with the ways in which our actions are, at bottom, all things considered, to be described. We might also put it in terms of their "real (or deeper) meanings." Authentic descriptions are informed by the situations in which we find ourselves, the various social roles we play in fact, the long-term and most often unforeseen consequences of our actions. They have to do with their unconditional and "final" dimensions. They are to be contrasted with the descriptions with which we rationalize our actions for the benefit of others (and on occasion ourselves) or adopt as the result of some passing mood or perception. We do not, because we cannot, invent our lives. In particular, it is misleading to say, as the concept of the autonomous self suggests, that our actions result from the "choices" we make. This way of talking separates the choices from the making of them and from the context in which they are made. It fails to recognize that the situations in which we find ourselves make "demands" on us in such a way that any two people finding themselves, perhaps impossibly, in the same situation, will, so far as they respond "authentically," undertake the same courses of action. On the autonomous way of construing choices, we cannot really take responsibility for our actions; in some deep sense, they are for the most part embarked on in ignorance. Genuine "choices" or commitments, on the other hand, are to be described in such a way that they cohere with what Bugbee calls a person's "destiny," with the sort of person she is, her character, and with the most adequately informed description of the world in which her actions take place. Autonomy recognizes no fundamental distinction between what I am doing at any moment and what I think I am doing, and hence no distinction between an "I ought" and an "I must." Authenticity insists on it.

## 9

In his dialogues having to do with moral questions, Plato always intends us to look beyond the often inconclusive nature of the discussion to the personal example of Socrates. Although we may not be perfectly clear about the fundamental moral concepts involved—courage, justice, temperance, and the rest—we are led to see how and why Socrates is a perfectly moral human being. In the same way, it is perhaps not too much to say that we have Henry Bugbee's example to guide us whenever we become perplexed about the difficulties and obscurities in his notion of authenticity and his view of the human condition. Who knows him and does not agree that his perception of the world, his relation to people and things, the style and grace of his thought and behavior bespeak an "authentic" human being? He is wonderfully original, of course. But more to the point, he is receptive, serious, and modest, listening and watching carefully, trying to catch hints of and then to act upon his own destiny. Happily for his friends and readers, students all, his own destiny, to the extent that we can comprehend it, has overlapped with ours.

## Notes

My colleagues James Allard and Sanford Levy made a number of useful comments. Embedding several of these comments in my discussion does not commit them to endorsing the rest of it. Hubert Dreyfus, as noted earlier, made me rethink my reading of *The Inward Morning,* particularly the distinction between self and other on which this reading trades. The editor of this volume, Edward F. Mooney, offered a number of valuable suggestions for reworking the discussion.

1. Henry Bugbee, *The Inward Morning: A Philosophical Exploration in Journal Form* (1958; reprint, with a new introduction by Edward F. Mooney, Athens: University of Georgia Press, 1999), 146.

2. Ibid., 103n.

3. A. L. Caplan, "The Morality of the Mundane: Ethical Issues Arising in the Daily Lives of Nursing Home Residents," in *Everyday Ethics: Resolving Dilemmas in Nursing Home Life,* ed. R. Kane and A. L. Caplan (New York: Springer, 1990), 39.

4. Lewis Beck, *A Commentary on Kant's Critique of Practical Reason* (University of Chicago Press, 1960), 125.

5. Immanuel Kant, *Lectures on Ethics,* trans. L. Infield (New York: Harper Torchbooks, 1963), 252.

6. Bugbee, 62.

7. Here I follow Robert Paul Wolff's discussion in *The Autonomy of Reason* (New York: Harper and Row, 1973).

8. Bugbee, 91, 146.

9. Ibid., 146.

10. Ibid., 183–84.

11. August Hecksher, *Woodrow Wilson* (New York: Collier Books, 1991).

12. Charles Taylor, *The Ethics of Authenticity* (Cambridge: Harvard University Press, 1992), 29.

13. Bugbee, 138.

# A Burden Tender and in No Wise Heavy

MICHAEL D. PALMER

> In general, respect seems to involve the focus of attention either on that which can inspirit us and call out our aspiration or on that which can offer us the resistance, the mettling condition, or the medium upon which the clarification and embodiment of spirit through action depends. Of course these phases of respect tend to intermingle, as when a man raising a crop may look upon his fields, finding them good, and then move in a vein of unbroken contemplation to meet the demands of a day's work. Thus the fields call out his love and exact his effort, and each of these phases of his caring for them permeates the other.
> —Henry Bugbee, "The Moment of Obligation in Experience"

Reading once again certain passages in *The Inward Morning* in which Henry Bugbee eloquently describes his South Pacific wartime experiences aboard a 137-foot minesweeper, I am reminded of Antoine de Saint Exupéry's experiences in the French air force during the same period. Describing their situations, both men resort to such unadorned expressions as "contingent," "senseless," "random." Speaking of the way in which in the Pacific Theater the U.S. Navy imposed its inscrutable plans on service personnel, Bugbee poignantly observes, "A motley of backgrounds and personalities went into each crew, a job-lot of men into each ship. These hitherto divergent life streams converging at random, to pour into the ship's life. None of us exercised much choice in landing aboard a particular ship." In a similar vein, Saint Exupéry recalls the frightful scene in France during the last days of May 1940: "When did anyone ever hear, among us, anything else than 'Very good, sir. Yes, sir. Thank you, sir. Quite right, sir.' Throughout the closing days of the French campaign one impression dominated all others—an impression of absurdity." If Bugbee's situation was dangerous, at times life-threatening, Saint Exupéry's (and that of his fellow airmen of the mere fifty reconnaissance crews available for duty in that dark hour) was desperate: "The whole strategy of the French army rested upon our shoulders. An immense forest fire raging, and a hope that it might be put out by the sacrifice of a few glassfuls of water. They would be sacrificed."[1]

What impresses me most about Bugbee and Saint Exupéry is not their lucid awareness of the senselessness of their wartime circumstances but the way in which they reflect on (and bring us to reflect on) how such circumstances might nonetheless yield some measure of sense. In particular, what captures my imagination is the way in which each grapples with the logic of responsibility. Neither man gives much credence to the customary understanding of choice. The usual conceptions of knowledge and control associated with ascriptions of responsibility are not central features of their thinking. And yet for both men—despite how the contingency of their respective situations invited hopelessness and cynicism—responsibility figures importantly in their assessment of what life is about. For example, Saint Exupéry, after returning unharmed from an especially dangerous sortie and while taking supper at the table of a French farmer, speaks movingly of the responsibility he feels for his countrymen. When he arrived at the farmer's house, the farmer, his wife, and niece were already seated around table sharing food. Saint Exupéry describes being made to sit down between the girl and her aunt and thinking that here is something besides his flight group that he formed part of. "Behind the silence of these three beings was an inner abundance that was like the patrimony of a whole village asleep in the night—and like it, threatened. Strange, the intensity with which I felt myself responsible for that invisible patrimony. I went out of the house to walk alone on the highway, and I carried with me a burden that seemed to me tender and in no wise heavy, like a child asleep in my arms."[2] Responsibility—a burden—tender and in no wise heavy—like a child asleep in my arms. What can be meant by such expressions? How shall we take the measure of them? In an attempt to interpret Saint Exupéry's portrait of responsibility, we shall make use of certain key concepts explored in *The Inward Morning*: faith, reverence, and generosity.

I

Responsibility is a central theme in *The Inward Morning*. In order to place us on location with respect to Bugbee's development of the theme, we begin with a review of "responsibility" as the term is customarily used these days. Moral and legal theorists commonly ascribe responsibility in two related but distinct ways, depending on whether our purpose is to control (produce, modify, prevent) an event or to hold someone accountable for an event. Consider the following statements that exemplify these purposes:

1. Frozen controls were responsible for the loss of 30 percent of the French reconnaissance planes in the early days of World War II.[3]
2. The sergeant was responsible for the death of the private.

The responsibility ascription in the first statement identifies frozen controls as *causing* the crashes of a certain percentage of French aircraft early in the war. We can make the same kind of ascription in a concrete statement such as "Frozen controls were responsible for the loss of the reconnaissance plane," referring here to a specific aircraft. Or we might similarly ascribe responsibility to animate things, as when we say, "The dogs were responsible for tracking mud on the new carpet" or "The patient with Parkinson's disease was responsible for spilling the glass of water." These kinds of responsibility ascriptions, which can be made to things as well as to persons, are commonly referred to as expressions of "causal responsibility."[4] When we make them, we are not assessing blame or attempting to hold someone or something accountable. Rather, we are identifying as responsible for something those things that we, the users of the information, will want to modify in order to prevent events unwanted or bring about events wanted by us.

We can ascribe causal responsibility to events (floods, crashes), things (aircraft, trucks), or persons (pilots, guards). When we make such ascriptions, however, we are saying neither that the events, things, or persons are responsible *to someone* nor that they should be held accountable for what happened. Moreover, since causal responsibility is always ascribed retroactively with respect to something that has already happened, it cannot be *assigned* or *assumed* (practices that are ordinarily future-oriented and often carried out in accordance with formal rules or procedures).

The type of responsibility that can be assigned or assumed (and that can be prospective, rather than simply retrospective, in orientation) is customarily called "agent responsibility."[5] Unlike causal responsibility, which as we noted can be ascribed to a wide range of events, things, or persons, only persons are capable of becoming agent-responsible. Moreover, in typical moral and legal contexts, persons can be held agent-responsible only under a limited set of conditions. Kurt Baier succinctly identifies them.

> Nobody can have responsibility for some past occurrence ascribed to him unless that occurrence can be attributed to a failure in his responsibility to society, that is, his failure in a task he could have performed and knew he was required to perform; he cannot be held responsible for it except by persons to whom he was responsible for his failure; he can be subjected to corrective measures only if he failed to give a satisfactory answer when held responsible; and there are only certain carefully circumscribed forms of corrective measures to which he may be subjected, for the sake of ensuring that he will not bring about socially unwanted events or prevent socially wanted ones, or for the sake of rectifying states he has already brought about.[6]

Two related points in Baier's remarks merit special attention. The first has to do with the notion of *task,* the second with the notion of being responsible *to someone.* In morality and law, agent responsibility typically involves at least two persons, one who is responsible for something and another to whom the first is responsible. Often the relationship involves one person performing (or being expected to perform) certain tasks. Task responsibility may arise within the confines of a formal relationship in which specific guidelines prescribe certain kinds of behavior and proscribe other kinds. Employees are task-responsible to their employers as are combat troops to their commanders and professors to their department heads. Within formal institutional contexts, task responsibility is commonly arranged hierarchically so that the supervisor of one or several persons may be task-responsible to another supervisor and so on up the line to the CEO of the corporation, the commander in chief of the armed forces, or the university board of trustees. Of course, in many moral contexts and some legal contexts, task responsibility need not be spelled out in organizational charts or job descriptions. Sometimes it arises in tacit ways determined by custom and tradition. Children are task-responsible to parents, and marriage partners may be responsible to each other in this way as well. And sometimes task responsibility arises only informally and in accordance with agreements (some of which may be tacit) that grow and change as the relationship evolves. Task responsibilities among friends often develop in this way.

Whether a relationship is or is not a formal one in which roles are overtly defined according to lines of authority and job descriptions, performing one's task counts as discharging one's responsibilities as an agent. By contrast, the task-responsible person who fails to discharge a duty is responsible for her or his failure. If the captain is the person task-responsible to the commander for making sure that all members of the flight group receive mission briefings, then if he fails to provide a briefing he must answer why he failed to do so. He is, we say, responsible, that is, answerable, to the commander for his failure. In order to clear himself, he must offer either a mitigating or exculpating excuse. If the explanation is inculpating, then his failure is culpable, and we will say he is responsible, that is, culpable, for his failure. The task of *holding him* responsible for his failure then proceeds to the next step, the taking of appropriate rectifying measures by the person to whom he is responsible: dressing him down, admonishing, reprimanding, warning him, perhaps even punishing him.[7]

Once we accept the proposition that someone (now regarded as an agent) has entered the realm of responsibility, the preceding account maps some of the basic territory of moral and legal responsibility ascription. But the prior question is, How do we become task-responsible? Is it by reason of holding a particular job with a certain job description? If so, the agent's task responsibilities extend only to the limit of her or his job description. By implication, if a certain task is not part of the agent's job description then she or he cannot justifiably be held answerable-responsible for untoward consequences when the task is not completed. In short, on this view, no one can have responsibilities that are not formally assigned.

In the ordinary ebb and flow of social interactions, being *assigned* responsibility is one way we become task-responsible. Saint Exupéry certainly recognized and accepted this arrangement when, as he tersely notes, "I was posted to Group 2–33 in November 1939." Being "posted" means being assigned a position and a set of responsibilities in a military setting. It has little to do with choosing from among available options, though it does imply being answerable-responsible. It also evidently has little to do with the kind of responsibility that, in Saint Exupéry's words, is "a burden that seemed to me tender and in no wise heavy, like a child asleep in my arms." To take up responsibility in this latter way requires a very different orientation of the self—one that cannot simply be assigned or commanded by another.

*Assuming* responsibility comes closer to describing the dynamic underlying Saint Exupéry's remark. One freely picks up the burden. But here, too, we must exercise caution. There are different ways to assume responsibility. Understood in its most generic sense, to assume responsibility for a certain task means nothing more than that one is not formally assigned that task. One undertakes it voluntarily—that is, one undertakes it with the requisite minimum awareness of what one is doing and with some level of control over one's bodily actions. In the sense now in question, one assumes responsibility for ordinary, day-to-day tasks, the range of informal and unspoken things that friends and neighbors regularly undertake for each other. But if responsibilities thus assumed are only occasionally regarded as burdens (to borrow Saint Exupéry's word) they are also therefore rarely morally weighty.

It becomes intelligible to say that Saint Exupéry *assumed* responsibility only if we are prepared to consider a deeper and more intense sense of what it means to assume responsibility. For the responsibility he felt toward the farm couple and their niece and the patrimony they symbolized, though not something he in any way resented or wanted to put away, is not precisely and strictly described as something voluntarily accepted. It seems to have devolved on him as a burden in precisely the way that our ordinary conception of assuming responsibility seems to miss.

> I looked at the beautiful niece beside me and said to myself, "Bread, in this child, is transmuted into languid grace. It is transmuted into modesty. It is transmuted into gentle silence." . . .
>
> I had made war this day to preserve the glowing light in that lamp, . . . for the particular radiation into which bread is transmuted in the homes of my countrymen. What moved me so deeply in that pensive little girl was the insubstantial vestment of the spirit. . . .
>
> I was moved. I felt mysteriously present, a soul that belonged in this place and no other. . . . Strange, the intensity with which I felt responsible for that invisible patrimony.[8]

Clearly, given the gravity and immediacy of the threat to his countrymen and the particular power of the moment, it makes little sense to apply the word "assume" in the same sense that, say, one assumes responsibility for making loan payments on a new automobile or agrees to water plants for a vacationing neighbor.

In the moral sphere, there is a special moment of assuming responsibility that seems akin to the type of responsibility described by Saint Exupéry. The moment I have in mind is one in which we feel ourselves constrained—not by an external authority figure but by the exigency of the situation. We may not particularly want to perform the task in question and would readily turn it over to someone else. It may be something for which we would not assume responsibility under less urgent conditions. But when no one else knows what to do (or even that something needs to be done) and we do know, and when we are in a position to perform the required action, then we may find ourselves *saddled* with responsibility. Responses to emergencies, when undertaken by someone not specifically assigned the relevant task responsibilities, are often instances of being saddled with responsibility.

Is Saint Exupéry's intense experience of acknowledging himself as responsible for the invisible patrimony an instance of being saddled with responsibility? Not precisely. The experiential texture of being saddled with responsibility is surely richer and more complex than the common form of assuming responsibility considered earlier. Part of what explains our feeling of being saddled with responsibility, when we do experience it, is our sense that the stakes are high (something out of the ordinary confronts us) and we (perhaps we alone) are able to respond. These factors seem consistent with Saint Exupéry's experience. But there are important differences as well. To be saddled with responsibility suggests something that runs contrary to our first inclination. It suggests internal conflict. When we are saddled with responsibility, we would prefer not to respond, even if in the final analysis we do respond. Saint Exupéry's feeling of responsibility for the invisible patrimony—the burden that seemed to him tender and in no wise heavy, like a child asleep in his arms—seems cleaner, less fraught with ambivalence, less conflicted than someone saddled with responsibility.

2

In the preceding section, we reached a kind of impasse. None of the three customary notions of agent responsibility examined there adequately explains Saint Exupéry's portrayal of the responsibility he experienced in the encounter with the farm family. Neither the notion of assigning responsibility nor the usual way of thinking about assuming responsibility adequately accounts for the kind of responsibility portrayed by Saint Exupéry. The experience of being saddled with responsibility bears some experiential affinities with what Saint Exupéry describes. But here too both the name ("saddled") and the core experience (inner conflict) fall short. What is needed is an account of responsibility that, like the experience of being saddled with responsibility, achieves a level of cognitive and affective intensity consistent with the realization that something is truly at stake in the situation and that culminates in action. But what is also needed is an account of responsibility that, unlike the experience of being saddled with responsibility, explains how the agent can think and speak univocally and act unhesitatingly, decisively, and with integrity. For assistance in clarifying and extending the discussion, I find it useful to turn to Henry Bugbee's exploration of responsibility in the journal entries of *The Inward Morning*. Doing so, however, requires that we reach down to a more fundamental ground than we can touch with the customary language of moral and legal responsibility.

For Bugbee, the logic of responsibility exhibits three phases. These phases are not isolated instants or discrete states of being but more like three movements of a symphony: distinct yet integrated and thematically unified. Bugbee sets them forth in a single, succinct sentence. "I confront myself, then, with a movement in thought, at any rate, from faith, into reverence, and into generosity (with its two moments of respect and compassion)." Of his own admission, this movement among three moments, schematized in this way, seems lame. "It invites one to a tidiness from which the experiential weight of these ideas is liable to drain away."[9] Perhaps if we attentively attend the movement of the sequence in the journal entries where they are worked out in the context of reflection on experience they will assist us in making sense of Saint Exupéry's portrait of responsibility.

We begin with faith. The first way to go wrong in attempting to grasp Bugbee's notion of faith is to take him as referring to anything like "articles of faith," propositions of belief, or ideological statements. Faith, for him, is less a *believing that* than it is a *believing in,* by which he means something like entrusting oneself. In the last analysis, faith is a kind of readiness, wholehearted openness, anticipation. In this respect, faith has a twofold reference. To begin with, it shows itself as "sensitization to intimations of finality in things."[10] Quite literally, to sensitize is to become sensitive. Sensitization has to do with learning how to attentively attend things and persons that present themselves in one's field of attention. Intimations are announcements. To be sensitive to the intimations of things is to notice them, to listen to them, to care for them. Finality is a certain character of things and persons. In their finality things and persons have a way of seeming settled, irrevocable, complete. And as such they carry authority (moral weight?) for those who reckon with them. To put the matter in slightly different terms, to be sensitized to intimations of finality in things and persons is to have prepared oneself to encounter them as *presences*.

Second, faith appears as a certain posture of the self that, when assumed, transforms the self. The opposite of faith—its denial, so to speak—is self-assertion and presumption. The latter is the mind-set that one retains ultimate control over his own actions and circumstance. The dialectical contrary of this mind-set is the belief that nothing one does matters, since all human initiatives eventually get subverted by other persons (one's competitors), blunted by the implacable forces of nature, or lost altogether in one's own death.[11] By way of contrast, faith is the posture of a person who neither presumes that he is the master of his own life (the autonomous agent) nor acquiesces to the view that he is completely subject to external controls and impositions (the heteronomous victim). For Bugbee, faith is finally an exercise in responsiveness, what Gabriel Marcel calls *disponibilité*—availability. The transformation of the self that occurs in faith is the transformation from agent to respondent. From the standpoint of responsibility this transformation implies thinking of oneself as responsive to a call in a way that is not arbitrary.

In the logic of responsibility, faith deepens into reverence. But reverence is a difficult concept. It can connote deferential honor, adoring awe, even amazement, for something or someone. But taken in any of these ways, reverence has the potential to emerge as a kind of aggrandizement of the thing or person. Bugbee intends neither this view of things and persons nor the implied corresponding diminution of the self. If "faith" identifies a posture of readiness, wholehearted openness, anticipation, availability, then "reverence" qualifies the direction, so to speak, of faith. If faith is an exercise in responsiveness, then reverence implicitly identifies *what* we are to be responsive to: things and persons. The denial of faith is self-assertion and presumption—the aggrandizement of the self. But faith, issuing in reverence, does not thereby warrant aggrandizement of things and persons; it warrants only opening oneself to them (extending one's hand to them, so to speak). The reverence that issues from this expression of faith will be the act of receiving or welcoming things and persons. "[R]everence seems to be a matter of accepting their ultimate gift, and not reverence for them."[12]

For Bugbee, the core meaning of reverence is what he calls "understanding-communion." The understanding element of this reciprocal pair he speaks of in various ways: "understanding of reality supervening upon the decisive act of informed will," "the flowering of human consciousness," "a discovery of 'raison d'être' which is no reason at all," "a funding of intelligibility," "the fulfillment of a life of reason worthy of the name." Reverence as *understanding*-communion seems to be a basic appreciation of the meaning of things and of one's placement among them. Such an appreciation is the product of contemplation, which itself is a work of solitude. Reverence as understanding-*communion* speaks of the nature of the interaction one has with things and persons: mutual participation (as distinct from domination), acts of sharing (as distinct from competing for or withholding), and rapport or intimate fellowship (as distinct from strife or indifference).[13]

Here I find Bugbee and Saint Exupéry in complete accord. The complex nexus of relations in reverence that Bugbee works out in his journal entries and brings under the title of "understanding-communion" is exemplified in Saint Exupéry's supper scene at the farmer's house.

> Silently my farmer broke the bread and handed it round. Unruffled, austere, the cares of his day had clothed him in dignity. Perhaps for the last time at this table, he shared his bread with us as an act of worship. I sat thinking of the wide fields out of which that substance had come. Tomorrow those fields would be invaded by the enemy.... To-morrow that wheat will have changed. Wheat is something more than carnal fodder. To nourish man is not the same as to fatten cattle. Bread has more than one meaning. We have learnt to see in bread a means of communion between men, for men break bread together. We have learnt to see in bread the symbol of the dignity of labor, for bread is earned in the sweat of the brow. We have learnt to see in bread the essential vessel of compassion, for it is bread that is distributed to the miserable. There is no savor like that of bread shared between men.[14]

Saint Exupéry's treatment here of sharing bread around the farmer's supper table is no mere description. It is essentially a contemplation on the meaning of things in context and of his participation with them. To paraphrase Bugbee, Saint Exupéry achieves understanding within the context of communion. There, in that place, with those unassuming people, reflecting on the wide wheat fields that are the source of the bread they share together his will is informed. About what?— The dignity of the farmer, the grace and modesty of the little girl, the meaning of bread shared with others as an expression of compassion and received as a gift symbolizing the dignity of labor. In sum, his will is informed about the invisible patrimony so mysteriously present to him. And it is this patrimony that finally evokes an intense sense of responsibility.

In the logic of responsibility, Bugbee tells us, reverence issues in generosity. The mark of generosity is abundance and ample proportions. The generous person is openhanded, magnanimous, prepared to recognize others and give them their due. If faith and reverence are intimately bound up with contemplation, generosity is their outward expression: concern with or responsiveness to things and persons. Or again, if faith and reverence are works of solitude in which we prepare ourselves to heed a fundamental call, generosity is the way we dwell in the world as respondents to that call.

For Bugbee, generosity expresses itself in two primary ways: *respect* and *compassion*. Both are ways of giving particular attention to another. Their place in the logic of responsibility—last in the sequence—implies that we must finally respond to others in some specific and concrete way. We see both moments in Saint Exupéry's description of those gathered at the table. The farmer is unruffled, austere: "the cares of his day had clothed him in dignity." In his demeanor and presence, the farmer evokes Saint Exupéry's respect. The niece, with a child's limited understanding and an inarticulate but felt grasp of the family's imminent loss and suffering, evokes his compassion.[15]

3

We have come full circle. Our earlier criticism of the way in which certain moral theorists speak of assuming responsibility is that it too often seems to be a routine if not casual affair. Assuming responsibility may then appear to be as simple as signing one's signature on a contract. Or if the situation is morally complicated and thickly textured, we run the risk of construing responsibility as something with which we are *saddled*. In this instance, we don't really want the responsibility but we accept it because we see no other satisfactory resolution. We accept the burden but we do so, as it were, under protest. Moreover, we keep very much in the forefront of our mind that we will give it up at the first opportunity.

What is evident in Saint Exupéry's narrative reflection is that many factors converged at the point where he declares his responsibility for "that invisible patrimony." The convergence of these factors makes his expression of responsibility more an acknowledgment of what he needs to do than a statement identifying an option available to him. Part of our debt to Henry Bugbee is that he helps us understand why this is so. If we conceive of responsibility as unfolding in accordance with the sequence he describes—"from faith, into reverence, and into generosity"—responsibility shows itself as both necessary and freely taken up. It is *necessary* in the sense that we ourselves are at once unconditionally claimed ("We are laid hold of") and also cannot realistically imagine abandoning that for which we feel responsible; it is *freely taken up* in the sense that, when we commit ourselves and our resources, we do so without mental reservation. Responsibility so conceived and so experienced is a burden willingly borne—a burden that seems tender and in no wise heavy, like a child asleep in one's arms.

How our friend and mentor, Henry Bugbee, embodies these ideals! What a debt of gratitude we owe him for teaching us!

## Notes

1. Henry Bugbee, *The Inward Morning: A Philosophical Exploration in Journal Form* (1958; reprint, with a new introduction by Edward F. Mooney, Athens: University of Georgia Press, 1999), 179; Antoine de Saint Exupéry, *Flight To Arras* (New York: Harcourt, Brace & World, 1942), 3, 4.

2. Saint Exupéry, 128.

3. In *Flight To Arras,* Saint Exupéry describes the constant problems he and other French pilots had with aircraft controls freezing while flying at high altitudes. I am only speculating at the actual percentage who crashed their aircraft as a result of losing control due to frozen controls.

4. Kurt Baier, "Guilt and Responsibility," in *Individual and Collective Responsibility,* ed. Peter French (Cambridge, Mass.: Schenkman Publishing, 1972), 47–53.

5. Ibid., 51

6. Ibid., 50

7. Ibid., 51.

8. Saint Exupéry, 124.

9. Bugbee, 220.

10. Ibid.

11. "Fate is the way of a man whose assumption of responsibility is an attempt to take charge of his destiny; no matter that he sets about this with right-minded convictions" (Bugbee, 146).

12. Bugbee, 219.

13. Bugbee, 220. Bugbee's treatment of contemplation in solitude is worked out in detail in "Loneliness, Solitude, and the Twofold Way in Which Concern Seems to Be Claimed," *Humanitas* (November 1974).

14. Saint Exupéry, 126.

15. Bugbee's most thorough discussion of respect appears in "The Moment of Obligation in Experience," *Journal of Religion* 32, no. 1 (January 1953): 1–15. One particularly notable passage is used as the epigraph for this chapter. Saint Exupéry, 126, 127.

# 4

# Faith, Love, and Lyric Evocation

Bugbee resists the familiar existential tropes of bad faith, absurdity, or nihilism. Although wilderness does not always play a clear supporting role in human affairs—it can devastate as well as elevate the spirit—a line exists between a wild that strips a spirit of hubris as a condition of a grant of life and a wild that humiliates or destroys one's spirit *simpliciter*. The ambiguous power of wilderness is no more or less than the uncertainly at the heart of faith.

David Toole amplifies the central themes of faith and compassion in Henry Bugbee's journal, tracing links between reverence, generosity, and redemption, and tying each to wilderness. John Lawry probes the theme of steadfastness in the face of suffering in his reflections on Bugbee's reading of the Book of Job, and Orville Clarke expands the theme of love. We move amid creation, among things calling for our affirmation. In a stance that is affirmative, we find power to bear *with* the burdens of the world.

Articulating the power of the wild is like confronting the sublime and finding apt response in lyric voice. The last essay in this group takes Henry Bugbee as a lyrical philosopher who tunes the themes of love, responsibility, work, and community to the places of his life, evoked in the memorable passages of *The Inward Morning*. As Bugbee avers, philosophy approximates a poem. Lyric can evoke trust and sympathy and bring us face-to-face with presences that are restorative and without which we would be lost.

# As We Take Things, So We Have Them
## Reflections on the Fragility of Nature

DAVID TOOLE

> The only valid tribute to thought such as Nietzsche's is precisely to use it, to deform it, to make it groan and protest.
> —Michel Foucault, *Power/Knowledge*

> Now for me philosophy is in the end an approximation to the poem.
> —Henry Bugbee, *The Inward Morning*

## 1. Faith

And the story seems something like this: as we take things so we have them; and if we take them in faith, we have them in earnest; if wishfully—then fantastically; if willfully, then stubbornly; if merely objectively, with the trimmings of subjectivity—then emptily; and if in faith, though it be in suffering, yet we have them in earnest, and it is really them that we have.[1]

As we take things, so we have them. Of all the places I might begin, let me begin here, the one passage I keep coming back to with slightly more frequency than all the rest. Let me begin here because here Henry Bugbee speaks most decisively to me, speaks most decisively to *us*, insofar as we are people in need of instruction about how to take in faith a world that we possess otherwise "in effigy"—or, to put it differently, insofar as we are people who need to learn to take in faith "the marred figure of what we should love," to borrow a telling phrase from T. W. Adorno. The phrase is telling because it suggests that what we must take in faith, what we should love, are not things as they come to us unscathed and whole but things that bear already the scars of abuse—things that we possess already in effigy.[2]

Rivers and oceans sick with pollution; whole mountains leveled for gold; whole forests leveled for profit; whole species gone—or worse, at least from the perspective of love, species still present, but perishing. This is the marred figure of what we should love, and yet we are reluctant to do so. Indeed, it is tempting, as Bill McKibben says, "to try not to love it too much, for fear, weak-kneed as it sounds, of getting hurt." It is tempting to declare, as McKibben does, that there "is no future in loving nature." Henry Bugbee reminds us, however, that such thoughts are those of a "stricken soul." For to withdraw our love from things, in whole or in part, is to abandon them; and in "abandoning the world we are lost; we are lost again and again. We may speak poignantly of the experience of being lost while we are lost; but we cannot be clear about our situation in so far as our thinking is dominated by that experience. Disillusionment with the world knows nothing of the sacrament of coexistence. It can find no place for the sacramental act." In abandoning the world we are lost, and so it is that we must make room for the sacramental act of taking things in faith.[3]

## 2. Wonder

To take things in faith is to come to the world in wonder, which is to say with "an alert openness, on our part," to "things in their importance"—the kind of alert openness that accompanies the practice of fishing, where we encounter the world "with our fingertips touching the trembling line." In wonder, says Henry, things come alive and "hold us in awe." To come to the world in wonder, however, is not yet to take things in faith. Before it arrives at faith, "wonder deepens into certainty." And certainty "pertains to the possibility of understanding reality as a participant in it, and not to knowledge . . . we can be said to possess." Indeed, certainty, insofar as it follows from wonder, "may be quite compatible with being at a loss to say what one is certain of." One might simply *be* certain, as Henry was one early morning on the Gualala River: "It is a glorious thing to know the pool is alive with these glancing, diving, finning fish. But at such moments it is well to make an offering in one's heart to the still hour in the redwoods ascending to the sky; and to fish in one place, for one fish at a time. On such mornings, too, one may catch nothing at all." The certainty of a deepened wonder is not the certainty of the catch but the certainty that comes to us in those glorious and fleeting moments when we find ourselves encountering the world with the expectancy of fingers on fishing line. Certainty as such arrives in these moments, leads us toward faith in things, and presses us to "make an offering" both to them and to the experience they have made possible.[4]

> Wonder becomes certainty, and certainty becomes sacrament, because wonder sets us to questioning which can only find conclusive answer in terms of a deepening of our response to things, which is the deepening, and not the allaying of wonder. . . . [T]he deepening of wonder is faith, and the deepening of faith is certainty. To this I would add that the deepening throughout is the deepening of our response to things. It cannot be an abandonment of them, an ignoring of them, a turning away from them.[5]

Rather, this wonder-become-faith-become-certainty becomes, as it deepens still more, reverence—a reverence of "things in their importance." To take things in faith is to encounter them first in wonder, and then to find that wonder has deepened past certainty into reverence—and not so much a reverence for the things themselves—for that would be idolatry—but for the "finality in things."[6] Consider, for instance, the biblical story of Job.

## 3. Reverence

Job, of course, was a man afflicted with great suffering: he lost his wealth, his children, and his health. So great was Job's suffering that when his friends came to comfort him they found him unrecognizable and fell, stunned, into a week's worth of silence. It is Job who finally breaks the silence when he curses the day of his birth and then declares: "I will not restrain my mouth; I will speak in the anguish of my spirit; I will complain in the bitterness of my soul." Job's complaint has its source not simply in his suffering but in the inexplicable character of that suffering; Job, after all, was a righteous man, and as such could not have earned this fate. Hence Job takes his case to the highest office and addresses his complaint to God. "Oh, that I knew where I might find him," Job says, speaking of God, "I would lay my case before him and fill my mouth with arguments. I would learn what he would answer me. Would he contend with me in the greatness of his power? No; but he would give heed to me." And indeed, God does, finally, give heed to Job, but not in the way Job might have expected. God does not address the specifics of Job's complaint; he does not offer an explanation for Job's suffering, nor does he address Job's questions about justice. Instead, God arrives in what Henry calls in another context "the imperative mood" and begins to question Job about the details of creation. "Where were you," he demands to know of Job, "when I laid the foundations of the earth?"[7]

> Have you commanded the morning since your days began, and caused the dawn to know its place? Have you comprehended the expanse of the earth? Can you hunt prey for the lion? Do you know when the mountain goats give birth? Do you give the horse its might? Is it at your command that the eagle mounts up and makes its nest on high?[8]

So it is that God responds to Job in his suffering, and then He says, "Shall a faultfinder contend with the Almighty? Anyone who argues with God, must respond." Job, for the first time since God's appearance, now has a chance to speak, but he is "speechless": "what can I answer? I put my hand on my mouth. I have said too much already; now I will speak no more." Face to face with divinity, Job does not, as he said he would, fill his mouth with arguments but instead falls silent, saying only, in the end, "I have uttered what I did not understand, things too wonderful for me, which I did not know. . . . I had heard of you by the hearing of the ear, but now my eyes see you. Therefore I will be quiet, comforted that I am dust."[9]

Job questions God about human suffering, and God replies with a display of the wonders of his creation, to which Job responds in silence. And as Bill McKibben notes, "It is not simply his smallness in the face of the infinite that shuts him up, it is his sense that infinity is somehow sufficient." Or as Henry has it, "When Job calls out for understanding in his affliction, the response speaking to his condition is simply in the terms of the things of this world. . . . If he is illuminated, it is hardly by reason of having been informed. . . . What holds up is creation, and in the discovery of creation faith is refined, deepened, and renewed. . . . And the story seems something like this: as we take things, so we have them; and if we take them in faith, we have them in earnest."[10]

In the end, it is the things of this world, as God parades them before Job, that sustain him in his suffering. When Henry speaks of a wonder that deepens past faith and certainty into reverence, he has in mind, in part, Job's encounter with God in the whirlwind. And when he speaks of reverence as an encounter with things "in their finality," Henry joins McKibben to say that what Job learns from the whirlwind is that "somehow infinity is sufficient"; somehow when we discover "the infinite importance of finite things," we come to rest in the comfort of faith.[11]

## 4. Wilderness

We find what Henry has in mind by "reverence" and "finality" displayed not only in the story of Job but also in those moments when we encounter what Job encountered. Indeed, it seems that much of Henry's work is an extended reflection upon one such encounter in his own life.

> It was in the fall of '41, October and November, while late autumn prevailed throughout the northern Canadian Rockies, restoring everything in that vast region to a native wildness. Some part of each day or night, for forty days, flurries of snow were flying. The aspens and the larches took on a yellow so vivid, so pure, so trembling in the air, as to fairly cry out that they were as they were, limitlessly. And it was there in attending to this wilderness, with unremitting alertness and attentiveness, yes, even as I slept, that I knew myself to have been instructed for life, though I was at a loss to say what instruction I had received.[12]

In the fall of 1941, Henry, like Job, encountered things in their "native wildness." And it was, he notes, in attending to these wild things, "in attending to this wilderness," that he received a lifetime of instruction, though he did not know then exactly what he had learned. And it seems that what he was at a loss to say in 1941, he begins to say almost two decades later when he says, in effect, that wonder, faith, and reverence are but ways of naming our encounters with wilderness.

And what exactly is it to encounter wilderness? It is in part to encounter a world unknown, to be involved in "a mystery intelligible to us only as such"; it is to "learn to take things in their darkness, their utter density and darkness"—for then "we stand upon the threshold of receiving the ultimate gift of things." Wonder, faith, and reverence are ways of naming our encounters not with things generally but with "things dense and dark." But such things are, as Heidegger reminds us, "modest in number"; they have, as Albert Borgmann suggests, "suffered a diaspora"; they live only at the margins of a world possessed in effigy.[13] Thus such encounters are rare. "That ours is a holy place has ever seemed to me true when I have been most awake, and I take it as a mark of awakening whenever it dawns on me again as true. But much of the time I cannot remember that it is true, and I cannot understand what such a saying might mean, if it were to occur to me to dwell on it at all. Amidst the noise of my thoughts things appear as an innocuous congeries of items, noted, and so what?" Most of the time, we are "at a loss to understand that ours is a holy place, a universe of things, a wilderness." Instead, "we cling to things and claim the right to mastery of them," and we thereby come to embody what Henry calls the "possessive mind": "And we might say that for the possessive mind, the other is merely an object; and that the characterization of the other taken as object amounts to taking possession of it in effigy."[14]

We find ourselves in possession of the world in effigy, and therefore we must learn of wonder, faith, and reverence, as Henry did in the fall of 1941 and as Job did in his encounter with the whirlwind. We must learn of wonder, not from books, nor from teachers, but from our encounters with things themselves—hence the importance of those occasions when we are "most awake" to the world and find ourselves called upon and invited to participate in the "universe of things." On such occasions, "We are laid hold of."[15]

In one of his last published essays, Henry poses the question, "how could it be that [things] might hold such force?"[16] How could it be that things, and things alone, might have the power to transform a world possessed in effigy into a world taken in faith?

> Only, it would seem, in some radical way; positioning us, as it were, with respect to our involvement in reality. . . . No doubt our situation is always a metaphysical affair. But wilderness, to the extent that it will not

permit one to take one's surroundings for granted, is a place which will not let us off the metaphysical hook. At the same time it establishes us in such a decisively lived relationship with our surroundings that it precludes subsumption of the lived relationship to any depictive representation of how we are situated in relation to our surroundings. . . . We are not there as seen by ourselves. . . . No, we are there on the spot with respect to the meaning of what we behold.[17]

In other words, all our powers of description come up short when we walk around the bend and find a grizzly bear standing in the trail. Even a "depictive representation" of the situation by the best of bear biologists will fail to capture the meaning of the encounter now underway. All bets are off; nothing can be taken for granted. To encounter a grizzly bear is indeed to be placed on the spot and radically positioned amid things; and this, according to Henry, is what our encounters with wilderness are like, which is not to say that all such encounters are as dramatic as the example. In fact, the drama of the example displays graphically something that is both more common and more subtle than an encounter with a grizzly bear: on certain occasions we encounter things in such a way that they overcome the nonchalance of our "so what?" and radically reposition us "with respect to our involvement in reality." Is this not precisely what happened to Job in the course of his encounter with the whirlwind? As God laid before him the whole of creation, fully arrayed in all its wonder-producing glory, did not Job find himself radically repositioned amid things? Is it not in wilderness that Job finds comfort? If "in wildness is the preservation of the world," is it not for the reason that in wilderness is the birth of wonder?[18]

But note that "wilderness" is not limited to encounters with grizzly bears nor even to the places they inhabit; rather, "wilderness is reality experienced as call and explained in responding to it absolutely." Wilderness is not a place but, like faith and reverence, a way of naming those moments when we awaken to the world in wonder, when we are most alert to the infinite importance of finite things. Grizzly bears are not a prerequisite for the birth of a wonder; other things will do. Indeed, any thing will do, as long as it shares with the grizzly bear the ability to focus our attention in a decisive way and thus to position us with respect to our involvement in reality. Any thing will do, but modest in number and dispersed to the margins of our lives, such things gather most readily in nature, and it is there we meet them most forcefully. It is there that we come to find, like Job, that wilderness "is the reality of faith." However, in our encounters with nature's "native wildness," what we learn of faith is also, and in an important way, unlike the lesson of Job's encounter with the whirlwind.[19]

## 5. Fragility

What Job encountered was the strength of creation as God had made it—the native wildness evident most clearly in God's description of Leviathan:

> Lay hands on it; think of the battle; you will not do it again. Any hope of capturing it will be disappointed. . . . I will not keep silent concerning its limbs, or its mighty strength, or its splendid frame. . . . When it raises itself up the gods are afraid; . . . Though the sword reaches it, it does not avail; nor does the spear, the dart, or the javelin. On earth it has no equal, a creature without fear. It surveys everything that is lofty; it is king over all that are proud.[20]

As God lists them, Leviathan is the last of his creations, and it stands forth as the ultimate example of nature's "indomitable wildness" (to borrow a term from Albert Borgmann). And yet it is just this unassailable character of God's creation that is absent from our encounters with nature. What we encounter is fragility and not Leviathan. Hence to say that wilderness is the reality of faith is not to say that in wilderness we find comfort, as Job did, in the "mighty strength" of things that are themselves untouched by suffering.

"And if in faith, though it be in suffering": when Henry uttered those words, the suffering in question was ours, and we found comfort in "the things of this world." Hence, what held up was creation. But once fragility replaces Leviathan as the dominant character of our encounters with things, then the suffering in question is not ours but theirs.[21] For Job, it is the wilderness that saves him from suffering; for us, wilderness itself is in jeopardy. And the fragility of wilderness has implications for what it might mean to take things in faith. Wonder now not only deepens into reverence, it is also altered by something like grief. We must speak, then, not of wonder that has deepened into faith alone, nor even of wonder that has deepened into reverence, but of a wonder, now altered by grief, that deepens into love. We must speak now of love in addition to faith and reverence because the finality we encounter in things is inseparable from their fragility, and only a wonder that has deepened into love is capable of sustaining us in the midst of a fragile world. For finality does not arrive for us, as it did for Job, in the commanding voice of divinity; rather, it arrives in the form of things as they "silently and gently press upon us" in their fragility, as they come to us in what Henry calls "the imperative mood."[22]

## 6. Love

It "may help," Henry tells us, "to bear in mind that the imperative mood is not the mood of assertion. It is the mood of affirmation, the mood in which we truly respond." It is the mood of things as they "question" us and "call upon us" with the beckoning darkness of their "inexhaustibility." Perhaps we should call it instead the interrogative mood. Except that the questions harbor within them demands; they place us under obligation; they have about them the tenor of necessity—and yet they do not *assert* themselves: "We learn of necessity in all gentleness, or not at all"—in gentleness, because though inexhaustible and infinitely important, things are yet fragile; they are, and inevitably so, perishable. "There is weeping and gnashing of teeth; there is stony impassivity; there is ribaldry and vacuous staring; there is confusion. But there is pure gentleness, and it is in this vein that perishing speaks." It is in this vein that experience "is permeated with meaning by invasion"—by the silent, gentle invasion of things in their finality. It is here that things demand our "consonant" response, which is the response of a wonder that has deepened into love.[23]

"What I seek to clarify," says Henry, "is a perennial meaning of things, by virtue of which, things are experienced not merely as old, or as new, but as ageless"—ageless and yet perishable. "For everything that strikes us through and through with wonder, deepening into love, should teach us not to confuse things in their eternity with some realm in which time's arrow is stopped." To confuse the finality we encounter as agelessness with the unending presence of things is not to love them but to cling to them. And as "we cling to them, as we fail to realize them profoundly, no doubt perishing strikes us as to be fought against with all our might. Perishing, accordingly, robs us of what we love, and our vulnerability lies in loving anything likely to perish." Or so it seems when we confuse eternity with permanence, but for Henry at least, it also seems otherwise: "at times another standpoint on perishing . . . has hinted itself to me. It has seemed on occasion that the very perishing of what we love might be an essential moment in the clarification of love of that which perishes."[24]

The very perishing of what we love: against that we fight with all our might, as we cling to things and call upon them "to bear witness to the finality of *our* insistence." But when things perish all the same and we lose the fight is it not then that we abandon them, failing to understand that finality is not for us to insist upon but for things to offer— and failing to see, too, that it is we who are called to bear witness? "Abstractly stated, man is a finite center of response. And now I would go on to say, he encounters personality only in relation to other finite centers of response. . . . The peculiar importance of personality seems to me to lie in the capacity of responsible beings to *bear witness* to the groundedness of the finite." To bear witness to things in their "groundedness": that, it seems, is what we are called to do.[25]

The question, Henry says, "is whether we can rejoice with things, or whether we find them simply inane." To take things in faith is to rejoice with them and affirm them, even as they perish: "We are taught finality in the once-for-allness of events, so clear in the presence of death, and in the givenness of things to which we reach out with infinite receptivity. Is there not a depth in which joy and sorrow meet?" Perhaps we should answer, no. But if joy and sorrow do not meet, then what hope do we have of reaching out with infinite receptivity to a fragile world; what future is there in loving nature?[26]

## 7. Generosity

A children's book called *The Giving Tree* comes to mind here; it tells the story of the relationship between an aged tree and a young boy.

> Once there was a tree and she loved a little boy. And every day the boy would come and he would gather her leaves and make them into crowns

and play king of the forest. He would climb up her trunk and swing from her branches and eat apples. And they would play hide-and-go-seek. And when he was tired, he would sleep in her shade. And the boy loved the tree very much. And the tree was happy. But time went by. And the boy grew older. And the tree was often alone. Then one day the boy came to the tree and the tree said, "Come, Boy, come and climb up my trunk and swing from my branches and eat apples and play in my shade and be happy." I am too big to climb and play," said the boy. "I want to buy things and have fun. I want some money. Can you give me some money?" "I'm sorry," said the tree, "but I have no money. I have only leaves and apples. Take my apples, Boy, and sell them in the city. Then you will have money and you will be happy."[27]

So the story begins, and the boy does take the apples. "And the tree," we are told, "was happy." But then the tree is alone once more, until, after a long time, the boy, now a middle-aged man, comes again, this time wanting not money but a house. The tree offers the boy her branches, and he takes them and builds a house. And once again, the tree was happy. Years later, the boy comes again, now an old man who wants to escape his life. And so the tree offers him her trunk for a boat so he can sail away. The boy cuts down the tree and takes the trunk and "the tree was happy . . . but not really." Finally the boy returns one last time, now a very old man. And the tree, long ago reduced to a stump, says, "I am sorry, Boy, but I have nothing left to give you." The boy replies that he does not "need very much now, just a quiet place to sit and rest." And so the tree offers him her stump as a resting place. And as the boy-become-old man sits down on the stump, the book ends, declaring one last time that the tree was happy.

My wife, who encountered this book as a child, informs me that she has always hated it. And she wonders why I like to read it to our children. I read it to them because it is a story, I think, about the generosity of things, about our tendency to fail to respond to that generosity in kind, and about the relationship between that failure and "the marred figure of what we should love," to recall the words of Adorno. The tree gives; the boy takes—and not in faith but in effigy. Somewhere in all this is a lesson about the fragility of nature and about what it might mean to take things in faith.

Though he never quite says it, Henry suggests that "the ultimate gift of things" is generosity. And "is it not," he asks, "'wound' in the reception of things given in their importance?" Do we not, in other words, learn of generosity only as we encounter the finality of things? And is not perishing part and parcel of finality? Like the giving tree, are not things generous, all the way to the point of perishing? And are we not called to respond to them in kind? In their "silent presence" things teach us of generosity; that is their ultimate gift.[28] It is the *ultimate* gift because generosity is "the mainspring of true action." If they do not spring from generosity, our actions are not true, and we prove incapable of fulfilling our calling as responsible beings, a calling we hear of only as we encounter finality: "if we fail to find finality in the world we will ultimately fail to find it necessary to do anything; and all that we have done will come to seem senseless." If our lives are meaningful, it is for the reason that we are moved by necessity. But we "learn of necessity," remember, "in all gentleness, or not at all." And gentleness, pure gentleness, is "the vein in which perishing speaks." Hence to encounter things in their finality can be only, in the last instance, to encounter them as they give themselves away. It is thus that we learn of the generosity of things, which becomes for us "the soul of necessary action." As Henry puts it, one last time: "from faith, into reverence, and into generosity"—the final resting place of wonder. Or better, the point at which wonder spurs us into the necessary action of bearing witness to a fragile world that is, nonetheless, grounded.[29]

## 8. Redemption

When I ask my five-year-old what he thinks of the story of the giving tree, he tells me that it is a sad story. When I ask him why, he speaks of the tree's apples and branches and trunk and proclaims that it was such a beautiful tree. These answers don't surprise me, of course, for his face tells me of his sadness before I even finish the story; and I know, because I know him, that this sadness is born of a wonder that has already deepened into love. And though it may seem odd, I read him the story precisely because I want to teach him that love is but wonder that has deepened all the way to that depth where joy and sorrow meet. He already knows of the joy, because he knows what it is like to climb a tree and to swing from its branches and to rest in its shade. There are several trees, just down the hill from the house, that I know he considers his friends. But he has yet to learn of the sorrow, though I know he senses it, close by, every time he sees a logging truck on the way to school. Of course, I don't need to teach him sorrow, the world will do that for me all too soon. But I do need to teach him what to do with sorrow.

Just last year, as my son ran around the house shooting pretend enemies, I stopped him once again to register my displeasure with his violent tendencies. And he informed me that it was OK to shoot these people because they were bad guys. When I asked of the nature of their offense, he replied, somewhat hurriedly, that they were cutting down the trees and killing the animals and blowing up the mountains, and then he ran off to shoot a few more of the culprits. I didn't stop him because, after all, I believe in his cause. But I'd rather hear him speak of beauty, which is what he does when he hears the story of the giving tree. For as long as his first response is to grieve over beauty lost, rather than shoot the bad guys, then he has, I think, encountered the finality of things and thereby proved himself capable of loving things and taking them in faith, though they be in suffering.

Henry sometimes refers to the experience of finality, to the reception of things in their importance as "aesthetic contemplation." Such experiences and encounters are "aesthetic" because, in the end, "there is no demonstrable conclusive meaning in the situation in which we live and move and have our being. And there is no demonstrable necessity about any course of action. . . . We cannot, therefore, make good the ideas of finality and necessity by demonstrating their relevance to anything which we represent to ourselves. These ideas must be thought out from the standpoint of unconditional concern." Precisely because there is no "proof" about the meaning of our lives or the necessity of our actions, nothing prevents us from taking things in effigy, nothing except beauty. But beauty can prevent us from possessing the world in effigy only if we already find ourselves at the mercy of an unconditional concern: "so far as our thinking is not actually centered in such concern and *informed with it* we are out of position for . . . the discovery of finality and necessity in anything."[30]

When my five-year-old speaks of the beauty lost when the giving tree is nothing but a stump, he does so, it seems, out of an unconditional concern for things, which is to say out of a wonder that has deepened into love. As he speaks of the apples and the branches and the trunk that the boy carts away, he seems to be quite cognizant of the gentle voice in which perishing speaks, and the fact that his first response to this voice is to speak of the tree's beauty indicates to me that he has already learned the final lesson of the story, which is that if we truly receive the ultimate gift of things, then we will be moved to bear witness to things as they perish. Most of this, I think, my son already knows, but what I must teach him now is that simply bearing witness to the beauty of things, even as they perish, is somehow sufficient for both their redemption and ours.

Speaking of Kierkegaard, Henry says, "that theme of the leap of faith beyond despair can be genuine enough, not as a *recommendation* but as the upshot of reflection based on experience. But should it not bear with it the recognition of a redemption into which finite things are assimilated, from which accordingly they are born anew?"[31] To take things in faith, then, is to move beyond despair—or better, to alter it—with the redemptive powers of an ever-deepening wonder.[32] To encounter things with wonder that has deepened into faith and reverence and love is to be "embraced by a significance that is all-embracive; as a significance found in [things] uniquely and originally it is the essence of their individuality; but as all-embracive, it sweeps us into ken with them as coparticipants in a universal situation"; that is, it sweeps us into "a universal significance which embraces them, and which, in embracing us, transfigures us and renders us whole." To be swept away with things into the embrace of this universal significance is not only to have taken things in faith and borne witness to them in their groundedness but also to have experienced redemption.[33]

Faith, sacrament, bearing witness, redemption: with the prevalence of such notions in Henry's work, we cannot be surprised to find him, at the end of *The Inward Morning*, admitting to the theological character of his thought: "It is at this point," he says, "that explicitly theological questions must be reckoned with by anyone whose sensitivity to the possibility of our groundedness has evolved within the framework of the Christian tradition."[34] Indeed, when I teach my five-year-old to embraces things, even as they perish, and bear witness to their beauty, so that both he and they will be transfigured and rendered whole by a mystery that transcends them both, am I not teaching him the lesson of the Cross? Do we not arrive at the Cross when we say that bearing witness to the fragile beauty of things is itself true, necessary, and sufficient action?

Henry tells us,

> We cannot *know* in advance what we must do. With whatever knowledge we truly stand forth, we stand forth beyond the frontier of knowledge, beyond, indeed, where we have been. Only so do we find out where we have always been, in all creation, a true wilderness. That is the home in which things other than ourselves are welcomed as guests, where innocence is sacred, and helplessness moves us not to abandon the helpless, in spite of our not knowing how to help.[35]

When helplessness moves us not to abandon the helpless, in spite of not knowing how to help: it is then that we encounter *true* wilderness, that we discover what it means to bear witness to things in the groundedness of their ageless beauty, and that we learn to take in faith and in love the fragile things of our world.

> As we take things, so we have them. And if in faith, though it be in suffering, yet we have them in earnest, and it is really them that we have.

## Notes

1. Henry G. Bugbee Jr., "The Philosophic Significance of the Sublime," *Philosophy Today* 11, no. 1/4 (spring 1967): 55–79.

2. Henry Bugbee, *The Inward Morning: A Philosophical Exploration in Journal Form* (1958; reprint, with a new introduction by Edward F. Mooney, Athens: University of Georgia Press, 1999), 165; T. W. Adorno, *Negative Dialectics*, trans. E. B. Ashton (New York: Continuum Publishing, 1973), 191.

3. Bill McKibben, *The End of Nature* (New York: Random House, 1989), 211; Bugbee, *Inward Morning*, 158.

4. Bugbee, 112, 86, 38, 164, 40, 175, 37, 36, 86.

5. Ibid., 162.

6. Ibid., 112, 220.

7. Job 7:11, 23:3–6; Bugbee, *Inward Morning*. Biblical references are from the New Revised Standard Version, unless otherwise noted.

8. These are questions selected from chapters 38 and 39. I have not used ellipses to indicate omissions because they proved too cumbersome.

9. Job 40:2, 40:4–5, 42:3–6. Quotations are from the NRSV, with the exception of the last sentence, which is from Stephen Mitchell, *The Book of Job* (New York: HarperCollins, 1979). The NRSV reads, "therefore I despise myself, and repent in dust and ashes."

10. Bill McKibben, *The Comforting Whirlwind: God, Job, and the Scale of Creation* (Grand Rapids: Eerdmans, 1994), 69; Bugbee, "The Philosophic Significance of the Sublime."

11. Bugbee, *Inward Morning*, 197.

12. Ibid., 139–40.

13. Ibid., 76, 163; Martin Heidegger, "The Thing," in *Poetry, Language, Thought*, trans. Albert Hofstader (New York: Harper and Row, 1971), 182; Albert Borgmann, *Technology and the Character of Contemporary Life: A Philosophical Inquiry* (Chicago: University of Chicago, 1984), 199.

14. Bugbee, 165–66, 165, 158, 165.

15. Ibid., 221, 155, 109.

16. Henry G. Bugbee Jr., "Wilderness in America," *Journal of the American Academy of Religion* 42, no. 4 (December 1978), 614–20.

17. Ibid.

18. "In wildness is the preservation of the world" is of course Thoreau.

19. Bugbee, *Inward Morning*, 128, 126. I owe the choice of the term "focus" to Albert Borgmann, who speaks of "focal things." For a helpful discussion of focal things that is indebted at some level to the influence of Henry Bugbee, see Albert Borgmann, *Technology and the Character of Contemporary Life: A Philosophical Inquiry* (Chicago: University of Chicago, 1984), especially, 196–210, and Borgmann, *Crossing the Postmodern Divide* (Chicago: University of Chicago, 1992), especially, 116–26.

20. Job 41:8–34.

21. Of course, in a certain sense nature remains indomitably wild, particularly as we encounter it in events like storms and earthquakes. But the fact remains, I think, that generally nature is not what it used to be, hence the transformation from Leviathan into "fragility." Once again, I owe to Albert Borgmann the choice of the term; he first alerted me, at least at the level of my reflection, to the fragile character of nature as we now encounter it; see Borgmann, *Technology*, 190–94.

22. Bugbee, *Inward Morning*, 137, 208, 117.

23. Ibid., 120, 221, 223, 68, 117, 138, 41, 208.
24. Ibid., 135, 137.
25. Ibid., 157, emphasis added, 215–16.
26. Ibid., 126, 231.
27. Shel Silverstein, *The Giving Tree* (New York: Harper and Row, 1964).
28. Bugbee, *Inward Morning*, 112, 139.
29. Ibid., 112, 159, 220.
30. Ibid., 113, 152–53.
31. Ibid., 197.
32. Thus it is not only that grief and despair alter wonder and turn it into love, as I said above, but also that wonder alters grief. Grief-altered wonder, and wonder-altered grief are flip sides of the same experience, which is the experience of loving things. For an extended discussion of wonder-altered grief, see my essay, "Wonder, Grief, and Tragedy: A Nietzschean Defense of Norman Maclean's *Young Men and Fire*," *Soundings, an Interdisciplinary Journal* 81, no. 1/2 (spring/summer 1998).
33. Bugbee, 219, 220.
34. Ibid., 215.
35. Ibid., 224.

# Henry Bugbee's Interpretation of the Book of Job

JOHN LAWRY

> At the core of personal life there seems to be something inviolately impersonal, akin in our fashion to the mode of being of rose, or rock—known and owned by all weather.
> —Henry Bugbee, "A Way of Reading the Book of Job"

One crucial question that needs to be asked is what is it Job heard in God's speaking from the whirlwind that brought him back to a desire for life and out of his earlier pleas to God to end his misery.

Rudolph Otto discusses something of this in *The Idea of the Holy* in his chapter devoted to the numinous in the Old Testament. He points out that Job's reasoning as far as concerns his friends is right. They are silenced by him. Job, however, after hearing the voice from the whirlwind, repents in dust and ashes. But it is inner convincement and conviction not mere impotent collapse and submission to merely superior power. Otto also points out that the inward convincement is not that which St. Paul insists upon in Romans 9:20—in which the clay is told it cannot question the power of the potter over the clay. Otto argues that the God of the voice puts "forward a theodicy of its own, and a better one than that of Job's friends, a theodicy able to convince even a Job, and not only to convince him, but utterly to still every inward doubt that assailed his soul."[1] I, for one, do not believe that Job's insistence on raising questions of justice are set to nought by God. But whether or not a theodicy is delivered in the voice, something momentous occurs through the voice, and Rudolph Otto gets us on the way to seeing what it is that Job sees after the speaking of the voice.

Otto thinks the opening sections of chapter 38 of Job lead us to expect God to say something like this: "'My ways are higher than your ways; in my deeds and my actions I have ends that you understand not': viz. the testing or purification of the godly man, or ends that concern the whole universe as such, into which the single man must fit himself with his sufferings." But nothing of the sort follows. There are no teleological reflections or resolutions even suggested. It is not the rational ordering of the heavens and the earth but its *mysterium* that is presented.

I shall not at this point discuss the dysteleological incidents and beings displayed in the epiphany in chapters 38 through 41 of the Book of Job. Suffice it to say, we should be reminded that the ostrich, and other examples, too, are as Otto says, "a crucial difficulty rather than evidence of wisdom, and it affords little help if we are seeking *purpose* in nature." The dysteleology is overpowering. "Nevertheless," he says, "with their mysterious instincts and their inexplicable behaviour, this very negation of purpose becomes a thing of baffling significance." The monsters: behemoth and leviathan—the mysterious in monstrous form—"these beasts would be the most unfortunate examples that one could hit upon if searching for evidence for the purposefulness of the 'divine wisdom.'" But they do "express in masterly fashion the downright stupendousness, the well-nigh daemonic and wholly incomprehensible character of the eternal creative power; how incalculable and 'wholly other,' it mocks at all conceiving but can yet stir the mind to its depths, fascinate and overbrim the heart." Otto goes on to say it is not simply the mystery that comes forth here: that would simply strike Job dumb not inwardly convince him. What more is there then? Otto says we see that this *mysterium* has an *intrinsic value*—a value that is *fascinating*. And this fascination is sufficient to assure us of the inward convincement of Job.[2]

Otto goes no further and leaves the matter at a psychological level of fascination that has intrinsic value. But we want to know why it is that what is displayed in God's speech is fascinating. We need it to be anchored in human nature, especially in Job's human nature. For help with that let us turn to Henry Bugbee's reading of the Book of Job.

We begin with Heidegger's quotation of a passage from Angelus Silesius: "The rose is without a reason (without a why), blooms because it blooms. It has no care for itself (or takes no care of itself), nor desires to be seen." Heidegger remarks on this passage:

> Short indeed, to speak truly, would be our thought, if we were to admit that the sentence of Angelus Silesius has no other sense than to indicate the difference in the ways in which the rose and man are that which they are (or ways in which they exist). That which the sentence does not say—and which is all important—is rather that in the most secret foundation of his being man exists truly only if he exists in the same way as the rose—without a reason.[3]

On Heidegger's interpretation of Angelus Silesius, Professor Bugbee has this to say: "At the core of personal life there seems to be something inviolately impersonal, akin in our fashion to the mode of being of rose, or rock—known and owned by all weather. It is through this in us that the elements seem most deeply to befriend us."[4]

Here something needs to be said about the things, as creatures in the world, as speaking to us as humans. We are apt to think that the things speak to us only in so far as there is a kind of personalizing of the things as creatures. I don't think Wordsworth would say this, but some interpreters have seen in *The Prologue,* his epic poem of his youth and learning, in those scenes of his walks in the Alps, that the craggy cliffs, windswept and bursting with secret springs, speak to him because there is something in the cliffs that *respond* to his *personhood.* Such views are again sometimes used to support general philosophical positions, usually thought of as romantically idealistic, that there is something in nature, however much it may, at first, appear otherwise, that partakes of the nature of self; that knows, feels, has desires; has plans and carries through resolves. In this sense we are adjured to get close to nature because it is our other self.

Speaking very crudely (and I apologize for the barbarisms I must commit to get the point across quickly), this romantic idealism supposes there is a "merely" *natural-part* of the things of the world (other than ourselves), but also there is a peculiar *self-part* of the things, and it is this part that speaks to the self-part of us. Notice that a view like this would hold that if there were no self-part in the things, then they would not speak to us. The world would then become without voice. In other words, this view holds that the world speaks to us only if there is "personality" in the world. Thus if we take personality out of the world (as, some hold, science does), then the world ceases to speak to us. But all this romantic idealism and its consequences run counter to what Heidegger and Henry Bugbee and Angelus Silesius are saying. The world does not speak to us in its personality but in its impersonality: in its inviolately impersonal reserve. We are not befriended by the world in that it speaks to us as a friend speaks to us. (Note how Job's friends speak to him, and they do not befriend him.)

As Kant drove home to us, it is essential ethically to think of ourselves always as *persons* in contrast with *things*. But if we think of our personhood as that by means of which we are grounded in the world, as one creature among others, then, by emphasis on our difference from things, we may come to think of ourselves as alien to the world and with little hope of access to it. We may become not merely moral agents (which we ought to be) but also we might become moralistic. Professor Bugbee, in his Job article, quotes D. H. Lawrence to the effect that one cannot idealize Mother Earth. And he goes on to say: "[It] is not in the direction of idealizing heaven-and-earth, and the things therein, that one is sustained by them. In this sense, making something of them is making nothing of them."[5]

God does not speak to Job of God's self as being teleologically concerned for humanity's ends in the world and enforcing a rule in which the things of the world work to our advantage, even though we, in our limited understanding, find it hard to discover God's concern. Rather, as Bugbee interprets the passage, God speaks of the world as impersonal and of inviolate reserve. In hearing God's speech, Job may have been answered—as Otto insists and Henry Bugbee suggests—but he has not been answered in accordance with his presuppositions, in terms of the charge he brought before God. He has been returned to a quickening desire for life and turned away from his earlier pleas that the Lord put him out of his misery. But there is a second theme, that of God's justice, and that needs to be addressed. Job is tasked and heaped by the problem of justice and *more important* that of suffering: why do the wicked prosper? and why does God ordain suffering for humanity? He does not simply complain of his undeserved suffering;

in chapters 21 and 24 he universalizes his charge and asks after the need for the unprovoked suffering visited upon all human beings.

I take it Job has believed in the proverbial wisdom with respect to justice (a view to be found in many places in the Book of Proverbs and most crudely stated in Psalms 37:25: "I have been young, and now am old; yet I have not seen the righteous forsaken or his children begging bread"). Such a view holds the following to be true:

1. Events as they affect a human are rewards and punishments. Joy and prosperity are reward and pain and misfortune are punishment.
2. The rewards and punishments are based on a principle of justice: you get what you deserve.
3. God is the being who adjusts events on the basis of justice to bring reward and punishment to humans.

But given the catastrophe in Job's life, he seems forced into an impossible dilemma, as Bugbee points out. He must either hold himself in contempt as having been guilty of some evil action, though he cannot discover what it was (as his friends insist he should do), or he must, if convinced of his righteousness, hold that people are punished by God without deserving it. This would lead him into an unbending defiance of God (as his wife counsels him to do). However, he refuses to be contemptuous of himself or defiant of God. But what is the alternative? It must be evident in what he hears from the voice in the whirlwind. What then does he learn? What alternative releases him?

As Henry Bugbee presents it, he sees things in their mode of being: their majesty, wonder, and inviolable reserve. That they have *no reason* for their being, but that being itself is the reason. Job, in sticking to his righteousness in the face of his losses, does not believe you get what you deserve. But as I read Professor Bugbee's paper, he is saying that before God speaks to him, Job is still caught up in believing that though joy and suffering are not distributed justly, nevertheless, they are distributed by an agent, God, and the agent consciously intends these rewards and punishment; thus that agent is not just.

Now, speaking in pedestrian terms, after Job has heard the voice from the whirlwind, he now sees things in their own right, and not as "cues" that we use to search for their significance as pawns brought into our lives to help or hinder us, he then no longer believes in points one through three above: that joy and suffering are reward and punishment, and are meted out to people by God. With this knowledge, he is released from the dilemma of contempt on the one hand and defiance on the other. Since he is not being punished justly, he need not scour his life to find some putative wickedness to explain his present misery. Since he is not being punished unjustly, he need not fall into defiance of God.

Now, on to some questions that have occurred to me, and to a number of students with whom I have read Professor Bugbee's paper. Assume that Job learns what Otto, Angelus Silesius, Heidegger, and Henry Bugbee (as I have interpreted them) claim he does from the voice in the whirlwind; assume he learns that at the heart of the being of things there lies not a reason but that they are *without reason,* without a *pourquoi,* without an answer for the "why?" either efficiently causal or purposive; assume the things of the world also speak to us of their impersonality and inviolate reserve, and that we respond to the world out of the core of our personal life, which is also impersonal and constituted by inviolate reserve, and that is the way we come home to the world—what place, then, is there for God? To put the matter simple-mindedly: has God spoken Elohim out of a job as God speaks to Job of the way in which he, Job, should see the world? And if we suppose that there *is* a place for God, in what sense can we say that this God is either just or merciful?

Some points need to be made with respect to the God who speaks. As I've mentioned to Henry Bugbee in our discussions of Job, I find it difficult to apply the notion of Being to what is said in biblical passages. The word is heavily Greek in its ontological origins and bears in it the mark of Greek detachment. It seems to me the place Being plays in the metaphysics of the Greeks, and of Heidegger, is played for the Jews by the *living* God. As for inviolability, I believe the God Job sees is indeed inviolable, but not inviolable reserve, nor impersonality, but inviolable *life.* This God does set many away from God's self in the Lord's majesty and unapproachability. Not in the sense of reserve but in the sense of *excess* of life. This is the same God who, when He is about to covenant with the seed of Israel, effecting the closest possible relation for a people, personal to its core, warns Moses that neither the priests nor the people are to approach close to Mount Sinai "lest he [God] break forth upon them" (Exodus 19:24). But this excess of life is always ameliorated, rendered approachable even in its risk (to the people) of its excess, by its *speaking* quality. Jeremiah and Isaiah object to worship of the things of the world (the things of the heavens, of the earth, and under the waters, if worshiped, were idols), because, as such, they neither spoke to the people nor heard their pleas. (See especially Jeremiah 10:6–14 and Isaiah 46:6–7.)

I, of course, am not saying Heidegger or Bugbee wants us to worship the things of the world, but I do wish to emphasize an aspect of the biblical sense of the Holy that is obscured by the notion of Being. No people have been more aware of the suffering inflicted upon humanity than the ancient Jews nor have been more conscious of the many ways in which the beings of the world can conspire against human well-being. Yet in the midst of all vicissitudes, they always searched for the way in which the things of the world, and its incidents, could be speaking to them as to what they were to believe and to do. And this insistence on *hearing* the speaking of the world had the most fundamental place in the ontology of the Hebrew scriptures. And this place was guaranteed to *speech* by the central claim, advanced in Genesis 1 and by the first chapter of the Gospel of St. John, that God does not create the world by a kind of first-cause artificing (as Aquinas claims) but, as St. Augustine insists in his *Confessions,* that God creates only by speaking. God creates the beings of the world to retain their aspect as things, even as they speak to us.[6]

I argue that it is the burden of the first lines of Psalm 19 to hold that the speaking of "day unto day" and "night unto night" is the source of our speech as creatures. (This follows the translation of the King James Version, a reading no longer customary. I believe the older reading can be defended but, given the necessary brevity of this essay, cannot present it here.) It is this creative speaking that we hear in our own speaking. Merleau-Ponty suggests in his *Phenomenology of Perception* and in *Consciousness and the Acquisition of Language* that our initial speech response to the world is a kind of singing of the world's praises.[7] The ancient Jews themselves support this interpretation of God's creative force by using the term most often employed to mean "word" (*dabar*) as also, equally, to signify "thing." Psalms 95 through 98 proclaim that our basic response to creation is joy. And in this joy, as the last five psalms (146–50) declare, we are brought to expressions of music and dance.

Now, I claim, it is this speaking quality of the world, of its being spoken by God, that Job claims to be his most acute loss in the midst of his suffering. This cry occurs in chapter 9. There he declares, just as the friends aver and God proclaims in the epiphany, the wonder and majesty of God's power: "Which doeth great things past finding out; yea, and wonders without number." But it is a sense of power that, for Job, in his collapse, has lost its speaking-hearing quality and has become unapproachable, impersonal, inviolate power, and nothing more. As he says: "Lo, he goeth by me, and I see him not: he passeth on also, but I perceive him not." In Exodus 33, Moses pleads with God to show him God's powers. God says he cannot do that if Moses is to live, but God will pass before him so Moses can see some part of the Lord's power. It is this seeing (perceiving) of God that is denied Job. God passes by him in God's unapproachable power, but there is no way Job can get to God to plead his case. As he says in chapter 9, God will not let him forget his complaint but will not let him present his case either.

Indeed, it is in chapter 10 that Job cries out, as he says, "in the bitterness of my soul." "Is it good unto thee that thou shouldest oppress, that thou shouldest despise the work of thine hands, and shine upon the counsel of the wicked? Hast thou eyes of flesh? or seest thou as man seeth? Are thy days as the days of man? are thy years as man's days?" Here, it seems to me, he is demanding an approach to God's person. He nowhere denies God's unconditioned creative power; indeed he insists upon it again and again throughout chapters 3 through 31 of the dialogue with the friends. But in chapters 9 and 10, Job is at his lowest point, expressing his view that he cannot come before God's presence (to come "before the face of God" is meant by the biblical writers or what English-speaking translators display as "presence of God"). However, even here, there is the briefest hint that Job is beginning to see that, in his suffering, he is being held by God to stick with his complaint, and thus God is not Job's adversary but his support in demanding that Job carry on with his complaint.

From chapters 9 and 10 on, even in the midst of Job's contention with God, there arises a sense in Job, ever more clear to him, that God is not maintaining God's unapproachability but is showing him how, in maintaining his ways before the Lord, he will find a way to come before the face of God.

Already in chapter 13 he comes to see that he has a status before God that his friends cannot claim: for he is not a hypocrite and his friends are. They have spoken wickedly for God in accepting a terribly low estimate of God's person. They assume he can be flattered. They know they are presenting weak, invalid positions, but present them in the hopes of currying favor with God. That is something Job will not do. He even goes so far as to say that this "shall be my salvation, for an hypocrite shall not come before him." And he says at the beginning of chapter 13 that he has seen all the wretchedness of humankind but still: "Surely I would speak to the almighty, and I desire to reason with God." He asks God to take God's hand from him and not let the Lord's dread make him afraid. And if this is allowed him, he knows he will be justified. He still has times when he lapses back into lamentation and says he cannot find the way to speak with God, but such occasions are increasingly interspersed with his eager pleas to God to speak to him. He says, "Then call thou, and I will answer: or I will speak, and answer thou me" (13:22). In 14:15 he says: "Thou shalt call, and I will answer thee."

Next consider 17:1–7. This appears to be simply a passage of lamentation. But these lines are followed by what, at first glance, appears to be an incongruity. "Upright men shall be astonished at this, and the innocent shall stir themselves up against the hypocrite. The righteous also shall hold on his way, and he that hath clean hands shall be stronger and stronger." If you think he is merely seeing the hardness of the world, and from that alone you draw conclusions about the world's governance, then this line is inconsistent with what has been said directly before it. But what if, in the midst of his calamity, Job is able to see something else at work on him, and other upright men will see the same. These matters will make the innocent and upright insist that hypocrites clear their speech of the cant that has been spilling from Eliphaz and his companions. In this insistence on maintaining his ways before God, one is not destroyed, not ground down but comes to be stronger and stronger (as Job is becoming).

This point of view, in which Job becomes stronger and stronger in his belief that he can come before God and be spoken to, is carried further in passages in chapters 16, 19, and 23. He insists there will be a witness for him who is either God or a redeemer who will take his case before the face of God, and he, Job, will see God, and God will not "contend with me in his great power"; rather God will pay heed to him.

Finally, in chapters 29 through 31, Job presents his last defense of himself in which he tells of the evils that he has not done and of his concern for the well-being of his servants and slaves, for they are human as he is: "Did not he that made me in the womb make him? and did not one fashion us in the womb?" But it is the final lines of chapter 31 that are the most revealing: "Oh that one would hear me! behold, my desire is, that the Almighty would answer me, and that mine adversary had written a book. Surely I would take it upon my shoulder, and bind it as a crown to me. I would declare unto him the number of my steps; as a prince I would go near unto him." As Marvin H. Pope, the editor and translator of Job for the Anchor Bible, says, "To wear or carry something on the shoulder is to display it proudly."[8]

God does rebuke Job, at the beginning of chapter 38, for darkening counsel and speaking words without knowledge; nevertheless, as God says in chapter 42 to Job's friends, God's wrath is kindled against the friends: "for ye have not spoken of me the thing that is right, as my servant Job hath." What was it Job said that was a darkening of counsel? What was it the friends said that was so much worse than anything Job said? And what is it God says to Job, not merely in the epiphany and the epilogue but all along during Job's debate with his friends?

In his debate with the friends, Job has spoken without knowledge, and Henry Bugbee has pointed out the sense in which Job was wrong. Job denies the claims of the friends' proverbial wisdom; especially he denies that one gets what one deserves. But Job holds God to be unjust (most clearly in 9:22–24). This implies that God is the agent of reward and punishment in human lives. And this implies the world is governed by Providence, Predestination, and Reprobation (as medieval scholastics claimed to be the case with God's governance); but the Providence etc. are skewed in that they are not laid out justly. I believe this is Job's darkened counsel. God scorns any teleological interpretation of His relation to nature (as Otto has pointed out), which interpretation is required by Providence, Predestination, and Reprobation.

And this, again as Professor Bugbee has said, releases Job from the dilemma of self-contempt or defiance of God. The friends have "kindled God's wrath" because they did argue deceitfully for God and refused to let Job present his contention with God.

What is the significance of what the voice from the whirlwind says to Job? It is neither impersonality nor inviolable reserve of Being. That would detach God from the world and Job from God. It is, rather, I hold, the overwhelming power of the living God. And this overwhelming power does not destroy the desire to live but sustains it, and when the desire seems lost in suffering, resuscitates it, brings it back to life, as it does for Job. Job had forgotten this and was lost (as he was in chapters 9 and 10) in that he knew of God's unconditioned powers but could not see God's person. Yet he *sees* God's person after hearing the voice from the whirlwind. That vision is not commensurate with impersonality of Being.

As for God's person as just, that is attested by what happens after chapters 9 and 10 in the move to Job's final statements in chapters 29 through 31. For here, I believe, God shows Job "the place of wisdom" in that the Lord is not Job's adversary in Job's suffering but Job's support in holding him to his complaint—insisting that he will be heard and answered by God's assurance that one can come before the face of God even in the midst of suffering. And if one holds to one's integrity, as Job does, he will come to "inward convincement" and the stilling of his anguish and affliction.

## Notes

1. Rudolph Otto, *The Idea of the Holy,* trans. John W. Harvey (New York: Oxford University Press, 1936), 78.
2. Ibid., 77–80.
3. Martin Heidegger, *Satz vom Grund,* cited in Henry G. Bugbee Jr., "A Way of Reading the Book of Job," typescript, III-7.
4. Bugbee, III-8.
5. Ibid., III-7.
6. See Thomas Aquinas, *Summa Theologica,* in *The Basic Writings of St. Thomas Aquinas* (New York: Random House, 1945), vol. 5, no. 1, question

14, art. 8, p. 147; see Saint Augustine, *The Confessions,* trans. E. B. Pusey (London: Dent, 1970), book 11, sects. 5.7, 7.9, pp. 256, 258.

7. See Maurice Merleau-Ponty, *The Phenomenology of Perception,* trans. Colin Smith (New York: Humanities Press, 1962), 187, and Merleau-Ponty, *Consciousness and the Acquisition of Language,* trans. Hugh J. Silverman (Evanston: Northwestern University Press, 1973), 81.

8. Book of Job, Anchor Bible, intro., trans., and notes Marvin H. Pope (Garden City, N.Y.: Doubleday, 1965).

# On Starting with Love

ORVILLE CLARKE

> Whoever has the *ordo amoris* of a man has the man himself.
> —Max Scheler, "Ordo Amoris"

The title of Henry Bugbee's major work is *The Inward Morning*. It is subtitled *A Philosophical Exploration in Journal Form*. The title itself suggests when or rather *where* this journal or journey begins; it begins, so to speak, with the first light of reflection, the dawning of the "inward morning." It is a spiritual journey. As such it begins at the only place such a thoughtful journal could begin: with the most immediate thought that occurs to one when one is thinking or reflecting. The first entry in *The Inward Morning* is most instructive in this regard. Here Bugbee compares the beginning of his reflection and musings with the spontaneous generation of a poem that accretes, as it were, from some initial perception or flash of insight. Observing with the poet William Carlos Williams that in the writing of a poem, "[o]ne perception must move instantly on another," he concludes: "Now for me philosophy is in the end an approximation to the poem, a structure built upon your own ground, . . . your ground where you stand on your own feet.[1] Where else pray could one begin? Granted. One can only begin in media res. You have to jump in right where you are and take your chances. You simply have to begin where you are. True.

But this leap of faith from within and upon one's own ground immediately raises a question: Is this a proper beginning or starting point for philosophical reflection? With what exactly is one beginning here? With oneself? Yes, of course; or say rather, with one's own *location*—here and now. In this same context, Bugbee cites with approval Dewey's conviction that "[t]he local is the only universal, upon that all art builds."[2]

Does this tell us what is local? I think not. Let us, therefore, change Dewey's remark slightly to read: "The *individual* is the ground of universality, upon that all philosophical reflection builds." That, I would suggest, begins to get at what Henry Bugbee has in mind as a starting point for *The Inward Morning*. It is, however, only a starting point, a first step and not the end of the journey. The personal and individual must be expanded inward and outward to meet the other. That is the supreme power of love.

*The Inward Morning* provides an answer to the question of the proper beginning of philosophical reflection—or rather, let us say, it *is* the answer in the form of thought "in the act of taking shape." That's an important point. However, without actually making the journey and riding it out to the end, one cannot truthfully say if it is a proper beginning or not. Bugbee does offer a more explicit—and, I believe, profound—answer to this same question in another essay entitled "On Starting with Love." Here the whole question of making a beginning of philosophical reflection is set in the context of whether one ought to start with love or violence. The issue is resolved insofar with the rather startling claim that "love must provide us with such measure of understanding as may be possible to us of love and violence"; in other words, a beginning is made with the recognition that love itself must provide whatever intelligibility there might be in our world. As Bugbee himself puts it: "What did I mean? Well, I meant that love enjoys priority in the order of intelligibility over the phenomena of love-and-violence, and to the effect that we simply can't be any clearer in our understanding of these phenomena than love unambiguously enables us to be."[3]

What Bugbee has come upon in his daily walks and reflections, not unwittingly I think, is the priority of what Scheler referred to as the *ordo amoris,* the order of love. According to Scheler—and here he reiterates the earlier insight of Pascal, "le coeur a sis raisons"—love is identical with the heart and to this extent is "a microcosmos of the world of values." Bugbee himself uses this order of love as a kind of reflective prism through which to glimpse something of the meaning of our being in the world. "In love and by virtue of love," he says, we come to know the emptiness and fullness of the world.[4]

Suppose we gaze at the world through this "optic of love." What shall we see? Can we truly behold the intersection of that emptiness and fullness of our being? And must we go it alone or do we share this mystery of Being with others?

Bugbee makes essentially two points: first, that our being in the world is a *rooted* mode of being, and second, that it is a being unto others. Both modes of "being-in," however, owe their possibility to love. His whole point, I believe, is that it is only in and through the light of love that we are able not only to glimpse something of the meaning of being in the world but also even *to have a world:* Without love we were worldless and alone. Enworldment then is a gift of love. Moreover, it is no accident of Being but happens, as we are told, "at the heart of our own agency and intelligence as *the principle of their animation.*" St. Augustine wrote: "Man loves." Why? Because that is what he is, or more nearly, *how* he is. Love is at the heart of Being. In this respect, the *ordo amoris* is that ontological (and even preontological) structure that enables us to discern, though perhaps through a glass darkly, the broad outlines of our human enworldment. More important still is the fact that it throws into relief a fundamental structure or feature of that enworldment, a structure Heidegger designates as Care or Concern *(Sorge)* but Bugbee prefers to call "responsibility." Responsibility is a term that indicates our concern with and responsiveness to other beings. It is this responsiveness that carries us beyond ourselves into relationship with those others: "Our responsiveness is ek-static."[5]

What do we see in this "optic of love?" Ourselves. Yes. But not just ourselves—alone but always in relation to other beings. What is reflected back to us in this reflective prism of love—which we ourselves are—is the existential fact that our being-in-the-world is always already a being with others, or as Bugbee says, our being in the world is "a being unto other beings in mutual existence with them."[6]

Enworldment is also and at the same time an "enfoldment" of man's being along with others: the world is a *mitseinwelt,* a world shared mutually with others. I think Jean-Luc Nancy makes this very same point in a beautiful and penetrating essay entitled "Shattered Love":

The "world" that is here in question is not an exteriority of objects, nor an environment or Neighborhood. It designates the mode of the putting into play of Being: through the *Dasein,* Being is being-in-the-world (thrown, abandoned, offered, and set free: that is what "in the world" means). If the world is *mitwelt,* shared world, Being insofar as it is "in the world" is constitutively being-with, and being-according-to-the-sharing. The originary sharing of the world is the sharing of Being, the Being of the Dasein is nothing other than the Being of this sharing.[7]

Being human then *is* this "being originarily with others" and that means finally being vulnerable and exposed to "the finite touch of the infinite crossing of the other" that we call love. But this is just where the real problem begins. Love finds us running scared, so to speak; that is to say, we never quite know fully how it stands with us or those others with whom we find ourselves. We are caught in a kind of "erotic ambiguity" that is an essential part of being human and being in the world. Our own being is called into question by the same structure that grants us that being. As Bugbee himself puts it: Our "worldly" concern and responsiveness involves us reflexively in a sort of mutual questioning of ourselves and others. What is ultimately at stake, he says, is "the mutual questionableness of being in the world—our own and that of other beings." This mutual questionableness is "at issue" or "at stake" insofar, that is, as it bears the whole weight of human concern, both for our own being and that of others it constitutes "the essence of being in the world."[8]

So where does this leave us? Does the order of love leave us high and dry regarding the question of the meaning of our being in the world? If we start with love where do we wind up?

If we start with love—and, indeed, Bugbee claims we cannot do otherwise, then inevitably we wind up exactly where we started, viz., at the intersection of the emptiness and fullness of Being—which is to say: *in-the-world.* But this does not leave us high and dry, existentially speaking; on the contrary, it leaves us right where we belong: at the core of our "being-in." The questionableness of being in the world, then, goes straight to what Bugbee calls "the heart of responsibility," that is, to human *concern* itself. Concern points back to the rootedness of man's being-in-the-world in "concern-with" other beings. This presumably is the ground of our being-in-the-world.[9]

In some respects Bugbee might seem to be merely recapitulating Heidegger's basic insight that Concern (*Sorge*) is always already "concern-with" (*Fursorge*). That, however, is not the case. The essay "On Starting with Love" does show the influence of Heidegger's thinking—it would be strange perhaps if it did not—but is a deepening and reworking of this thought. The most significant difference concerns the question of whether Fursorge or "concern-with" is itself fundamental or given from the ground? Is Fursorge itself rooted in some still more fundamental phenomena? Bugbee thinks so. When he speaks of love, for example, he means something fairly straightforward, something basically human and down to earth. Love is simply the responsiveness (and this means more than merely "concern-with") of one human being to another that always takes place under what he calls "a governing simplicity." In Bugbee's words: "That is the simplicity of spirit—as it is given, in all manner of incarnate ways, *coming right down to the everyday,* whatever the walk of life in which we may happen to be engaged." In this sense it is love that grounds concern and thus opens up and makes possible a human world: "Our being in the world is a radical, a rooted mode of being even as it is also a being unto other beings in mutual existence with them. Therefore we and our relationship with them stand under qualification through the radicalization of concern."[10]

Heidegger is for the most part silent about love and consequently never presents it as having any real ontological bearing on man's being. Fursorge (concern-with) is as close as he ever gets to mentioning it. Why is not entirely clear. Perhaps Jean-Luc Nancy is right in saying that he was prevented from summoning love by the fact that Fursorge always starts from an "I" or from an ego-center and moves toward the other. In this respect human concern-with is and remains egocentric and never quite reaches the other. It is not an act that cuts across and radically alters the "I" in its movement toward the other, not that mysterious crisscrossing of "I" and other that occurs in human love. Fursorge more nearly resembles the classical ideal of a noble and spiritual kind of love that would hardly sustain the bonds of a human and shared world.[11]

In any case, love is not the primordial bonding surface of the human world. That is reserved in Heidegger's thinking for temporality

*(Zeitlichkeit)*, which is taken to be the "preontological" structure of Dasein's being-in-the-world and thus the ground of finitude itself: Dasein is Time. Temporality is also the source and ground of human Care *(Sorge)*: Dasein is a being-toward-death *(Sein-zum-Tode)*. The question remains, however, whether temporality and the awareness of death is enough to bond human beings in a shared world? Is Concern itself primordial and "given from the root"? Bugbee thinks not. He probably would not quibble at all with Heidegger concerning the radical finitude of Dasein or human beings; in fact, he states explicitly that finitude is "the condition in which we come knowingly to share with other beings through dependent participation with them in the world." This sharing always occurs "under the conditions of finitude." However, he goes on to point out that the sharing of a common world is rooted in some deeper structure that he calls "a world-constituting principle *underlying concern itself.*"[12] Now if we understand this correctly, then concern, though fundamental to our being human and being in the world, is not the most primordial structure. What is then? What is this world-constituting principle underlying concern?

Bugbee states outright that it can be nothing other than love. Love and love alone grants to human concern that "enabling power" that lets us stand forth into relationships with other beings and without which we should stand *alone*. In his own words:

> It is from the love that comes to us as reflexively given that we become truly concerned with beings occupying our attention, feeling no less than the fittingness of their call as a claim upon us; not as a claim inherent in them or conferred by us, but as intrinsic to their mode of being in the world with us. Their claim is, as it were, substantiated in that which discovers itself to us reflexively as grounding ourselves. It is by virtue of love as thus coming to us that we are able to receive other beings into our concentrated, undivided, undistracted attention. "Love" as naming our mode of concern in attending to them is reflexively grounded in love as coming to us. The latter, *love as fore-given, is also forgiving of ourselves.*[13]

Love then grants and begets more love. But what does it mean to speak of love as "fore-given" and "forgiving" of ourselves? What else but that our humanity and with that our essential limitations are given ahead of us as possibilities *in and through love:* "Finitude receives defining."

The essay "On Starting with Love" is a kind of "phenomenology of love" that affords the reader a perspective on a structure or phenomenon more primordial than temporality. Time is a possibility only for a being who is always already outside itself in-the-world. Without the *"ek-stasis"* of love, time would simply be a mindless blur in the infinite void of nonbeing. Bugbee is right, therefore, in speaking of love's "gracing us." What we are graced with is what he so gracefully describes as "the non-self-sufficiency of finitude in principle."[14] That and that alone is the ground of our humanity.

We owe a debt of deep gratitude—and, yes, of love—to the man and philosopher who almost alone among contemporary thinkers has given us such profound insight into the very foundations of our human essence and being. What Henry Bugbee has discovered—I had almost said "uncovered"—in the essay on love is something that only a few philosophers but all mystics have always known: that the *ordo amoris* is the ground of the *ordo humanis*. To be human is to have a world and to be able to share that world with other human beings. Love alone makes that possible. Love therefore is the "enworlding" power of Being: it is what gives in the *es gibt* of Heidegger's ontology. What is given is the gift of our humanity. We are singularly *graced*.

## Notes

1. Henry Bugbee, *The Inward Morning: A Philosophical Exploration in Journal Form* (1958; reprint, with a new introduction by Edward F. Mooney, Athens: University of Georgia Press, 1999), 33; italics mine.

2. Ibid., 33.

3. Ibid., 232. The whole question of a proper beginning is in some respects a kind of tour de force. One simply begins as Bugbee makes clear in the very first journal entry, where he writes, "What is needed, I have concluded is a record based on just one principle: Get it down. Get down so far as possible the minute reflections of day to day thought. Get down the key ideas as they occur. Don't worry about what it will add up to. Don't worry about whether it will come to something finished. Don't give up when faced with the evidence of miscarried thought. Write on, not over again. *Let it flow*" (34).

Henry Bugbee, "On Starting with Love," *Humanitas* 2 no. 2 (1966): 150. To find a philosophical parallel to this claim of the ontological—and even "preontological" priority of love, one would need to go all the way back to Plato's *Symposium* where the Idea of Love constitutes the fundamental source of intelligibility for all Being. The only modern equivalent I know of is found in Pascal's *Pensees* and to some extent in Max Scheler's work *The Nature of Sympathy*.

4. Max Scheler, "Ordo Amoris," in *Selected Philosophical Essays,* trans. David R. Lachterman (Evanston: Northwestern University Press, 1973), 100; Bugbee, "On Starting with Love," 150.

5. Bugbee, "On Starting with Love," 157; italics mine.

6. Ibid., 155.

7. Jean-Luc Nancy, *The Inoperative Community,* chap. 4, "Shattered Love," in *Theory and History of Literature,* vol. 76, ed. Peter Conner (University of Minnesota Press, 1990), 103.

8. Ibid., 102; Bugbee, "On Starting with Love," 152. I cannot resist slipping in a personal existential note of my own here. Not only is our being questionable but it is also damnably ambiguous. We grope our way through the world forever in the throes of what the U.S. novelist Thomas Wolfe so graphically described as "the monstrous fumbling of all life." But what can we do? What can we finally expect or hope for from this life? Nothing. Or perhaps only to be "modestly happy" as one of my students once put it. Without love, however, even this is not possible. Love is our only saving grace. As Sheldon Kopp said, quoting Auden, "We must love one another or die."

9. Bugbee, "On Starting with Love," 155. Bugbee's idea of "responsibility" differs fundamentally from Heidegger's concept of Concern *(Sorge).* In Heidegger's view Concern is a basic ontological structure of Dasein and is existentially given, whereas, Bugbee maintains that human beings can choose to be responsible or to be concerned. The difference here is freedom of choice. The life of concern is not forced upon human beings.

10. Ibid., 156, 155; italics mine.

11. Jean-Luc Nancy, 104.

12. Martin Heidegger, *Basic Writings; From Being and Time to The Task of Thinking,* ed. David F. Krell (New York: Harper and Row, 1977), 61; Bugbee, "On Starting with Love," 156, 157; italics mine.

13. Ibid., 157; italics mine.

14. Ibid. The full context of this quote is the realization through love that we are "incapable of inherent reality" and are thus laid open to both the emptiness and fullness of the world. The one thing needed to realize the fulfillment of our being is the one thing that prevents its realization.

# When Philosophy Becomes Lyric

EDWARD F. MOONEY

> A voice often comes to me, and always says the same thing: "Socrates, make music and compose."
> —Plato, *Phaedo* 60-e

We all need some sort of homing device, an indicator that reminds us where we came from and how to return home. When this device gets dropped as an automatic mechanism from our evolutionary inheritance, when we no longer have the wonderfully reliable and mysterious sense of place that migrating geese or whales possess, then we make do otherwise, largely culturally, with equally mysterious and hopefully reliable charts and paths to get us home. Sometimes an especially tuned text, arriving in the mail, will point the way.

Henry Bugbee says that philosophy is a meditation of the place. If so, then philosophy becomes a meditation of the place we now inhabit, with respect to whether it can be our home or is in fact our home. And if lyric meditation rings true, we find the faithful place from which we came, to which we return, to our loves and celebrations and sweet consolations, as well as to each grief and pain and anguish lying there. Meditation knows dusk and gloaming as well as openness to light.

Let's say that coming home, through a lyric meditation of the place, is finding our place but also common ground, returning to a common source. Still, this does not mean, for Henry, that we forget the variety, the special detail, of all the particulars along the way. What we share, our most shared source, is presence to particulars, not generalities. So he would have us stop at each bend in the river, at each pool, at each eddy—and there to watch for glitter, for color of leaves, and there to listen for the whisper of trees on the banks where feet have purchase and good standing.

And if (as Henry has it) philosophy approximates the poem, then the texts and meditations that lead us to the place will be poetic texts and meditations. A lyric philosophy will lead us home, or remind us of the home we've left, or reveal in flash of insight that where we stand is now where we belong.

Thirty years ago *The Inward Morning* came upon me as convincing as a sudden pelt of sleet. I was stopped cold. Here was a thinker absolutely on track—speaking ever so eloquently, so precisely, in a language I barely understood. I can still find myself moved, bewildered, heartened, by a lucid piece of Bugbee lyric prose—glittering like morning light in the glassy splendor of boughs, bent low under an ice storm's gentle gift.

The mainstays of my philosophic background—Kierkegaard and Nietzsche, Hume and Kant—seemed barely relevant to my floundering. This was terra incognita. And a triple wonder, at that: the wonder of the vast terrain, where landscapes, ships, and philosophic streams and sloughs seemed to intermingle wildly; the wonder of the smaller things presented to me then and there within this vastness: this bend of oar, this branch of willow, this line from Pindar. And the wonder of my eerie entanglement in this terrain and its particulars—up to my ears and flailing.

I composed a list of passages and concepts to which I could return, when lost. This accumulating index gradually became a trail of twigs and stones, familiar signposts as I made my way through wilds crowned by nameless peaks, cradling ever-changing rivulets. Then sometime in early summer 1969, I traveled to Montana to meet the author, face to face. Now I return to face the question I faced then: Can the circle of philosophy be widened to include lyric, religious philosophy, philosophy with a poetic, musical openness toward spirit or the sacred? I'll be answering YES, and painting in broad strokes on an oversized canvas to illustrate.

I suspect you'll wonder if I'll be doing epistemology or environmental ethics or even philosophy of religion. Or you might wonder more generally whether what I offer is literature or philosophy, love of nature or love of truth? But I'm out to blur these boxes, if not bash them, gently—without kicking up too much mud. Lyric should take us clean out of the corrals, clean out, and into the open, where the niceties of professional compartmentalization can be set aside.[1] I remember Stanley Cavell distinguishing between his daytime student writing and his wilder after-midnight journals.[2] In his remarkable career that contrast seems gradually to have disappeared. I admire the exploratory candor and inventiveness of his searching voice, however idiosyncratic and untamed it might sound, defying genres and corrals, left and right. You just can't harness his sliding, backing, devilishly spinning paragraphs. Perhaps because of their journal format, Henry Bugbee's thoughts, though also on the loose, seem more immediate, in both their anguish and their joy.[3] They're on the mark and nontranslatable, glancing, uttered in a moment of birth as they become his own unique and fully recognizable voice. In composing my own mind in response to his reflective journal, I've found myself working to avoid three pitfalls, and I've named them: they're the philosophical vices of Dryness, Divide and Conquer, and Impatience.

1. Against Dryness: Our ideals, or what matters, must be delivered in terms that evoke their presence. When we talk about ideals or moral or aesthetic or spiritual matters, we may speak dryly. But if we do, if we fail to evoke the presence of places of moral or aesthetic or spiritual importance, then those scenes and the spirit or ideals that animate them, dry up—whatever nominal assent we mumble. Lyric is one way to evoke the presence of what matters. If we fail, if the presence of what matters dries up, then we, and our students and our sisters and our citizens, for good or ill, will be fed from other sources inimical to what reflective philosophy can provide.

2. Against Divide and Conquer: Our ideals, or what matters, must be delivered whole, and not in terms of rivalries and battle lines among the disciplines. The strategy of divide and conquer often makes good

analytical sense. But Balkanization is not always the way to go. In retrospect, we can see the unintended damage Kant exacts in erecting great administrative divides amongst a university's faculties, which then protect their fond preserves and serve as staging grounds for raids on adjoining territory. It's a pity he breaks apart art, morality, science, religion, politics, and everyday life, divides their territories and names their defensive ramparts so convincingly that we can now hardly see the world otherwise than as so divided up. But to parcel out the common tasks of understanding and reconciliation into a multiplicity of distinct disciplines or institutions nips wholeness, connection, in the bud. Why should art and ethics, spirit and community, sky and earth, be taken up in ways that increase their distinction from each other? The cure is lyric in philosophy, which aspires to wholeness, linking streams of life within a single resonating verse.

3. Against Impatience: Let the tumblers fall into place. Then the bolt can slide, the door can open. We rush into answers before we're ready, before we know the true dimensions of what we face, and we take quietude, patience, as a vapid refusal to participate or pull one's load or be resolved. We must await the truth to dawn, and on her terms, in her time. We cannot force her arrival as suits our needs or timing. I trust my discussion will avoid these vices.

What follows is a kind of divertimento, like Mozart's K. 563, scored this time for Henry's voice, my voice, and another. There are five movements, the first called Love and Strife, the second, Trust and Danger, the third, Affliction and Release, the fourth, Death and Purity, and the last, Philosophy and Inward Mornings. Each starts as a meditation and evocation of a place: the place of Diotima, the place of Melville's boatmen, the place of Job, a place on the North Fork of the Trinity River, and a place for lyric philosophy.

## 1. Love and Strife: The Place of Diotima

Philosophy has not always been indifferent to the lyric or religious. The pre-Socratics had their gods and hymns.[4] But perhaps that was extra baggage. There's some clear shift as Socrates comes on stage. In one disguise, he's there expressly to debunk the lyric and religious. The figure of a skeptical antagonist stands before us, the philosopher badgering his public with demands for rational justification of any position whatsoever. But Socrates has another side, one pertinent to our topic.

Think of the *Symposium*. There we find him late for the party, delayed by the grip of a trance. Later, when he's fully present, he rises to speak on the evening's topic, which is love. Perhaps his earlier solitary withdrawal into the quiet of a doorway was a kind of meditative preparation. In any case, as he begins to open up, the persona of a rational skeptic has been put aside. For one thing, he instantly gives credit for his insights to someone else, relying here on the authority of another whose credentials he's had no time to check. His tale, he says, was told to him by a priestess — as I imagine it, beside a village well — with no confirming witness present. And more to our surprise, he claims for these newly adopted insights not ignorance but knowledge. Love, apparently, is the one thing Socrates knows about. In his ignorance, he needs instruction from another. What he learns of love he owes to a woman who wears her authority on her sleeve and whose wisdom subsequently gently oversees and guides his rich and intimate account. His sense of love is a gift from Diotima whom he encounters at a fount where earth and water mingle, where looking down one sees one's face, and also heaven's vault.[5] It's here that lyric words of love spring forth.

It is not like Plato, however, to let this rapture last too long. This lyric transport to the divine unknown (or known), laid out secondhand by Socrates, is barely done when it is broken up. The vision of love leading us to Truth and Beauty might have been given more time to settle in. But reality has other plans, for if we turn the page, strife breaks up the party. A drunken Alcibiades barges in, braying all sorts of threats and accusations. His rage is tweaked, it seems, by Socrates himself — Socrates has jilted him. His most cunning advances have been rebuffed. How dare this balding sage, so far from youthful beauty, presume to reject him — a hunk, a king of homecoming parades? Thus Plato has the all-but-divine Diotima countered in his dialogue by the all-too-human intoxicated Alcibiades, who leads down to pandemonium.[6] Yet both speak of their daimon, love. A wildness reigns about this table and its loquacious guests.

What is the link between the unearthly even somewhat barren

frosty wilderness of Socratic love and the riot of willful desire that possesses Alcibiades? How can creation, a universe, hold steady in its hands both the speech of Diotima and the disruptive rant that follows? Can the wisdom of Socrates delivered as a voice by crystal wells, tame the violent, wine-stained spleen of this late-arriving party-crasher? Whose call shall we heed? If reality is completed by our answers to this tense standoff, how shall we answer—and thus complete reality?

This is exactly the sort of bait Henry Bugbee would rise to take. We should glide up on the matter, as Henry does in his essays and throughout *The Inward Morning*.[7] He ties love and lyric and the religious, looping them through sympathetic references to Meister Eckhart, through discussions of celebration and rebirth, of idolatry and grace, and through narratives that move us to the quick, move us to respond commemoratively, affirmatively.

Lyric in Henry Bugbee's work sounds the wonder of a world, but not through dodging strife or fracture. Creation is wilderness, an uncharted world where the abundant presence and passing eternity of finite things stand forth destinate and dense with meaning. But the itch of Alcibiades remains. Can love and wholeness claim day—and the dusk or night?

This question resounds in Henry's distinctive voice. We sense him struggling to hold within a single world-worth-being the savage terror of a kamikaze raid—and the saving testament of falling snow.

> I think of the suicide planes which I *witnessed;* oh! they still call out to me, and what I make of them, of the lives perishing in flames, is still unfinished business which I feel I shall have to take upon myself until my dying day. What, what, indeed can I make of them? Oh, I must be answer for these men. Men I never knew. Living men. How can I find answer except as I can articulate a true prayer? Is it not true that we were not enemies? And who will believe this, how can it be believed?[8]

## 2. Trust and Danger: The Place of Melville's Boatmen

Henry Bugbee wilderness is not a solitude apart from communities of trust. Think of those portraits of ship life on the Pacific, where relentless danger, numbing fatigue, celebration, and mutual dependence are tightly interwoven. But let me lay the terror of those suicide planes respectfully aside—without neglecting the need to answer to and for them, even perhaps in prayer. I'll take up a more manageable page from Melville that works on parallel themes.

In a particularly hair-raising passage from *Moby Dick* we are presented with a fourteenth-century British conqueror who demands as tribute to his victory six citizens to be hanged.[9] The French mayor and five others step forward with halters around their necks, at the ready, noosed. This fright snaps us alert—to our mortality. What follows is a whale chase:

> Men in frail longboats, far at sea, hard at work. With luck, a harpoon strikes, and all is burst alive and into risk. A hemp line, an instant earlier coiled neatly aft within its barrel, springs out, around the loggerhead, and forward, jogging by each boatman's oar and by his rowing wrist. The hooked whale runs and dives. Rope smokes, racing over oars and through its bow notch, pulling boat and crew at break-neck speed. It was called a "Nantucket Sleigh Ride," a time and place of boisterous, dangerous fun. A bracing, pitching, soaking ride, all right. Yet that whale in harness was deadly serious, and the line he pulled was deadly—terribly ready to snake out a wayward loop to noose an oarsman's foot or wrist, flinging him and boatmates fast into the deep.[10]

That's a philosophic image of the place, as much as Diotima's place with Socrates beside the well—or the opening in which a snowflake falls to melt in moving waters. It's a place of danger that might open toward despair. Our world contains the possibility of hanging. The Melville chapter ends thus:

> [T]he graceful repose of the line, as it silently serpentines about the oarsmen before being brought into actual play—this is a thing which carries more of true terror than any other aspect of this dangerous affair. But why say more? All men live enveloped in whale-lines. All are born with halters round their necks; but it is only when caught in the swift, sudden turn of death, that mortals realize the silent, subtle, ever-present perils of life. And if you be a philosopher, though seated in the whale-boat, you would not at heart feel one whit more of terror, than though seated before your evening fire with a poker, and not a harpoon, by your side.

We are indeed wrapped toward death.[11] But the boatmen's image also contains strains of joy, common bonds, and the thrill of racing free beneath the sky. If there's doubleness here, the aspect of doubt, danger, or despair need not utterly prevail.

When we succumb to images of distrust and violence we are easily cleaved by cynicism. Just as feedback loops of love breed love, loops of distrust breed more distrust. We must think candidly and anxiously of Alcibiades and of the danger of that smoking rope. Yet these images have no exclusive claim to truth. Frames of distrust or suspicion can be met with possibilities of trust and generosity; frames of violence or horror, met with compassion and respect. If pictures hold us captive, it is only other pictures that can set us free.[12]

The beauty we can see is and will be cracked and marred. Yet we're not just captive spectators: we work in ways we can against the triumph of the worst. And this includes imaginative, philosophical work. As Gillian Rose puts it in a startling book called *Love's Work,* "keep your mind in hell, and despair not!" Attend to evil, but do not despair. The "true prayer" Bugbee sought in the awful memory of a death-bound pilot is part of love's work, the part that keeps us from despair. And celebrating fellowship and grace and splendor is good reflective work, as well—good philosophy, I'd say.[13]

You'll note I've left out all mention of rational or reasonable appraisal and subsequent free choice. In this, I follow Iris Murdoch's lead. Neither in our lives nor in our thinking can we hoard our trust, awaiting propitious, even guaranteed, investment, with all rational warrants secured in advance. Goodness involves perception more than calculation.[14] There is no place of safety, as Melville's boatmen know, from which to calculate. And a Hobbesian attitude of fearing the worst and sounding alarm can breed the worst—and trust will never flower.

As Melville has it in his boatmen's narrative, we are not on separate islands vying for protection, or not always that, but navigating a common sea. This is the heart of Henry Bugbee's social philosophy, though he doesn't call it that. In *The Inward Morning* there is work with fellow seamen, work with rowers in an eight, and in Melville there are working whalers in their longboat. These are pictures of community, of necessary mutual trust and risk in work. Care and trust and responsibility are here—inescapable and all the way down.

As I see it, this Melville image counts against any contract theory of society, for it reminds us that whether the setting is Hobbesian or Rawlsian, we must have trust already in place—trust, say, that others will heed contracts or bargain in good faith. Thus trust, and acknowledgment of the personhood and responsibility of the other, must precede any negotiation of contracts. We are always already somewhat faithfully in a boat, even as we ponder whether to jump ship or switch crafts. We are never utterly weightless, boatless, or if we are, no resolve can make the least bit of sense, whether for the good or for the worse.[15] It's worth noting too, against contract theory, that it has no place for the underappreciated communal virtues of praise and generosity and acclamation, virtues central to Henry Bugbee's philosophy. Is it not true that we acknowledge praiseworthy persons and actions before we devise rules to encourage the sustenance and legacy of such persons and acts?[16]

Such communal values and working fellowship are surely of central importance. So if we come across a philosophy like Henry's, that bypasses zealous skepticism and adversarial distrust, that brings moments of celebration, joy, and commonality to the fore, then we should be won over on this ground alone. If he shows up danger, he also shows up trust and wholeness and a depth of generosity. This makes a philosophy to take to heart. And lyric holds the heart.

Philosophy is a meditation of the place—the place of Socrates and the place of boatmen on a drunken sleigh ride. And next comes the place of an outraged Job, ready to curse the very bowels of creation. This is the third stop on our itinerary.

## 3. Affliction and Release: The Place of Job

Henry finds a comity between the sacred and the everyday. Grace and gracefulness, renewal and redemption, release from bondage and accommodation to suffering display this commingling. These concepts cross back and forth over sacred-secular divides, and in crossing back and forth, underwrite a lyric-religious philosophy. Consider their place in Job.[17]

Affliction and misery are all too familiar—yet we hope not so commonplace as to numb compassion. Job's unmitigated affliction strikes us terribly—as it strikes Job himself in round upon round of wounding disasters. In short order he loses his fortune, his family, his health, his friends. We witness killing blows to body, mind, and spirit. His wife and erstwhile companions recoil in fear and self-righteous judgment. In his troubles, none remain to stand by him. His "friends" are there as empty shells or worse—they peer with vacant curiosity or interfere with blame. Would that they would work with him in his fragility!

Instead he's left alone in tatters by his ash heap. But Job does not despair. He rises up. We watch his fierce counterattack, as he demands reasons for his pain. His rage boils over giving strength to the fist he shakes at heaven in frank and fearsome protest. And yet for all its power, Job's story does not end in this rebellion—despite its righteousness. For we are witness also to a wrenching transformation of that protest and of the pain that feeds it—a sudden quieting. He is reborn to wonders of creation as he responds in the closing blizzard, the howling, lyrical Voice from the Whirlwind.

The voice from the storm is not bent on crushing Job but on delivering him to something else, delivering him to the religious dimensions of his cares, the very depths of his cares. This demotes matters of the justice of his pain and dilutes pain itself. The blizzard seems to offer an occasion for true prayer. But who could believe all this, that in his outrage, Job might be quieted, without humiliation, and that his pain might become bearable?

The voice with such power to transfigure Job's suffering into quiet and readiness for prayer had been preceded by the voice of Elihu, a mysterious figure, perhaps a Diotima, who reminds Job that wisdom and understanding will not come in a lawyer's brief, will not come from forcing one's way by protest and argument into a hearing before the Lord. The bench of Justice is vacated. Instead, as Elihu foretells, wisdom comes in *dreams,* and in *visions,* and in *songs in the night.*[18]

Job must lower his fist and his voice—and listen—not to an explanation but to something like a song in the night. And then the Voice from the Whirlwind arrives to roar and whisper in his ears. Job hears no justification of his pain but a summons to partake of a grandeur that sweeps around and through him, a call to complete his reality in new and sustaining terms.

In poetry unsurpassed in power, fury, and sudden gentleness, the

Voice commends to the sores and fissures of Job's consciousness soaring hawks, plummeting hail, and starry skies. To his ringing ears and smarting eyes it presents creatures of the deep and denizens of the meadows, one by one. And as Job's listening awe increases, his afflictions recede.

True, he's overwhelmed by the Lord's spectacular parade of the particulars of creation. But he is not overwhelmed in the way a stronger force subdues, and hence defeats, its enemy. He is overwhelmed as great music might overtake us, sweep our will and power—but not our strength—to one side. The Lord asks knowingly:

> Canst thou command the dawn?
> Like clay, the shape of things is changed by it;
> They stand forth as if clothed in ornament! [19]

Job becomes open to radiant particulars that are intimate: they enter the heart. Simultaneously they are strange, uncanny. They hold us at arm's length, even in their intimacy. Perhaps this is to ensure that any lurking claim we might harbor to master or control them stays properly subdued. Job's questions about the justice of his plight are swept aside. Here he is, recipient of creation, reality itself, delivered despite his protest—delivered point blank.

We can hear this tale of suffering, protest, and release toward a world transfigured in a roughly secular register. We stress what is NAMED by the Lord—rather than what the LORD names. We don't need to stress the obvious unfairness of Job's afflictions—given a human scale of justice. We have Job "melt away" before the grandeur of creation, rather than abase himself before a tyrant's bullying power. (The Hebrew permits: "I melt away," which surely bests the humiliating and self-loathing "I repent [or abase myself] in dust and ashes."[20])

In this vein, we can make sense of the gifts of this world being gifts, without being sure how, if at all, to picture a Giver. In my view it is the great strength of both Henry Bugbee's writing and of the Book of Job itself that we can see and hear the wonders of creation—with no assurance whatsoever about what we should say (if anything) about the source of these wonders.

We sense our capacity to receive a world of radiant particulars, partaking of the sacred and the everyday, while the topic of their source is discreetly set aside, a tolerable and appropriate mystery. I can know Melville's lyric world—while he recedes in mystery. I can know the lessons of moving waters—while the source of these lessons, their origin, recedes in mystery, the mystery of how waters speak or teach, the mystery of how mere words, mere blocks of print, speak or teach in *Moby Dick*. Gilbert Ryle reminded us of this years ago. Without lacking one whit of confidence that our thoughts, apt or inept, have in fact arrived, their presence quite indisputable, nevertheless, we never catch their source, or the explicit process of their deliverance, in the moment. As he has it, this source is and forever will remain "systematically elusive."[21]

At one point in *The Inward Morning* Henry Bugbee asks how he could ever assimilate the wisdom he has gained from moving waters or do justice to its profundity. The fact that instruction is given is beyond doubt, even as its basis is eclipsed. The fact of instruction and the mystery of its source are grounded in testimony, in witness, in the power of voice attesting and confessing and bearing witness. This assumes, of course, an expressivist view of language and the self, and assumes holistic ways in which they complicate themselves—not in reflecting reality but in bringing it to birth through sensitive attention and articulation. Such a view has begun to appear back in the academic pastures and corrals, say in the work of Charles Taylor on language and ecology. But here I'd like to keep my voice closer to the open winds and tangled watersheds.[22]

### 4. Death and Purity: The Place on the North Fork of the Trinity River

In *The Inward Morning* lyric testimony to the religious sometimes rises as a closing reflection on an arresting narrative. You may recall the swollen river carrying an anonymous camper from a pool along the bank of the Trinity River under a boom and then into the rush of smothering downstream rapids. He is swept under an overhanging willow branch. At the last moment he clutches at the trailing, tangled shoots and clings for life. The branch holds, he holds, and he is swept in a wide arc toward the safety of a muddy bank. Henry arrives at the spot on the run, grasping the hands of the young man and gazing on him with compassion and relief. At that moment, each registers the nearness of death, the vulnerable strength of a will to live, and a gratitude for the gift of willows. There's also, at least for Henry in retrospect, a sweeping gratitude for release into a world reborn at the very instant it passed the brink of perishing. Henry gives us this story in words as resonant as the realities they convey. These realities come as a call for response. As we take them, so we have them.

This capacity to complete reality in answer to a call is an aspect of our reception of great music.[23] When it has us in its grip, the reality of a conductor's score, or of a wooden fiddle, or of acoustic rebounds recedes toward insignificance—as we take music, so we are taken up by it. It becomes completed in our response to its call. This can become all too evident if the smooth flow of resonance is disrupted, not allowed to complete itself: a doorbell rings, a siren wails, shattering our capacity to respond affirmatively.

Our capacity to complete reality in answer to a call provides the bridge we need between the contingent particularity of voice and locale and the universality and necessity philosophers have always sought. In answer to a call, we offer up a voice from where we stand, in hope of resonance felt as necessary as it impacts a wider, potentially universal community of listeners. In response, I have faith that my voice *does* answer to the necessary, and will be heard by others as such. I have faith that the capacity of each to answer for all is universal.

We return now to the narrative of the North Fork. Take the words that follow Henry's account of the young man swept unaccountably from certain death to safety. He writes: "Not a word passed between us. As nearly as I can relive the matter, the compassion I felt with this man gave way into awe and respect for what I witnessed in him. He seemed absolutely clean. In that steady gaze of his I met reality point blank, filtered and distilled as the purity of a man."[24] I'm struck again that these words must stand or fall on their own. Apart from the massive fact of cultural acquaintance with our language and traditions, if these words persuade, their power must rest on the testimony of the speaker, and on the accumulated respect we have gathered for the authenticity of his voice.

Hume will grant us compassion, and Kant will grant us dignity. But both would surely balk at "meeting reality point blank," unmediated by some "conceptual scheme" or current paradigm or habit. And both would surely balk at the idea of meeting reality "filtered and distilled as the purity of a man." For the lesson of our times—or so it's bandied—is that only we humans, through our technical manipulations, can filter and distill—that reality itself, in this regard, is dead or dormant. It just IS, containing no powers of vital becoming, of filtering or distilling itself, even in our presence—let alone powers permitting it to be reborn.[25] But I fear the towers of meaning we construct are falling down about us. If there is purity of voice in things, it cannot be there merely tailor-made, cut to our own taste and fashion.

Think of exemplary persons, saints and shopkeepers, scientists and daughters, singers and comforters, whose lives themselves are direct testimony to value, without which, I suspect, we would have no purchase on awe, respect, or compassion, no inkling what purity might mean, or of what it might mean to be taught by moving waters.[26] Our footing here depends on trust in the truthfulness of some avowals that are first personal, through and through.[27] If lyric provides comity between the religious and the everyday, there is also reciprocity in *The Inward Morning* between vivid narrative depiction and more abstract philosophical reflections.

In music to which we have given ourselves over time, we can hear premonitions of a complex central section in the simplicity of an opening bar. Likewise, giving ourselves to pages of *The Inward Morning* allows us to hear premonitions of a complex closing in the midst of an opening narration. In fact, the simple narrative becomes deepened and the complex closing strikes us with new simplicity. There we find the pages themselves filtered and distilled, yielding purity anew.

Try rereading the passage we've considered, in Henry's words, straight out. Perhaps in its opening you'll hear its closing, and in its waters see the sacred everyday, and in its particulars hear its universal resonance—and relevance. The passage ends, you'll recall, with Bugbee's remembering that "In that steady gaze of his I met reality point blank, filtered and distilled as the purity of a man." The pure reality of the man is the reality of Job, a Job cleansed by the storm, cleansed by the rapids of affliction and rescued into the wonder of a world reborn as a place of perishing, passing, and bountiful particulars.[28]

Reflecting on this meeting with reality point blank, Henry continues: "I think of Meister Eckhart's 'becoming as we were before we were born.' I think of what Conrad says of the storms visited on sailors far at sea as chastening them."[29] These reflections too resonate with our companion Job—suffering, protesting and resuscitated—a Job cleansed absolutely by the swirling voice from the storm. I think, too, of the incapacity of Job's erstwhile friends to comprehend his affliction, their readiness to cast blame, and the ease with which his danger might have slipped into irremediable despair. Job came close. Would that he had had a human hand reach out to him, in his tatters, on his bank of ashes, and an eye watching with compassion! Would that Job in melting before the music of creation had had a witness who could see his becoming as he was before he was born—could see the fullness of reality there, point blank, filtered and distilled as the purity of a man.

## 5. Philosophy and Inward Mornings: The Place of Lyric Philosophy

Henry Bugbee's view of the religious is rooted in his conviction of the splendid significance, even the sacredness, of moments and things that we encounter day by day. Here is an author who can carry us with absolutely no smoke and mirrors toward the animating center, a place where divine and commonplace are in communion. As he has it, the true mystery, which a religious stance embodies, is not acknowledgment of or belief in some Other World or God or Righteousness. On the contrary, the center is already here before our noses: "The genuine religious mystery . . . is none other than that of the existence of things, of ourselves, and of all finites."[30] It is not the science, nor the utility, nor the brute and obdurate resistance of finite things and others but the trembling mystery of these to which *The Inward Morning* is addressed and by which it finds itself informed.

There's a rhythm to these reflective Henry tales, encounters with trees and wild seas: adagio or allegro. They're tales that open up as song, emerging from an infinite expectant quiet before the exhalation of a word. And they carry forward into verse a stillness, a patience—a poise of breath awaiting its successor sound.

Here is Henry reflecting on Job's plight, giving us Job's stillness, his quiet in affliction:

> Tuesday, January 15, 1963
>
> No wind stirs. At Zero Fahrenheit the flakes of snow are not at all large. Incredibly light and unwaveringly they fall. A myriad of them fills our meadow round the house. One sees them best looking at the trees beyond. Their falling accentuates the still-standing trees, the dark trunks.
>
>> And the still of the trees is the nearness of falling snow.
>> Occasionally, in the meadow, a weed nods and lifts again.
>> The low fire on the hearth is even more discreet.
>
> Tuesday, February 12, 1963
>
> No great pressure of anything to say.
> Doubt with respect to so much of past thought.
> ... a reticence almost to speak at all.[31]

Perhaps from silence, or perhaps from waste or welter, words skip like stones in rhythm, melody, or color, or mourn the incandescence of a setting sun, or sound the stopping wonder of a harvest moon.[32] Lyric brings us there to them in sempiternal resonance. We're quieted, invited to take in a scene as if it were born again that instant: born through words at one with world, expertly joined, both—just then articulate.

Lyric testimony gives voice to the very things its songs enfold. The truth to which it aspires is truth not of statements or propositions but of the realities it conveys, delivered directly to us, point blank. True generosity, true care, true flux and perishing. And it is realities indeed we seek, not just words to stand in for something else. So lyric philosophy lies toward the margin of a philosophy modeled on science or the law, for its testimony is far removed from the construction of a lawyer's brief or a physicist's proof—however elegant either may be in their own terms and in their own right.

Of course testimony, like any other speech, can fail, drum helplessly on deaf ears. As Henry Bugbee has it, "We cannot rub each others noses in immanent reality by argument," and neither can we be assured our witness will be heard. But that is an inevitable risk when philosophy goes lyric. And its track record in presenting essential, existential truth is none the worse for that. We must know in our bones or not at all that at its height, testimony ascends to truthful song, verse that joins persons and their worlds.[33]

Here is his encounter with Robert Oppenheimer: "I can remember hearing Robert Oppenheimer on an occasion, when he was casting about for a way of communicating the 'beauty' he found in the things he had investigated. Those with whom he was talking wanted to go on talking about quantum theory; how little they reckoned with the look in the man's eye as the meaning of his life's work suddenly overtook him anew, and he stammered with gratitude for the magnitude of the gift, in the appalling newness of essential truth. How shall we find a word to say it?" The contexts for revelation of essential truth, then, are several and ever-surprising. The occasion might be fraught with drama of Job-like proportions—a matter of ultimate affliction, abandonment, and at last the restoration of a world. Or it might be a midsize occasion, as in Robert Oppenheimer's sudden stammering attempt to assimilate the force of a life's work bearing on him. Or it might be the size of a sudden realization of danger of a man at sea gripping a rope-looped oar. Or it might be a miniature, as in catching sight of a snowflake in graceful fall upon a cabin stove.[34]

As in life, our endings should return to our beginnings. So I return to Socrates wondering over the voice that said "Socrates, make music and compose." I wonder if he took that voice to be telling him that his life would have been better spent making music. Perhaps he mentions it for another reason, though. Perhaps he's telling us that the voice came to him, regularly, and he in fact tried to have his life become a tribute to it, an answer to it—he's telling us, that is, that despite any appearances to the contrary, he lived his life devoted to this voice, devoted to music and composition. What would it be to have thought and life answer to music?

Architecture has been called frozen music. We could alter this image to our advantage: when music freezes, it becomes architecture. And if we ever had to choose between music frozen and music fluid there's no doubt which we'd have. The music of our best architecture aspires to erect a frame to outlast floods and fires and ravages of time, a frame aspiring to immortality. Yet the power and eternity of liquid streams is something else again. Music is the most passing of the arts, yet none the less for that. Lyric, as music, is not depleted by its being transitory, caught in passing. Its power lies in how it passes, how it grows and builds, winds down and disappears into a silence not alien to itself but all its own. It creates its own life, and its own wake and aftermath. Which is its eternal glory or sadness—its lightness or heaviness—all spun out as flow.

If modern philosophy returns to the great hope captured in Descartes's or Kant's architectural aims, to build a lasting edifice on strong foundations with integrity to span the ages, then we will sadly gravitate toward an impersonal, weightless language, and become weightless ourselves. We will become a static reflection of the remote cables of logic and engineering that at best aspire to the frozen eternity of geometry. But a lyric philosophy will aspire elsewhere, aspire to embrace the prospects of a contrasting and fluid eternity, to embrace the fragile perishability of flowing streams and simple calling sounds.

## 6. Endings

Let me try to gather up some loose ends—even though my idea has been that loose ends are best gathered in lyric. Here are some relatively static ideas—three of them—to pocket.

First, for all the celebration of a world receptive to our love and fellowship and walking, there's still—and will be—an Alcibiades, a smoking rope about to hang us, Jobs in affliction, men perishing in flames. Second, the way to face this dispiriting, horrific, clanking mess is not by looking for rationales or reasons but by caring despite the mess. Rubbing out disorder through philosophical or theological towers or crafty explanations will come to naught. We proceed in courage, perhaps in prayer, against the sharp grain of suffering, denying neither loss and devastation nor our capacity to complete reality for the better against the power of the worst. Third, lyric philosophy, by celebrating what's good and light while leaving room for inevitable dark helps us through these trials by gathering a coherent, yet perishing world. It provides a moral and linguistic voice to raise up a world and lets us be lifted by it.

Lyric becomes, as Henry has it, a meditation of the place and in extremis true prayer that opens to the impossible—and unbelievable: the redemption of an ice-bent bough of birch. Relinquishing the world as a cognitive or practical possession, it allows us to be thankful recipients of a world-well-worth-being, the only world we have, a world of persons given to our care, and things given to our awe and wonder, our gratitude and surprise.

Here is a fitting and characteristic Henry benediction, attesting to steadiness and perishability:

> It is well while looking at rocks
>     to have the roar of a river in one's ears.
> Or to see still-standing trees
>     through falling snow.[35]

## Notes

1. Charles Taylor makes the contrast between moral thought in the academic corrals, ethical thought in the open, and thought attentive to the spiritual forest beyond in *Iris Murdoch and the Search for Human Goodness*, ed. Maria Antonaccio and William Schweiker (Chicago: University of Chicago Press, 1996), chap. 1.

2. Stanley Cavell, *A Pitch of Philosophy, Autobiographical Exercises* (Cambridge: Harvard University Press, 1994), chap. 1. Cavell was Bugbee's student at Harvard in the 1950s.

3. The contrast between a distance one must assume in providing an autobiographical overview and the immediacy possible when one publishes a journal may be relevant here.

4. See, for example, Jan Zwicky's path-breaking and painstaking study "Bringhurst's Presocratics: Lyric and Ecology," *Terra Nova* 1, nos. 1 and 2 (1996), and her earlier and equally original *Lyric Philosophy* (Toronto: University of Toronto Press, 1992).

5. I take full responsibility for placing Diotima by a well; in defense, what more likely place for this auspicious meeting?

6. See Martha Nussbaum, "The Speech of Alcibiades" in Nussbaum, *The Fragility of Goodness* (Cambridge: Cambridge University Press, 1986).

7. See, for example, Bugbee's essays "The Philosophical Significance of the Sublime," *Philosophy Today* 11, no. 1/4 (spring 1967): 55–79, and "On Starting with Love," *Humanitas* 2, no. 2 (1966): 149–63.

8. Henry Bugbee, *The Inward Morning: A Philosophical Exploration in Journal Form* (1958; reprint, with a new introduction by Edward F. Mooney, Athens: University of Georgia Press, 1999), 225–26.

9. Melville, *Moby Dick,* many editions, chap. 60, "The Line."

10. I recently learned of an occasion Henry Bugbee used this passage. He had just been hired at Harvard a few years after serving on a navy minesweeper in World War II. At the first philosophy faculty meeting, new hires were to rise and say something about their interests — C. I. Lewis, Quine, and others, as I imagine, in intimidating attendance. Another new hire, Morton White, stood and performed with good grace, citing his interest in Dewey. Bugbee rose to read with great passion the boatman's noose Melville passage, paused, and then declared "That's Philosophy!" More than one auditor must have wondered what had become of philosophy at Harvard. But I take it Bugbee's point was quite serious: not only is the Melville passage an eloquent piece of philosophical reflection, its lesson is apt, namely that a philosopher, though he be seated by his fire, will know that strange mix of impending adventure and impending doom as vividly as the boatman will. The philosopher must have *immediate* access to the vitality that lies but a hair's breadth from hanging.

11. If you prefer Heidegger, we are "beings toward death."

12. On keeping philosophy alive to human fragility, see Nussbaum, *The Fragility of Goodness,* and especially Nussbaum, *Love's Knowledge* (Oxford: Oxford University Press, 1990).

On frames of trust and mistrust, see my *Selves in Discord and Resolve: Kierkegaard's Moral-Religious Psychology* (New York: Routledge, 1996), chap. 7.

13. I owe the phrase "marred beauty" to David Toole, who borrows from Adorno. See his essay in this volume. On moral imagination and the good, see Iris Murdoch, *The Sovereignty of Good* (New York: Schocken, 1972).

Gillian Rose, *Love's Work: A Reckoning with Life* (New York: Schocken, 1995). The quote is an epigraph from Staretz Siloun and reappears on 105. On theme of celebrating fellowship, grace, and splendor, see Rose, *Love's Work,* throughout.

14. See Murdoch's *Sovereignty of Good.*

15. See my criticism of MacIntyre's picture of a "criterionless leap" as an adequate way to grasp Kierkegaardian stage-shifts, *Selves in Discord and Resolve,* chap. 2.

16. See Annette Baier's "Trust and Anti-Trust" and "Trusting People" in *Moral Prejudices* (Cambridge: Harvard University Press, 1995); Keith Lehrer's *Self-Trust* (Oxford: Oxford University Press, 1997); and Stanley Cavell's essay

"Moments of Praise" in praise of Fred Astaire (forthcoming). In the present context we can argue (1) that "reason as argument" needs to be supplemented by "reason as interpretative-elaboration," (2) that a display of exemplary *persons* whose depth and voice *fronts* any claim to worth needs to supplement other sources of access to worth, preceding our familiar list of warrants *backing* claims to goodness; (we may, of course, subsequently break down an exemplar's presence, testimony, and witness discursively, and thereby find the conviction that we have a true exemplar either weakened or strengthened), and (3) that the time is ripe for celebration and acclamation of exemplars, of testimony and witness, and that this work is fully philosophical.

17. In speaking of lyric-religious philosophy, I am alluding to Henry Bugbee's sense of openness to the "ground of our being," or openness to Zen-like "moments of illumination," or openness to our "ultimate concerns"—each of which would call for a suspension of insistent self-preoccupation. In speaking of crossing "sacred-secular divides," I'm borrowing from the title of Albert Borgmann's fine book *Crossing the Post-Modern Divide* (Chicago: University of Chicago Press, 1992), an image that befits a Missoula writer.

On the Book of Job, see my *Selves in Discord and Resolve,* chap. 3, and "Repetition: Getting the World Back" in *The Cambridge Companion to Kierkegaard* (Cambridge: Cambridge University Press, 1998), as well as John Lawry's essay in this volume.

18. Job 33:15, 35:10.

19. Job 38:12–15, amended from the Herder translation found in *Dimensions of Job,* ed. Nahum Glatzner (New York: Schocken, 1969), 149.

20. See Herbert Fingarette, "The Meaning of Law in the Book of Job," in *Revisions,* ed. Alasdair MacIntyre and Stanley Hauerwas (South Bend: University of Notre Dame Press, 1981), and Terrence Tilley, *The Evils of Theodicy* (Washington D.C.: Georgetown University Press, 1992), 96, for discussions of appropriate translations of Job's final utterance marking his "quieting."

21. Gilbert Ryle, "The Systematic Elusiveness of the 'I'," *The Concept of Mind* (London: Hutchenson, 1949).

22. Bugbee, *Inward Morning,* 139; see Taylor's essay "Heidegger, Language, and Ecology," collected in *Heidegger, A Critical Reader,* ed. Hubert Dreyfus and Harrison Hall (London: Blackwell, 1992), and his *Philosophical Arguments* (Cambridge: Harvard University Press, 1955), chap. 6.

23. See Albert Borgmann's essay in this volume.

24. Bugbee, *Inward Morning,* 172.

25. What of the apparent exception posed by the popularity of evolutionary theories, where life emerges from the frothy seas? As that process becomes distilled statistically, it too approaches the model of the mechanical, of selec-

tive push-and-pull, and hence ultimately dead. Spirit, aspiration, conviction, or election become "folk-psychological" terms to be set aside as ultimately weightless.

26. Bugbee, *Inward Morning*, 83.

27. I discuss exemplars, and the mysterious artistry by which they communicate their being first-personally, in "Exemplars, Inwardness, and Belief: Kierkegaard on Indirect Communication" in *International Kierkegaard Commentary, Concluding Unscientific Postscript,* ed. Robert L. Perkins (Macon, Ga.: Mercer University Press, 1997).

28. Bugbee, *Inward Morning*, 171, 2. Kierkegaard's notion of "repetition" invokes the rebirth of a world as gift; see my "Repetition: Getting Back the World."

29. Bugbee, *Inward Morning*, 172.

30. Ibid. 160–61.

31. Bugbee, "A Way of Reading the Book of Job," typescript.

32. Robert Alter opens his new translation of Genesis (New York: Norton, 1996) with God beginning to create the earth "from welter and waste," which surely bests the too-abstract "from chaos" or "the void."

33. Bugbee, *Inward Morning*, 99.

34. Ibid., 169, 121. We might think a meditation of the place requires that we remember the poet and the wildness of rivers—and exile the physicist. But this would conflate the rise of natural science with an allied but conceptually separate hubris. In reflecting on Oppenheimer, Bugbee finds a compatibility, even a union, in one man, of a most exacting mastery of theoretical approaches to the material world with a most Job-like wonder at the mysteries of creation.

35. The closing lines of Bugbee, "The Philosophical Significance of the Sublime."

# 5

# Celebrations: Human Voice and Moving Waters

Philosophy is not worked out by anonymous scribes from no place in particular. *The Inward Morning* presents its author as his thoughts unfold, in walking, in seeing and remembering, in witnessing. It is easy to think of the author as "Henry," for he makes himself available to informal address. Cyril Welch remembers him as his teacher at the University of Montana. Gary Whited evokes Henry as a mentor and fishing partner. And the novelist David James Duncan celebrates Henry as a neighbor whose very being teaches grace and generosity of spirit despite the trials of his final years. Thus we come full circle to the praising epigraphs that open this collection. We see the writer, teacher, and companion through the presence he imparts to others, a gift to those who share his paths through wilderness.

# Henry Bugbee as Teacher

CYRIL WELCH

For the most part, we hitch a ride. As an undergraduate, I myself had been riding more than three years in mathematical work. Not only the rigor (a right way of doing things, rooted in the matter itself) but also the autonomy of agency enthralled me. Still, when I paused one day to ask my favorite mathematics teacher where my work would lead, how I could pursue graduate work in the field, he replied that I would eventually have to engage in original research. Original! His remark brought the truth home to me: I had been hitchhiking, with no sense of either beginning or end.

In the middle, then. Middles can intimate the pressing possibility of beginning at the beginning: the very instability of puberty, for instance, or the paradigm crises of scientific work, situations where the middle ground no longer provides the security to work on toward apparent endings without recuperating beginnings anew. Also in classrooms: in retrospect, I detect intimations in Mr. Dodge's freshman English, Mr. Bier's short story course, Mr. Karpat's course in totalitarianism (where we read Russian novels), and Leslie Fiedler's lectures on the Bible as literature. Hearsay, however, as words of others become, or de-come, unless we can rearrange them at their origin. Through no fault on their part, these men were the drivers, I the passenger. And I knew it, perhaps because my work in mathematics had clarified the difference between indicators of origins and engagement within them.

Winter quarter, 1960, at the University of Montana. Still in the middle. Mr. Marvin, my teacher in the history of philosophy, suggested I enroll in philosophy of religion, taught by the new chairman of the philosophy department, Henry Bugbee. Hume's *Dialogues,* Tillich's *Dynamics of Faith,* Kierkegaard's *Sickness unto Death,* Buber's *I and Thou*—we students had to puzzle through these ourselves: the class hours offered no exposition or explanation, only—only!—a voiced engagement in the origins of those works, dissolving them so that they could rise freshly again as responses to their origins. No longer would works simply indicate, invite, leaving me in the vestibules.

It was his voice. A voice directly addressing what we listeners also had to address. Addressing the speaker genitively, the listeners datively, the matter itself accusatively, the books vocatively. As in all great works handed down to us for contemplation, such a voice bypasses forever the question whether someone else's sayings are correct or not.

Not that, at the time, I understood. In my other work I had already learned the chief mark of understanding: the ability to assemble and reassemble, retrace another's sayings, keeping the words, my own now, in tune with their source. The voice baffled me, the source eluded me. All the more because I perceived no solid ground on which I could move, no histories to which I could revert, no formal argument I could mime. Listening to that voice, you either began at the beginning or missed the flow entirely. Or rather, not entirely. Even the most skeptical, the most middle-bound, sensed that an origin resonated within that voice. Perhaps the utter lack of middle ground in the voice itself released it from the conventional fetters of competition: I never knew anyone to take offense at Henry Bugbee's talks.

Unlike many others, I persisted. Voluntarily, I composed a one-page retracing, submitted it, arranged to meet him in his office, pressed him on one thing and another—I don't recall what. I do remember him steadfastly deflecting my reductive efforts. Accustomed both to patterns of intracalculative thinking and to neat taxonomies of philosophical positions, I would rephrase his sayings in isolation from their origins. And he kept starting over again from the beginning. Without the faintest sign of impatience (although he could, I later learned, become impatient with peers insisting on reducing great works of our tradition to middle ground).

Henry Bugbee baffled many of us—but in a way essential to any creative endeavor. Used as I was to the milder frustrations of mathematical work, I might not have pursued the matter with him over the next years had it not been for an evening's conversation with another student of his. Bill Dougherty, several years older than I, a chain-smoker with an aloof manner, commented one day in the university library that the high mark I received in philosophy of religion acknowledged only my organized work, not insight. Shortly after that occasion, he came over one evening for supper. And undoing the conventional tedium of social conversation, he took me through the Hindu story of "The King and the Corpse," as available (I later found out) in Heinrich Zimmer's book of that title. "Imagine you are this king," Bill said, "and this mendicant has brought you a fruit every day for many years." At each juncture of the story Bill demanded that I decide what I myself would do. Each fruit, as it turns out, conceals a jewel. This initial revelation leads to strange engagements at night, on a funeral ground where the dead are cremated and criminals executed. Bill's account, his questions, appealed to my talents for step-by-step decision making; I now had to respond, not just listen. I don't recall how, exactly, Bill guided me through the labyrinth of prima facie contradictory conditions: the rotten fruit containing, unnoticed, a gem; the hero of high station willing to engage in a lowlife adventure; the patient holy man engaging in the ultimate evil; the unresolvable twenty-four riddles to which the king must nonetheless proffer whatever solutions he can imagine; the ultimate resolution through ignorance; the subsequent violence.

A decisive inkling. An origin only makes sense, comes within hearing, as it originates us—gets us going, jump-starts those who acknowledge it. Every effort to sneak up to an origin, to address others about it without allowing oneself to be addressed by it, simply chases it away, leaves us with indications, invitations, procrastinations—unresolvable conundrums. Any flow, be it that of drum playing, horse training, or careful talking, utterly depends on our acknowledging such origination. Intellectual work likewise, although here the peculiarly modern emphasis on constructing a free-floating middle-ground detracts from the need to begin, encourages old and young alike to hitch a ride, to continue along the established itinerary without having either to begin or to end. We intellectuals may learn to say many clever things, organize many essential thoughts, discern many barely evident consequences, but our work really takes hold only when it embodies a beginning, reverberates with its own origin, ours only on trial.

Many who listen to Henry speak, even more those who read his *Inward Morning,* discern the possibility of a contemplative life attuned to, redolent with earth and air, fire and water. Myself as well. The voice, lurking even in the script, entices us into a walking life, introduces us to the shame of merely hitching a ride. Stepping out, we discover the exigencies of individuality, as well as their opposite, the comforts of anonymity. Unlike Thoreau's and Whitman's, Bugbee's voice resounds directly out of the person who in fact walks. This personal touch accounts, perhaps, for Henry's power to diffuse the resentment that the irony in other thinkers easily arouses.

Over the next two years I studied other works with him, either as enrollee or as auditor in his courses: Robert Henri's *Art Spirit* and John Dewey's *Art as Experience,* Oriental works such as the *Bhagavadgita* and the *Tao Te Ching,* Van Gogh's *Letters* and Zimmer's *The King and the Corpse,* Augustine's *Confessions* and Marcel's *Mystery of Being.* In the hours we met, we approached these works only indirectly, and some of the most memorable and influential moments consisted of citations from other works entirely. Already speaking out of an origin, Henry Bugbee's mere mention of another work would immediately confer upon this unknown a resonance drawing us to the bookstore or to the library. Works became testimonies, speaking from beyond the genres and the -isms academics have invented for them.

For me, Henry Bugbee's voice first ignited the faith that works of all kinds await us—await our willingness, shape our ability to respond to their, to our own beginnings. This faith reopens our literary tradition. True, each must begin at the time and place where one happens to be, and one finds oneself by finding the elements of that time and place, by participating in their various configurations. And Henry's voice always instantiated such beginning. But its greatness, at least for me, has consisted more in the propagation of this singular faith that human beings can and ultimately want to begin, rather than simply ride along. Also that the power of the traditional great works lies in their beginnings rather than in the ride they offer.

I could comprehend a mathematical proof, once I worked through it myself and in my own way, because I had learned to ask *why* at each moment of development. In contrast, prose works—histories, novels, essays—I could never comprehend outright. Some of my peers could: they could read through a book, listen through a lecture, in an even line, retaining the lateral structures as forming a two-dimensional whole that they could summarize and criticize with ease. Impossible for me. I needed the third dimension: coherence of line and plane became evident only when each line issued from an origin and only then, as a kind of afterthought, intertwined to form a two-dimensional web. Only the third, the epiphanic dimension fully addresses the question *why*. And as in mathematical work, this third dimension takes shape, ever tentatively, only as we participate in the origin; summaries and criticisms lock us into the first two dimensions. Henry Bugbee's voice unlocked the two, spoke out of the third.

Still, we first find ourselves in a middle. In the midst of its elements, mowing a lawn or building a fire, investigating a problem or discussing a novel, we rightly assume that our pressing task is to comprehend the line of development, some segment of the trip, a multiplicity of lateral contributions to the moment. This assumption easily carries over from productive and practical affairs into the life of contemplation. Yet comprehension compromises contemplation. From its temporal beginning in ancient Greece, philosophy emerges as the contemplation of αρχη. Comprehension commits us to the middle where origins appear, ghostlike, as hearkening to an elsewhere, an elsewhen; mysterious things, long lost, to which we refer. In exact correlation, our middle position invites us to refer to *endings* as elsewhere and elsewhen, as productive or practical applications. In the name of comprehension, the middle usurps both beginnings and endings, engenders a groundless procrastination. Contemplation shatters this illusion: this we must learn, and I doubt if I would have learned it had I not chanced upon a pure instance of it.

Just as we are born with a name that we must still earn, so too we start out with a kind of comprehension, an overview that will prove lethal unless we start all over, at the beginning, and earn it—earn it not by attaching imagined beginnings and arbitrary endings to it, but rather by abandoning, by rediscovering the middle as but an outgrowth of origins—so that these very origins become the endings, the culminations served by the outgrowth. All great thinkers from Plato to Heidegger have *said* as much. In Bugbee's words we could *hear* it.

In subsequent years, my sustained work in logic has driven home the difference between modern and classical semantics. We moderns find ourselves enmeshed within a triadic structure: our words take on meaning as they embody concepts referring to instances. In contrast, classical semantics is dyadic: we address each being as a duality of presence and completion, and our words take on meaning only as they embody our participation in the tension between these two aspects of the being. In modern scientific work and its attendant communication, we define our concepts and apply them retroactively to what we encounter. In classical philosophical work and its attendant dialogue, we define a being recollectively as a result of our participation in its emergence. Modernity has developed as a gradual, a painfully won battle between these contrasting modes of speech. And has obscured an even more originary mode.

Archaic semantics is strangely monadic. Out of some middle, not from it, an origin addresses us, and we answer. Our own speech takes on meaning as this answering. Here, the culmination, the end or purpose of talk, is none other than the origin itself, its reemergence. Apart from its epiphany, our ephemeral response *with* it, the archaic makes no sense. Try to *study* archaic semantics, and it becomes triadic: scientific study not only requires the employment of concepts covering instances but commits us to detecting them. Devise techniques to engage others in archaic semantics and it becomes dyadic: dialectic engenders the assumption that there is a better way to formulate our speech, that we must embark on this journey of improvement. Works of a modern or of a classical bent tolerate, provisionally, an acquiescence in the middle. Without any whisper of the archaic, they leave us there. Henry Bugbee's voice amplifies this whisper into a resounding call.

In April 1980 Henry came to Mount Allison University to speak about Homer's *Iliad* and *Odyssey*. For some years he had been reading these works with his students in a special humanities program at the University of Montana. By chance, Liliane and I had undertaken a private study of them in the previous year: she on the similes, I on the recurrence of words such as *telos*—strictly middle-ground work. For two hours early one afternoon Henry drew strand after strand of these works back to their life-giving, meaning-giving beginnings, converted both familiar and unfamiliar episodes into resounding culminations.

After the talk, the three of us embarked on a long walk along the Acadian dikes and under the red sandstone cliffs by the Westcock Marsh, here at the tip of the Bay of Fundy. I asked Henry if he was planning to commit some of his thoughts from Homer into writing, so that I and others could return to the event, reenact the script. He trudged on for a moment, raised his eyes to the horizon, and remarked that a distant promontory looked promising. And off we hiked in that direction.

Writing throws us back onto our language. The writing life engages us in the metalanguages of modern or classical semantics. A precarious engagement, since a metalanguage has an epiphenomenal, a ghostly life of its own that allows us to forget the archaic language whence the reflective forms issue and whither they must return for their substance. In its purity, archaic language engenders direct response: self, thing, world all emerge in unison for the duration. Such language remains, resounds, resonates originally in oral presentation. Henry Bugbee's work belongs first of all, at least for those fortunate to have worked with him, to the oral tradition. Without his voice, I for one would never have embarked on the literary life. Without voices like his, our entire literary tradition falls silent.

# Henry Bugbee as Mentor

GARY WHITED

> Only as things are dense and opaque do they stand forth in the light of eternity, and take the light. . . . But the agile mind and the distraught soul militate against true perception; for true perception requires stillness in the presence of things, the active, open reception of the limitless gift of things.
> —Henry Bugbee, *The Inward Morning*

When I reflect on Henry's work, I am moved to speak out of my own experience. This is Henry's own way, time and again. As I look back over my life, I see a path marked, at its best, by a theme central to Henry's work as I understand it. It is this: To see our life as a response to what lays claim to us and, as best we can, to remain true to this in order that the meaning and purpose of our life, and of the things that touch it, might dawn on us. My own path has taken me from the beginning of my life on the prairie to the study of philosophy to the writing of poetry and the practice of psychotherapy. I will leave it to others to comment on the ways in which Henry's work fits into the history and community of philosophy. For myself, I think I can best express my gratitude to Henry and my regard for his work by describing my own path in its relationship to Henry as mentor.

In so many ways Henry's presence in my life came as a gift, the full meaning of which I am uncovering more even as I write this. Two images of Henry come to mind. The first is of Henry beside a trout stream, fly rod in hand, working the breeze and the brush behind, finding the distance to just the place near that hole where a big trout had caught his eye. The second is of Henry in a classroom working a myth, a tale, a story, or a philosophical text that had claimed his attention much as the trout had. Casting for thoughts in the dialogue between himself and his students on the one hand, and between himself and the text on the other, Henry was poised to engage in philosophic inquiry as he knew and loved it. He had been laid claim to.

The second of these images evokes my first encounter with Henry thirty years ago. I was, at that time, in my third year as an undergraduate and puzzling over my decision to continue to study philosophy. Course work had become dry and had begun to feel arbitrary. Then I walked into Henry's class on Eastern philosophy. What unfolded there was an initiation into philosophic thought as a drama in which concepts could seamlessly weave together with characters and events as they unfolded in stories. An argument or the explication of an idea could take an unexpected and compelling turn as it led us along its way. Particular details could emerge as redolent of the universal. The arbitrary could always give way to the essential. A sense of destiny could emerge in the flow of our thinking, as in the unfolding of our lives.

My own clear desire to pursue philosophy returned during that first encounter with Henry. The next term I did an independent study with Henry on the work of Gabriel Marcel, Henry's friend and colleague in Paris. In that work I learned that the theme of "being claimed" by something in action and in reflection was a core idea for both Henry and Marcel. (See the account Henry gives of Marcel's theme of *l'exigence ontologique* in his essay by that title.) This theme has been a guiding force in my life and work ever since. It has drawn me from full-time academic philosophy into the writing of poetry and the practice of psychotherapy.[1]

Though my work as a psychotherapist has been touched by my encounter with Henry, it is in my work as a poet that I have been most deeply influenced by him. In the opening lines of *The Inward Morning,* quoting William Carlos Williams, Henry says, "Now for me philosophy is in the end an approximation to the poem, 'a structure built upon your own ground . . . , your ground where you stand on your own feet.'"[2] I like this passage, I suppose, because I have taken to writing poems over the years and like to think that I have not left the realm of philosophy behind in doing so. But there is another reason: in the writing of a poem, I feel I have the best chance of authentically recollecting those occasions when I have been claimed by something and of discovering where I am in relation to the world and to my own past. The place where I stand comes into focus.

I remember an afternoon conversation with Gabriel Marcel. Henry had arranged for me to visit Marcel when I made an excursion to Europe. Marcel was delighted to receive a student of Henry's, whose work he admired enormously. He invited me into his place at 21, rue de Tournon. His living room was filled with books and records. Every wall was covered, floor to ceiling, with bookshelves. We made our way in silence among stacks of records and books to a small sitting area. Marcel seemed quite small as he sank into a large stuffed chair. However, as we talked about many things of great concern to him, his stature and his voice grew. From this place surrounded by things he loved, he was actively engaged in efforts to gain the release of imprisoned Russian writers, in the current Parisian theater scene, and in speaking out against the Vietnam War, which was raging at the time.

When we turned our attention to philosophy, he was emphatic about the importance of the "place" from which one's philosophy emerges. "Sartre's philosophy," Marcel quipped, "comes from a sidewalk cafe, while Bugbee's comes from beside a trout stream." Henry shares with Marcel this sense of the importance of place in a person's philosophy. He speaks eloquently of this as he reflects on his days before the war.

> During my years of graduate study before the war I studied philosophy in the classroom and at a desk, but my philosophy took shape mainly on foot. It was truly peripatetic, engendered not merely while walking, but through walking that was essentially a meditation of the place. And the balance in which I weighed the ideas I was studying was always that established in the experience of walking in the place. I weighed everything by the measure of the silent presence of things, clarified in the racing clouds, clarified by the cry of hawks, solidified in the presence of rocks, spelled syllable by syllable by waters of manifold voice, and consolidated in the act of taking steps, each step a meditation steeped in reality. What this all meant, I could not say, kept trying to say, kept trying to harmonize with the suggestions arising from the things I read. But I do remember that this walking in the presence of things came to a defini-

tive stage. It was in the fall of '41, October and November, while late autumn prevailed throughout the northern Canadian Rockies, restoring everything in that vast region to a native wildness. Some part of each day or night, for forty days, flurries of snow were flying. The aspens and larches took on a yellow so vivid, so pure, so trembling in the air, as to fairly cry out that they were as they were, limitlessly. And it was there in attending to this wilderness, with unremitting alertness and attentiveness, yes, even as I slept, that I knew myself to have been instructed for life, though I was at a loss to say what instruction I had received.[3]

This is as clear a rendering of "being claimed" as I know in Henry's writing. He is claimed in a way that guides him to an understanding laid down, as Henry says, "in the bones," and recalled later into reflection and articulation.

Many of my poems emerge from recollections of the prairie of eastern Montana where I grew up. What claimed me there in that place is what has all along guided me in trying to make sense of things. It is for me, as I understand Henry, the ground where I stand. The prairie—its extreme weather, its subtle beauty, its spaciousness, its people, its inscrutable way of hanging together—is what has shaped much of what I think and what I am drawn to think about. And here again I am led by Bugbee's voice. "There are times when one seems to come to himself, to recollect himself, and only then does the granary of experience pour into present reflection at a fundamental level. No one has helped me so much as Marcel to form an idea of this strict connection between recall to oneself in one's true mode of being in the present and the depth of recall in which reflection may become concretely continuous with the past."[4]

For me the "granary" is my prairie experience. It is where I come from, it is where I stand most profoundly, even though I have not lived there for the past thirty-five years. The question of what lays claim to me always points me toward this place. The presence of prairie came to me first as a boy walking Shadwell Creek to play, to feed the cattle in the winter pasture with my father, to gather the milk cows on summer evenings, to muse and reflect in the unwitting way of a child. I see that presence of prairie in particular images: the grass being moved always by westerly winds, the large clay butte standing west of our place on the creek, the elm trees and chokecherry bushes lining the creek where magpies dart up and down, black-and-white, on hot summer afternoons.

The meaning of things past comes as a gift:

> [r]eflection it seems, must earn the gift of the essential meaning of things past. It is as if experience must continue underground for some time before it can emerge as springwater, clear, pure, understood. And reflection is a trying to remember, a digging that is pointless if it be not digging down directly beneath where one stands, so that the waters of his life may re-invade the present moment and define the meaning of both.[5]

There is trust in this recollective process. And it seems to me that the trust Henry requires and finds in philosophic reflection is indistinguishable from the trust that poetry requires. He speaks of this early in his journal: "If there can be concrete philosophy, give it a chance. Let one perception move instantly on another. Where they come from is to be trusted. Unless this is so, after all is said and done, philosophy is arbitrary and idle."[6] And in the very next entry:

> Let it flow: Fluency is the stylistic counterpart of the way present experience is invaded with authentic meaning. Basic meanings are not anticipated; they dawn on one. This is the point of keeping up the flow: If one works out the thoughts, the perceptions that press upon him with the demand for completion, as they lead to one another, in time the actual themes of his philosophy may have a chance to define themselves. Such a philosophy will not be set up like the solution of a puzzle, worked out with all the pieces lying there before the eye. It will be more like the clarification of what we know in our bones.[7]

I remember many afternoons sitting with Henry while he guided me through my study of Marcel's book *The Mystery of Being*.[8] We would begin with whatever end of a thread presented itself to us, and follow where it led, weaving in and out of war stories, fishing stories, reflections on other philosophers' writings, and often hearkening back to the *Bhagavad-Gita* or *The Book of Tao,* from our earlier work together. As I look back on these conversations now, I see that I was being mentored by the same voice that had spoken in these early passages from *The Inward Morning*. I was being initiated into a style of philosophic reflection grounded in experience, in recollection and in trust.

Working out the themes of a poetic voice is not unlike working out the themes of a philosophic voice. The trust required in both is manifold. There is trust that our own voice emerges intact out of a knowing that is as close to us as "our bones." There is trust that our perceptions and recollections come from a reliable place and that our voice can be attuned to that place.

I learned a hard lesson about trusting my own voice when I went to graduate school in the East. I was drawn to the work of the pre-Socratics, Parmenides and Heraclitus in particular. The sense that all things are interconnected, often in ways invisible to us, but nonetheless always so, grew directly out of my prairie experience—and it is this sense that drew me to the central theme of unity in Parmenides's poem. The first draft of my dissertation was, in design, a dialogue between Parmenides's poem and a phenomenology of my early experience on the prairie. In the course of rewriting, however, I lost faith in the enterprise. Perhaps I was too self-conscious to use all that recollected material from my past, or perhaps I thought I needed to speak in a more acceptable "philosophical" voice. In any case, in the final draft, I dropped most of the recollections, which I believe Henry had liked very much in his reading of the first draft.

Shortly after Henry read the final version, I returned to the University of Montana to teach. I'll never forget that first meeting upon my return. Henry was standing in his home office holding my dissertation in his hand, the usual smoking pipe clasped between his teeth. In a pensive tone he asked simply, "What happened?" At the time I do not think I took in the full import of Henry's short question. Over the years what he meant has slowly, and somewhat painfully, dawned on me. What Henry saw was that I had suppressed my own voice, and with it, my trust in the ground I stood on as a source for philosophic reflection.

Trust, so central to Henry's work, is the stance in which things come to us as gifts. He writes, "As I image the matter, philosophical truth overtakes us from behind in so far as we are at its disposal." Later in the same vein: "[I]n reflection . . . our position is not sound except as we are at the disposal of what we cannot command. I see that our conception of truth might be deeply affected in those moments when life comes to us as a gift."[9]

Poetry and philosophy are companion paths. At least I feel invited by Henry to think so. Throughout *The Inward Morning* he moves eloquently back and forth between poetic voice and philosophic voice. The philosophic voice is perhaps to be distinguished as more discursive, but at bottom, the urge in each is the same—to be moving toward an understanding, returning always to what has been given in experience.

Poetry for me has been a listening, a recollecting, through image and line, of the story of my early life on the prairie. This story is not fixed in its meaning but more like a river in relationship to which my life unfolds. The meaning of this prairie story and the meaning of my life are to be discerned in their relatedness, as I recall concretely my experience of the prairie pressing itself upon me "from behind":

> The things of the prairie, I loved them as a child
> without knowing I was loving. I had no name
> for this delight that leapt from my eyes,
> went out to meet these things;
>
> The glistening spittle from cows' mouths on their way
> to water, their afternoon grazing behind them, cuds chewed,
> walking in their swaying way along the same dusty path
> that always led to water;
>
> The creek moving by twists and turns
> down along its way to the Yellowstone River,
> its coolness in summer, its shelter in winter,
> holding me no matter how I came to it
> from the barn where I spent hours lost in details;
>
> The imprint of a hammerblow that missed the mark
> when men were building this barn I gaze upon
> years beyond its making. In haste one brought
> his hammer short of the mark, and the clean look
> of this board forever changed;
>
> Above it, near the rafters, spider-spun webbing,
> each strand carrying years of dust since one day
> when not just any spider, but that very one, moved
> by what moves spiders, came upon this joint of wood,
> made web to capture prey to live upon, to spin again
> the weapon fine and enough.

And now I unroll each memory, discover afresh
my love of earthly things that give themselves fully
into my loving, not spent in their giving,
but some way added to;

an exchange of things inviting us
and our love calling them out,
then forgetting giving way to remembering,
bringing us back again and again
from the river time to the river joy.

I remember going fishing with Henry. Henry had heard about a glacial lake from a friend who was willing to share the secret—which is how Montanans learn of unexpected fishing treasures. We hiked along the Middle Fork of the Flathead River, about a nine-mile hike from an old logging trail where we had parked. After hiking most of a day, we forded the river at the foot of a mountain and camped for the night. In fresh morning light we headed up the steep mountainside, our sixty-pound packs riding us hard all the way. We were spent by the time we arrived at the notch that opened out onto Castle Lake, nestled in among trees and rock cliffs on one side, open shoreline on the other.

In the midmorning warmth the rainbow trout were feeding on some new hatch. It was a beautiful sight, and I watched as Henry's eyes caught the gleam of those trout leaping from broken water, one after another after another. His face lit up as I had never seen a face light up. He dropped his pack, unfurled his rod and reel and made for the water, a smile creasing his face, his whole body drawn by some invisible force. It wasn't sport or mere hunger that drew him. He'd been claimed by those water creatures as soon as he came through that notch into sight of them dancing their feeding dance, choreographed as if for him to behold. They rose and fell in the full embrace of sunlight that glistened on their backs, arching out of the water for a split second, pulling this man to them.

During this visit to Castle Lake Henry taught me to fly-fish. After a couple of sessions, I had the basics and could make my way with it, and it was splendid. Yet even more splendid was the sight of Henry, knee-deep in the lake, right arm rhythmically casting the long yellow line that settled in a whisper onto the water, followed by stillness as he slowly drew in the line, watching every move of the water's surface. It seemed at times that he could see underwater, knew just where a trout was waiting, as if the fish had called to him. When a strike came, there'd be a sudden snap of the rod, a flurry of activity as he played the fish, landing it or losing it, then stillness again. He'd stay near the water all day in dialogue with the trout, whether they were biting or not. Toward sundown he'd come back to the campsite with just enough fish for supper and, if ever a man was, grateful to be alive.

Here was a man for whom the world arrived as a gift, to be relished and trusted in its own terms. As I watched, it seemed a spell of delight and grace was cast over him that bore the mark of something eternal passing, for a moment, through time.

## Notes

1. Henry G. Bugbee Jr., "L'Exigence Ontologique," in *Library of Living Philosophers,* ed. Paul A. Schilpp (Evanston, Ill.: Open Court, 1968).

2. Bugbee, *The Inward Morning: A Philosophical Exploration in Journal Form* (1958; reprint, with a new introduction by Edward F. Mooney, Athens: University of Georgia Press, 1999), 33.

3. Ibid., 139–40.
4. Ibid., 56.
5. Ibid., 140.
6. Ibid., 34.
7. Ibid., 34–35.

8. Gabriel Marcel, *The Mystery of Being,* vol. 1, trans. G. S. Fraser (Chicago: Gateway Edition, Henry Regnery, 1964).

9. Bugbee, *Inward Morning,* 55–56, 70.

# Five Henry Stories

DAVID JAMES DUNCAN

*for Sally Moore*

I

Language has vertical limits. Not just any speaker can pack up his speech and tote it at will to a higher elevation. Where there is a will, there is as often a major embarrassment as there is a way. Like a gymnast on parallel bars, the speaker or writer who successfully conveys exaltation must possess sufficient mental muscle to hoist himself above the level of everyday verbiage without appearing to strain. Even more importantly, and again like the gymnast, he must be able to lift all of himself, all himself. It is not histrionic or rhetorical coaching, number of advanced degrees, height-of-pulpit, tone of voice, thickness of thesaurus, number of books published, or any such contrivance that truly lifts language: it is personal integrity. It's the ability to find one's own words and to imbue them with the physical momentum, intellectual clarity, and psychic depth that only the actual deeds of a life can provide. If Martin Luther King Jr., in his renowned Washington, D.C., speech of 1963, had said "In my heart I know I'm right," and if Richard Nixon, in his resignation speech a decade later, had said, "I have a dream," the world would have remembered King's heart and forgotten Nixon's dream. It is not just words that make words memorable.

This principle, I believe, is one reason why so many people, often decades after the fact, remember with precision and pleasure some statement that Henry Bugbee once made to them. I too remember, in unusual detail, the first time I heard Henry speak. It happened like this:

In July 1993, after four decades in Oregon, I moved with my family to Missoula, Montana. A few weeks into that first Rocky Mountain summer I listened to a program on the local NPR affiliate devoted to Norman Maclean's justifiably famed novella *A River Runs through It*. I confess that I usually take pains to avoid literary educational opportunities, my entire working life being one relentless such opportunity. I tuned in this show not for literary reasons, but out of regard for my esteemed new neighbor, the Big Blackfoot River. I was pleasantly surprised, though. Two of the Maclean commentators turned out to be astute, and just to keep things tense and interesting, the third was a crackpot.

My apologies to this fellow for calling him a crackpot. Especially if he's reading this, and turns out to be big, mean and handy with his fists. All a crackpot is, by definition, is a vessel that won't hold water. I often don't. What brought the word to mind in this case was the fellow's claim that Maclean's novel was just a slick literary "cover-up attempt." He loved that term, "cover-up." He said that Norman was "covering up"—with useless love, useless hindsight, and uselessly beautiful prose—the fact that the Macleans had been a dysfunctional mess of a family. He said that Norman and his father oppressed every woman they knew, denied every complex thing that ever happened to anyone, and utterly failed to own up to the brother, Paul's, need for psychotherapy and an alcohol treatment center. As several call-in contributors patiently pointed out, in Paul Maclean's day there *were* no therapies or treatment centers besides the whiskey bottles and gambling halls he so faithfully tried. The cover-up expert never budged from his position, though he was finally buried by a barrage of far more articulate comments in praise of Maclean's classic.

The radio show changed gears, then: two local fishing guides and a retired fly-fisher–philosophy professor came on the air, not to philosophize ("Thank God!" I thought) but just to chat about the mystique and growing popularity of fly-fishing. No sooner had the radio host and fishing guides launched their discussion of fishing, however, than the old professor fooled them by veering off topic in order to make some of the most insightful comments I've ever heard on *A River Runs through It*. The show ended with the old professor's comments—as it should have: they were authoritative and climactic. Then a couple of weeks later, as often happens in small towns, some friends invited me over for dinner—and there the old professor sat.

His name, of course, was Henry Bugbee. And as soon as we were introduced, I told him how much I'd enjoyed the show—especially his contribution to it. Henry thanked me and said that he too had enjoyed the broadcast. He then confessed that, to be honest, he had a very inexact recollection of what his contribution had been. I should point out that this was before his stroke or his brain disease struck: the inability to remember his own most animated words has been a lifelong attribute of Henry's. He is one of these people who zeroes in on the flow of a conversation and goes with that flow, beautifully. But he so loses himself in the process that, though he's left with a profound sense of what we might call the "hydraulics" of the situation, he retains little memory of the specific and often wonderful things that he himself so often says.

This is a fine way of maintaining one's humility. And it is, of course, the Gospel's way ("He that loseth himself shall find it"). But I happen to be the sort of fellow who remembers most of the clever things I say! Where does this leave me spiritually? Envious of Henry, for starters! So I decided, there at the dinner party, to try and mess with the old prof's humility by quoting him to himself, showing him how bloody insightful he was, and seeing whether I couldn't puff him up a bit. . . .

I pulled out all the rhetorical stops (though I did confine myself, with a secret sigh of regret, to the truth). I told Henry that he had evoked the famous oatmeal scene. Little Paul Maclean, age five or six, sitting at the table before a heaped bowl of oatmeal, silently refusing to even taste this food that the Scots, as Papa Maclean puts it, have been happily consuming for thousands of years. Paul is not swayed by this. But his father will not excuse him. The rest of the family finishes eating and leaves the table. The little boy sits there, looking small and vulnerable. Both parents peek in on him from time to time. Paul doesn't complain, doesn't squirm, doesn't display emotion at all: he just sits before the ever-more-monolithic-looking oatmeal, refusing to touch it, till we realize, with his parents, that he is willing to sit there forever. Paul never does submit.

It was a scene, in the Robert Redford movie, that one could easily describe as cute. But on the radio, as Henry conjured it, the stand-off felt darkly prophetic. There was tacit violence in this father-son impasse—a frightening intractability on both sides. And Henry had summarized this intractability, thus: "For all the love and admirable qualities of the father, it was, one felt, his dogmatic stance that prevented grace from flowing in the son."

This sentence rang in me like a bell. It underscored everything I love about *A River Runs through It:* why the story feels so tragically inevitable; why the book speaks to every pious mother and father and renegade daughter and son I've ever known; why Paul's death is so shattering to the father especially, for through it we see how his greatest strength—his rock-solid faith—somehow became a mere rock, a deadweight, when he tried to will it to his son. Above all, Henry's statement helped me see why Paul's fly-fishing is so central to this story, so haunting, and so tantalizingly beautiful: in this willful young man in whom the flow of grace is otherwise blocked, fly-fishing is the one pursuit, the only pursuit, in which we literally do see "grace, flowing in the son."

Well, back at this dinner party I said something like what I've just written. And Henry's reaction amazed me. His eyes filled; he seemed half overcome. With a radiant smile and in a voice close to a gasp, he said, "You did that very well!"

I pointed out that all I'd done was parrot him back to himself, but Henry adamantly refused all credit. And the more I thought this refusal over, the more impressed I was with it. The trout we catch in these hard-fished Montana rivers have often been caught by some previous man or woman: we are no less alone on the river, and the trout is no less beautiful, the day we catch it ourselves. Here was a man with no sense of proprietorship in the presence of true words. In one sense I been a parrot, but in another sense I had plucked Henry's insight off the radio show and taken it to heart. Henry recognized and honored this second capture as the solo philosophical event that it indeed was. He was loving his neighbor's insight as one loves one's own. He was being a father whose nondogmatic stance let grace flow in a son.

2

I've walked around Missoula with Henry a few times since his stroke and brain disease struck. "Walk," in fact, is an exaggeration. Henry, the lifelong mountain-climber, totters along while I hold his arm, struggling to find a gear that allows my longish legs and restless nature to mesh with his knee brace and cane.

During these walks I've watched a lot of Henry's old acquaintances greet him. Henry's part in these exchanges is always the same: he smiles beatifically at a known face (and to this day—summer 1996—he still seems to know them all); he then extends a firm grip and a good word. The reactions to his greetings are more complex. Some of the old friends speak to Henry as if he has transcended the physical and become a holy guru. Others speak as if he's become a toddler or a tragic but likable village idiot. And a few others, whom Henry clearly recognizes as they approach, pretend not to notice him, and duck away before close proximity forces them to draw either positive or negative conclusions about his condition.

My conclusion is that I still love Henry's close proximity. My feeling is what better end than the one we're seeing for a philosopher who believes as Henry has believed? He hasn't lost anything we won't all be losing. According to our mutual hero, Meister Eckhart, Henry hasn't lost anything that was ever truly his: he has just started returning some things that, as he always insisted, were only his on loan in the first place. What strikes me about Henry Bugbee to this day is what wonderful tools he was loaned, how well he has used them, and how lovingly he still uses the ones that haven't yet been returned.

I don't wish to sound wiser than I am. I'm no master of detachment. In the three years of our friendship I've become exceedingly attached to Henry's unexpected phone calls, his warm, high-pitched voice, his sometimes fumbling, sometimes gorgeously meticulous word choices, his fish stories; I love the way he looks at Sally when she comes in the door; I love the solar smile he turns on his friends and leaves on, full-beam, till they have no choice but to realize that this is no social smile, no rote response: this is what it feels like to be seen and loved for a moment. If Henry has to return these gifts before he checks out completely, I'm going to be sad, I'm sure.

Yet almost everything I know about this man is an antidote to sadness. Henry has lived the kind of life that makes it impossible to mourn his failing without betraying the entire life. Because of this, you see a beautiful struggle in Henry's family and friends these days. An awareness that Henry is leaving—and a natural urge to grieve—is cut by a simultaneous awareness of, and wish to honor, the fact that Henry has stood lifelong by an ancient tradition holding that the loss of a loved one is not so much an occasion to mourn as an occasion to be true to love.

"To give thanks lyingly," said Jalaludin Rumi, "is to seek the love of God." In the eyes of those who greet Henry as his mind and body fail, I'm touched again and again by the lying thanks, the seeking of love. I see panic in some eyes, too, of course. When those who live the life of the mind see a friend taking gentle leave of the mind, there is bound to be some terror. But while I'm still able to remember the names, I side with Rumi's "lying thanks," Eckhart's "emptiness," Zen's "no-mindedness," Christ's "poverty of spirit." This mind of mine was never mine to start with; in sleep and in dreams I lose it every night. Henry, in his present state of mind, reminds me of that Chinese, or maybe Japanese, roshi, his name now lost to me, who when asked, "What is my real self, O master?" answered, "Mountains and rivers and the great earth." He reminds me of that Japanese, or maybe Chinese, poet, who when asked, "What is self?" answered, "Rambling in the mountains, enjoying the waters." He reminds me of Jim Harrison (finally a name I can remember!) who in "Cabin Poem" writes,

> I've decided to make up my mind
> about nothing, to assume the water mask,
> to finish my life disguised as a creek,
> an eddy, joining at night the full
> sweet flow, to absorb the sky,
> to swallow the heat and cold, the moon
> and the stars, to swallow myself
> in ceaseless flow.

Henry reminds me that though I once knew the names of the makers of all the above statements, what difference do the names make if the statements are true? A man once given to speak and write sentences such as "there is a stream of limitless meaning flowing into the life of a man if he can but patiently entrust himself to it" is near the end of his life of patient trust. Those people we encountered in the street— the ones who ducked away—make me want to shout after them: "Come back! Don't be pathetic! There's nothing scary or sad here! A wonderful old man is falling slowly to pieces. Come say hi to him and his pieces while you've got the chance!"

When I saw Henry the other day, a circuit crossed at one point and he called me "Mike." I say, close enough. I say Henry is finishing his life disguised ever more perfectly as a creek. I say, call me David, call me Mike, call me Ishmael, and give me, please God, the courage and grace to adapt the same disguise. The courage to become mountains and rivers and the great earth. The courage to make wilderness my true home.

3

Some teachers never retire, simply because they can't. Henry of course for instance. Almost every philosophical poker hand this old sharp plays in *The Inward Morning* can still win the pot. This is the upside of standing by Eckhart's "emptiness," Zen's "no-mindedness," Christ's "poverty of spirit." I guess the downside is loss of tenure and retirement benefits. But in poker and spiritual life, unlike academic life, you must return all your cards to the dealer. In fact, if you try to hold onto a card in poker, they might beat you up or shoot you.

The reason Henry can't retire, then, is that there's nothing to retire: when you align yourself with emptiness and truth, then spend your life teaching that alignment, what you taught goes right on teaching itself whether or not you're even alive, let alone whether or not you've retired.

I experienced the perennial nonretirement of Henry Bugbee last December, when I was invited to spend three days, in my capacity as a novelist, with forty college students at a small college in Oregon. These were *Christian* college students, mind you, with a Christian plan for my visit. What they wanted me to talk about, "openly and honestly," was my "personal faith." This presented an immediate problem: the phrase "personal faith" is oxymoronic; as soon as you talk about personal life, personal finances, personal anything, it's no longer personal. To compound the problem, I was also asked to speak "openly and honestly" about my experience as a church-goer. The rub here was, I don't *have* any experience as a church-goer. I was raised in one of those fundamentalist denominations the preachers called a "fold."

But from the day I first heard a trout stream give a sermon, I heard the word "fold" as the move one makes in poker when one's cards aren't worth a damn.

Bivouacked, then, among the forty young Christians, with a single evening to prepare remarks on "personal faith" and "personal churchgoing" in order to earn my personal honorarium, I felt disturbingly cognizant, for the first time in my life, of a slight vocational resemblance to Pat Robertson. What a relief, in relation to this nadir, to suddenly recall a card hand played by Henry in *The Inward Morning*, having to do with wonder.

I didn't have Henry's book with me, but I seemed to remember him saying, or at least giving me the feeling he said, that the tenets of religious belief are not intended to be the termination of wonder: they're intended to be occasions for it. This felt like a desirable entry point into my "personal faith" topic, in that it at least put an end to any resemblance between me and Pat Robertson. I also recalled Henry saying that wonder is not something we grasp but something that grasps us. This reminded me of how grace operates. It also reminded me of why I was balking at the topic of "personal faith." Isn't faith worth having precisely to the degree that it is not personal? The degree to which it is a gift rather than a personal invention? The degree to which it grasps us, rather than us grasping it?

By now I had a headache, based on the fact that I was supposed to talk about a kind of faith in which I have no faith. The skies opened, though, and the headache closed, when it occurred to me that I could answer the "personal faith" question by simply begging that question, and speaking instead about something in which I *did* have faith—namely, this word beloved by the never-retiring Henry: the word "wonder."

I grabbed my pen and legal pad and set to work, finding it incredibly helpful not to have Henry's book with me, in that it freed me to crib his thought with shameless abandon. The next day I gave my forty Christian charges a talk on three words that have fed my faith. I began with Henry's word, like this:

> For the same reason that I can't talk about fish without talking about rivers, I can't talk about faith without talking about the element in which

faith is born. That element is mysterious. It may be a mistake to pin it to any one word. But the English word that captures this element best, for me, is the word, *wonder.*

My earliest conception of the meaning of this word was a feeling that would come over me, as a little kid, when I'd picture the shepherds on the night hills above Bethlehem. Even when these shepherds were made of illuminated plastic, standing around in Christmas dioramas on my neighbor's lawns, their slack-jawed expressions of wonder appealed to me. Years later, having become literate enough to read a Bible, I learned that these shepherds were also "sore afraid." But—a personal prejudice—I didn't believe in their sore afraidness. I believed the star in the East smote them with sheer wonder, and my experience of wonder is that, once it smites you, you're smitten by wonder alone. Fear can't penetrate till wonder subsides.

Wonder is my second favorite condition to be in, after love—and I sometimes wonder whether there's even a difference: maybe love is just wonder aimed at a beloved.

Wonder is like grace, in that it's not a condition that we can grasp: it grasps us. We do have the freedom to elude this grasp. We have the freedom to do all sorts of stupid things. By deploying our sophistication, cynicism, fear, arrogance, judgmentalism, dogmatism, rationalism, we can evade wonder almost nonstop, all our lives. I'm not too big on that gnarly old word, "sin," but the deliberate evasion of wonder does bring this word to mind. It may not be biblically sinful to evade wonder. But it's artistically and spiritually sinful.

Wonder is not an obligatory element in the search for truth. We can seek truth without its assistance. But seek is all that we can do. There will be no finding. Till wonder descends, truth is unable to reveal itself. Wonder may be the aura of truth. Or something even closer. Wonder may be the feel of truth touching our very skin.

Like grace, wonder defies rational analysis. Discursive thought can bring nothing to any object of wonder. Thought at best just circumambulates the wondrous object, like a devout pilgrim circles Golgotha, or the Bo Tree, or Wounded Knee, or the Kaabah.

Philosophically speaking, wonder is crucial to the discovery of knowledge, yet has everything to do with ignorance. By this I mean that only the admission of our ignorance can open us to fresh knowings—and wonder is the experience of that admission. Wonder is unknowing, experienced as pleasure.

Punctuationally speaking, wonder is a period at the end of a statement we've long taken for granted, suddenly looking up and seeing the sinuous curve of a tall black hat on its head, and realizing it was a question mark all along.

As a facial expression, wonder is the letter O our eyes and mouths make when the state itself descends. O: God's middle initial. O: because wonder Opens us. Wonder is anything taken for granted—the old neighborhood, old job, old life, old spouse—suddenly filling with mystery. Wonder is anything closed, suddenly opening—anything at all opening—which alas includes Pandora's box. This brings me to the dark side of wonder. Grateful as I am for this state or condition, it does have a dark side. Heartbreak, grief, and suffering rend openings through which the dark kind of wonder pours. I have so far found it impossible to be spontaneously grateful for these openings. But when, after long struggle, I've been able to turn a corner and at least *accept* these openings, wonder has helped me endure the heartbreak, suffering, and grief.

Wonder is not curiosity. Wonder is to curiosity what ecstasy is to mere pleasure. But wonder is not astonishment, either. Astonishment is too brief. The only definable limit to the duration of wonder seems to be the limit of our ability to remain open.

I believe it is wonder, even more than fidelity, that keeps marriages alive. I believe it is wonder, even more than courage, that conquers fear of death. I believe it is wonder, not D.A.R.E. bumper stickers, that keeps kids off drugs. I believe, speaking of bumper stickers, that it is wonder, even more than me, who I want to "HUG MY KIDS TODAY," because wonder can hug them when I'm clear over here with you, and keep on hugging them, long after I'm gone.

### 4

I have watched—with a mixture of amusement and dismay—several adoring former students work hard to turn Henry into a guru; an infallible font of truth; the Daniel Boone of their inner wilds. I would like, in gentle reaction to this tendency, to point out that I dedicated two pages of prose to Henry in my last book, *River Teeth,* largely out of perverse delight in how un-Henry-like my working methods are.

In *The Inward Morning,* Henry urges us to, "Get it down. . . . Get down the key ideas as they occur. . . . Write on, not over again. . . . Fluency is the stylistic counterpart of the way present experience is invaded with authentic meaning. Basic meanings are not anticipated: they dawn on one. This is the point of keeping up the flow."

Beautifully put. But as a fisherman-writer I've learned that though rivers move in Henry's way, they move another way, too, shaping a stone, a shoreline, a cliff-face, by working it, working it, working it, again and again. The river may say, "Write on, not over again," but the eddy in the river says, "Write over again, not on." My two-page piece in *River Teeth* was created after a morning spent reading *The Inward Morning,* including a sentence that went something like, "We hear nothing so clearly as what comes out of silence." I then went fishing, had a beautiful though not atypical experience with a trout, and that night made a few notes on this experience. The next day, and on and off for weeks afterward, I worked those notes into finished prose, eddying back through the two pages an easy twenty times to get my final draft. I then dedicated those pages to a man who flows on, not over again.

I'm not out to expose serious differences between Henry and me. But I am out to befuddle Henry's would-be "worshippers" by pointing out that individuality is a gift, that differences are healthy, and that I for one prefer deep, difference-filled friendship to the guru-disciple relationship—even if the Friend happens to be God.

I write rough drafts, reflections, and letters to friends on the momentum of a flow, as does Henry. But a written story, to my mind, is different from a written thought-flow: a written story is a work of art—and as a longtime maker of such stories, when I hear the phrase "work of art" I am wildly more aware of the first word than the third. As a story-maker I believe, with novelist Milan Kundera, that "deleting a paragraph calls for more talent, cultivation and creative power than writing one does." But as a pilgrim and thinker I feel, with Henry, that the integrity of the moment is torn when we use this power. Milan Kundera also asks the question, "If a [human] life can be a work of art, what use are works of art?" And he asks it rhetorically—as if the answer is self-evident. This novelist-aesthete considers works of art more artful than human life can possibly be. I would argue (against Kundera and, I believe, *with* Henry) that a human life becomes a constant work of art, that this art puts mere literature in the shade, and that in men and women such as Eckhart, Mira Bai, Bodhidharma, Rumi, Socrates, Kabir, and Julian of Norwich, Human Life as Art has indeed been achieved.

In Henry's honor I'll let these thoughts shoot downriver in the flow, rather than spin them into an eddy. But let me also include the little story, inspired by and dedicated to Henry, reached by eddying rather than by riding the flow.

### A Door

Clark Fork River, late September. My knees in a patch of forget-me-nots. The light reddening: waning sun. I'm working a glide: silent water. And kneeling pays. A fish begins rising not two rod-lengths away. I flip out a mahogany-colored mayfly. The take, my strike and the leap are each instantaneous. A trout and my face are suddenly side by side, the only sound on earth the pulsing of its body.

We hear nothing so clearly as what comes out of silence. The trout's airborne pulsing is like a single spoken word in an empty room. There is no bottom-of-the-boat indignity in this airborne thrashing. Trading water for sky, meeting no fluid resistance, the trout's swimming becomes a spasm of speed, its whole heart and fear and body producing a sound like doves taking flight. It leaps again. I hear wings again. It leaps again. And now I feel them. My heart lifts; body vanishes; mind flies into a jubilant spasm, and I suddenly know a litany of things I can't possibly know: that the souls of trout too leap, becoming birds; that trout take a fly made of plumage out of yearning as well as hunger; that an immaterial thread carries a trout's yearning through death and into a bird's egg; that the olive-sided flycatcher, using this thread, is as much trout as bird as it rises to snatch the mayfly from its chosen pool of air; that Tibetans, using this thread, locate departed lamas in the forms of little boys; that the flycatcher that was the trout was the mayfly that was the river that was the creeks that were last year's snowpack that was last year's skies . . . and that leaps are exhausting. Still kneeling in forget-me-nots, I forget. Played out, the trout turns on its side.

I step into the river, ease the fish into my hands, unhook the fly. The trout streaks for the depths with every appearance of purpose. I stand in the shallows with nothing of the sort.

There are no rises on the glide now. My one trout's leaping has spooked things for a time. If I were a younger man I'd say the show here was over and rush, before light failed, to the next likely water or showing fish. But there are desires the vaunted energy of youth conceals. What I often want now is to be more present where I am. There are tricks to this, as to any kind of fishing. Here is one. When trout rise in rivers the rings drift quickly downstream. For this reason a river fisherman must cast not to visible rise-rings but to an invisible memory of where rings first appear. I've heard this called "the memory point." And I knew of this point when I was young. What I did not know, then, was that one's best casts to it are not necessarily made with one's rod. Leaning mine against an osier, using eyes alone, I cast to a memory point now:

In the last hours of a September day you can't see down into the Clark Fork. The sun is too low, the light too acutely angled. In the last hours of day the river's surface grows reflective, shows you blue sky and red clouds, upside-down pines, orange water-birch, yellow cottonwoods. Deer hang as if shot, by their feet, yet keep browsing bright grasses. Ospreys fly beneath you. Everything is swirling. In a snag, way down deep, you might spot a flycatcher. It's hard to believe these clouds and trees, deer and birds, are a door. It's hard to believe that fish live behind them. Yet it was the clouds at my feet the rainbow troubled by rising. It was into this false sky that I cast the mahogany mayfly. It was out of inverted pines and cottonwoods that the trout then flew, shattering all reflection, three times speaking its leaping word.

Not every cast hits the memory point. But when one does, this word just goes on speaking. It says that death is like the Clark Fork late in the day. It says true words are eternal. It says eternity passes through doors as it pleases.

## 5

I'm going to end with a little story that I shall *not* rewrite.

One warm evening last May, Henry and I were sitting in lawn chairs on a rocky point, overlooking the run-off-swollen trout stream that runs through my backyard. (I confess I just typed the word "bag" for "back," and made a correction.) This was the first time I'd seen Henry since his stroke. The hundred-yard walk from the house to the rocky point was a slow, serious undertaking. The stroke had clearly returned a few pieces of my friend back to wherever they'd come from.

As we sat above the fast green water, I told Henry about some of the spectacular seasonal changes I'd witnessed on the creek that year; I chanted a litany of encounters with local wildlife; I filled his ear with a few fish stories that had taken place in the eddy right before our eyes. Henry listened but seemed a little subdued. I stopped babbling and let the creek take over.

The evening was beautiful. I was relieved by the cessation of my own voice. The sun was warm. I was sinking into things, giving myself to the day—when I noticed something odd going on with Henry. He was seated directly to my right. And he had begun to slump way over on the right side of his chair. The ground beneath our chairs was rough and rocky. He kept slumping further. Fearing he would fall, I surreptitiously placed my foot on the aluminum base of his chair and held it firmly down.

Henry lowered his right arm to the ground. I couldn't see what he was doing, felt a little embarrassed to even look. I could hear rocks being stirred around. I could feel the chair sort of writhing as I held it down with my foot. I wondered if his body and right arm were having some kind of poststroke spasm. I hoped to hell that in sitting by that creek, as in reflection and prayer, my "position was not sound unless I was at the disposal of what I cannot command."

I was about to ask Henry if he was all right when he straightened, and the chair came back into balance. He did not look at me. Instead he leaned slightly forward, briefly studied the surface of the swollen creek—then his right arm flashed. A large, flat stone I hadn't even known he was holding sailed down over the green eddy, hit the water, bounced up in a crown of sunlit spray, hit the water, bounced up again, hit the water again. A triple skip! From a bad angle. Over rough water (a rough *eddy*, no less) by an eighty-one-year-old guy who'd just had a stroke. On the authority of a life spent skipping skippers, I tell you: this throw was an *ecstasis*.

I turned. Henry was still just studying the creek, but his "innocence" was a big sham now. His lips were pursed slightly. The slow turn of his head, toward me, was eagle regal. And the look in his eyes as they met mine, then turned—without smiling—back to the creek. . . I tell you. . . I tell you. . . It was even better than the lines "The readiness to receive is all. Without that, what can be given?" Better than the line "I trust in the remembrance of what I have loved and respected." Even better than "The work of the love of wisdom, then, is the reflective amplification of truth as it may only be given to us in serving it, and each day anew."

When I look to the day I'll see Henry's face no more, I feel waters rise in a place behind my face and feel a cracked place in my heart. I've learned from experience, and from the dark kind of wonder, that those are the waters of life, and that trees and flowers grow from these cracks. As long as we remember to ramble in the mountains and enjoy the waters, how can we ever truly miss our wonderful friend?

This chapter appeared in a slightly different form as "Four Henry Stories" in *Orion* in spring 1998, pp. 24–33.

# Contributors

Albert Borgmann, University of Montana, is the author of *Crossing the Postmodern Divide* and *The Philosophy of Technology*.

Gordon G. Brittan Jr., Montana State University, is the author of *Kant's Philosophy of Science*.

Orville Clarke, University of Wisconsin Green Bay, writes on Heidegger and Eckhart.

Daniel W. Conway, Pennsylvania State University, is the author of *Nietzsche and the Political* and *Nietzsche's Dangerous Game*.

David James Duncan, a novelist residing in Montana, is the author of *The River Why, The Brothers K,* and *River's Teeth*.

Andrew Feenberg, San Diego State University, is the author of *Critical Theory of Technology* and essays on Japanese culture and philosophy.

John Lawry, professor emeritus, University of Montana, writes on philosophy of religion.

Alasdair MacIntyre, Duke University, is the author of *After Virtue,* and *Whose Justice, Whose Rationality?*

Edward F. Mooney, Sonoma State University, is the author of *Selves in Discord and Resolve: Kierkegaard's Moral-Religious Philosophy*.

Michael D. Palmer, Evangel College, writes on ethics and philosophy of religion.

David Rothenberg, New Jersey Institute of Technology, is the author of *Hand's End* and editor of *Terra Nova: A Journal of Nature and Culture*.

David Strong, Rocky Mountain College, Montana, is the author of *Crazy Mountains*.

David Toole, University of Montana, is the author of *Waiting for Godot in Sarajevo: Theological Reflections on Nihilism, Tragedy, and Apocalypse*.

Steven E. Webb's interests range from Romanticism and the American Renaissance to Kierkegaard and Heidegger.

Cyril Welch, Mount Allison University, New Brunswick, is the author of *The Art of Art Works* and *Linguistic Responsibility*.

Gary Whited, a psychotherapist and poet from Brookline, Massachusetts, taught philosophy at the University of Montana and at Emerson College in Boston.

George Huntston Williams, professor emeritus, Harvard University School of Divinity, is the author of *Wilderness and Paradise in Christian Thought*.

# Index

Abram, David, 28
absolute authority (absolute importance), 37, 59, 66, 67
absolute presence, 85
absurdity, 151
active receptiveness, 12f, 46, 69, 158, 168. *See also* openness
Adorno, T. W., 177
affirmation, unqualified, 37, 42f, 45, 47
Alcibiades, Plato's, 3, 208f, 211, 221
analytic philosophy, xiv, 20, 33, 120, 123, 207
Anderson, John M., ix, 16 (n. 1), 76
anonymity of autonomy, 136
apophatic terms, 38
architecture, 221
Aristotle, xvi, 3, 104, 117
authenticity, 129–48, 216
autonomy, 129–48; and alienation from nature, 134
Ayer, A. J., 123

Bacon, Francis, 116
bad faith, 68

Baier, Kurt, 153
Beck, Lewis, 134
bells, 95f
*Bildung*, 84
Borgmann, Albert, 107, 145, 172, 182 (n. 19)
Buber, Martin, 230

calling, 84, 161, 172, 213, 216
Camus, Albert, 22
Cavell, Stanley, 206, 223 (n. 16)
certainty, 168f
claim, 236, 239
co-existence, 94
Coleridge, Samuel Taylor, 39, 42
commitment, xvii, 64, 104. *See also* unconditional commitment
communal values, 212
communion, xxi, 159
compassion, 158, 161, 211, 216. *See also* love
completing presence or reality, 50, 59, 67, 69, 93, 97, 100, 209, 213, 216, 221
Conrad, Joseph, 218

continental philosophy, 123
contract theory, 212
co-participation, 159
creation, 78, 171, 209, 214. *See also*
  voice from the whirlwind
creative love, 63; response, 40, 69;
  speaking, 190
creativity, 89
cynicism, 151

death, 42, 201, 211. *See also* perishing
delayed presence, 52f
democracy, 84f, 130, 132, 141, 146
Derrida, Jacques, xiii
Descartes, René, 104, 116, 221
desert, 75, 77
desert Fathers, 79
destiny, 48, 104, 137, 139, 147f, 237
devices, 107f
Dewey, John, 82, 104, 197, 232
dignity, 216
Diotima, and Socrates, 13, 208f
Dreyfus, Hubert, 123, 141

Eckhart, Meister, xvi, 76, 209, 218, 249f
Emerson, Ralph Waldo, 40, 42, 82
empiricism, xvii, 82f
emptiness, 250f
enworlding, 198, 202
ephemerality, 45, 93, 95, 104
equality, 145
*Erlebnis*, 84
essential truth, 33, 35, 70, 95, 220
eternity, 37, 43f, 176, 220, 244, 257
ethical realism, 34
ethics, xvi, 65
exemplars, 148, 224 (n. 16), 225 (n. 27), 229–59
existentialism, 19, 21f, 32, 142

experiential philosophy, 83
*extasis*, 96f, 100

faith, 32–70, 158f
Faulkner, William, xvi
fellowship, 212, 221
finality, xix, 32, 37, 87, 99, 115–17, 123, 147, 158, 169, 179
Fishing Satori, 41, 46, 48
flow, 7, 12, 21, 220f, 230, 237, 240, 254f
forgiving, 201
fragility, of wilderness, 174
Freud, Sigmund, 10, 93

garden, 75, 108
generosity, xxi, 158, 160, 176f, 211
gentleness, 175
grace, 39, 202, 209, 248, 251
gratitude, xxi, 38, 40, 216
Greeley, Horace, 14
grief, 174, 179, 204

Havel, Václav, 23
Hegel, G. F., 13, 117
Heidegger, Martin, xviii, 4, 13, 83, 86f, 92, 101ff, 109, 126, 172, 186f, 189f, 198, 200, 202, 234
Heine, Heinrich, 4
Henri, Robert, 232
Heraclitus, 241
Hobbes, Thomas, 211
Hocking, W. E., 82
Hölderlin, F., 102f
holy, 35f, 38f, 46, 77, 109f, 190
home, 8, 14f, 27, 51, 76, 204, 251
Homer, 234
homocentrism, 104
Hume, David, xix, 3, 104, 205, 216, 230

humility, 145
Husserl, Edmund, 82

idealism, 33
idolatry, 169
imagination, 50f, 211
immersion, 5f, 10, 84, 87, 97ff, 104, 109
individuality, 124
infinite, 37; infinite importance, 171
instrumentalism, 134
intimacy, 35

James, William, xvii, 82, 84
Job, book of, 169f, 184–94, 212–15, 221
joy, 38, 176, 178, 190, 206

Kant, Immanuel, xix, 4, 92f, 104, 116f, 122, 124, 130, 187, 205, 207, 216, 221
Kierkegaard, Søren, 43ff, 104, 180, 205, 230
Kundera, Milan, 255

Lawrence, D. H., 187
Lewis, C. I., 104, 223 (n. 10)
love, 175f, 196–202, 208f, 211, 221; and respect, 34, 39, 60, 65, 67, 69, 97. *See also* compassion
lyric, 48, 98f, 204f, 207–22

MacIntyre, Alasdair, 140
Maclean, Norman, 246
Marcel, Gabriel, xiv, xv, xx, 76, 81, 83, 85ff, 94, 131, 159, 232, 238, 240
Marker, Chris, 29
market economy, 133
Marx, Karl, 13, 117
materialism, 104

McKibben, Bill, 168, 171
Melville, Herman, 77, 210f, 215
Merleau-Ponty, Maurice, 190
Mill, John Stuart, 104, 117
Miller, Arthur, 104
moral worth, 131
Mozart, Wolfgang Amadeus, 207
Murdoch, Iris, 211
music, 21, 190f, 205, 214, 216f, 220f
mystery, religious, 32–70, 218
mystic, 44, 202

Naess, Arne, 26
Nancy, Jean-Luc, 198, 200
natural science, 224 (n. 25), 225 (n. 34)
necessity, 97, 122, 124, 146, 162, 175, 178, 216; moral, xviii, xix, 65, 140
Nietzsche, Friedrich, xiii, 4, 13, 117f, 205
Nishida, Kitaro, 81f, 85f
no-mindedness, 82, 87, 250
nothingness, 28, 86
numinous, 184

objective/objectivity, xvii, 33, 58, 61, 64, 67, 85, 107; objective/subjective, 88, 99, 135
Oedipus, 129, 144
Olafson, Frederick A., 70 (n. 7)
omnirelevant truth, 46, 125
openness, 28, 205. *See also* active receptiveness
Oppenheimer, Robert, 220
Otto, Rudolph, 184, 187, 189

paradise, 75
Parmenides, 241
participation, 35, 69, 172. *See also* immersion

Pascal, Blaise, 197
patience, 207, 218, 250. *See also* active receptiveness; openness
perishing, xxi, 168, 175, 216f, 222. *See also* death
phenomenology, xxi, 6, 19, 83, 85
philomorphic language, 99f, 104
Pindar, xvi, 205
place, xxi, 5f, 86, 94, 96, 204, 238
Plato, xvi, 3, 99, 104, 115, 148, 234
pluralism, 126
Plutarch, 49
poetry, 19f, 196, 205, 236f; poetic dwelling, 101f, 104
positivism, 84
postmodernism, 125
poverty of spirit, 250f
pragmatism, xiii, 87, 122
praise, 190, 212, 224 (n. 16)
prayer, 211, 213, 222
presence, xv, 32–70, 158, 205
pride, 137
Proust, Marcel, xvi

Quine, W. V., xiii, 118, 223 (n. 10)

rationalism, xvii, 82
Rawls, John, 103, 117, 123, 212
realism, 5, 33
rebirth, 36, 209, 216f
recollection, 48–70, 240
redemption, 178f, 212
relativism, 62
religious calling, 48; transformation, 53
respect, 158, 161, 211. *See also* love: and respect
responsibility, xv, xix, 67, 130–48, 150–62, 178, 198f, 211
responsiveness, 159. *See also* active receptiveness; responsibility

revelation, 34, 107
reverence, 38f, 158f, 169–71
rights, 132
Roquentin, and Sartre, 61
Rorty, Richard, 120
Rose, Gillian, 211
Rousseau, Jean-Jacques, 44f
Rumi, Jalaludin, 250
Russell, Bertrand, 104
Ryle, Gilbert, 215

sacred/sacrament, 122, 126, 143, 205, 212, 214, 217f; of co-existence, 94, 168. *See also* holy
Saint Exupéry, Antoine de, 150–52
Sartre, Jean-Paul, xiii, xv, 23, 62, 77, 142, 238
Scheler, Max, 197
Shakespeare, William, xvi
silence, 38
Silesius, Angelus, 186f, 189
Socrates, 3, 141, 148, 207, 220
song, 26, 190, 213, 218. *See also* lyric; music
Sophocles, xix
Spinoza, xvi, 92f, 104, 115, 146
St. Augustine, 190, 198, 232
St. Francis, 79
St. Paul, 184
Stace, Walter, 104
Stoics, 13, 104, 146
subjective, 33, 60, 67, 86. *See also* objective/objectivity: objective/subjective
sublime, 41
Suzuki, D. T., 81–83, 87, 108

Taxco, Mexico, 96
Taylor, Charles, 143, 215, 222 (n. 1)
technology, 101, 104f, 107f, 110, 116, 120

temporality, 201
testimony, 126, 215f, 219, 232
Thales, 3
theodicy, 184
Thoreau, Henry David, 3–16, 62, 77, 82f, 232
Tillich, Paul, 230
transcendence, 107, 109
transcendentalists, American, 10, 14
true perception, 41, 43, 46
trust, 63, 67, 209f, 240f, 244, 250

unconditional commitment (unconditional concern), xviii–xix, 140, 144, 180
understanding-communion, 159
universality, 115–17, 124, 180, 216, 237
utility, xix, 79, 84, 100, 122, 129, 218

van Gogh, 62f, 232
vocation, 88. *See also* calling
voice from the whirlwind, 171, 173f, 184–94, 213f. *See also* Job

voice, 6, 15, 84, 123, 144, 180, 206, 220, 230, 235

walking, 3–16, 197, 221, 232, 248f
wasteland, 76f
Weil, Simone, xiii
Whitman, Walt, 232
wilderness, 10f, 13f, 16, 26–28, 75–79, 98, 100, 110, 129, 143, 171–74, 181
Williams, Bernard, xix
Williams, William Carlos, 19f, 196, 237
witness, bearing, xviii, 66, 69, 176, 180
Wittgenstein, L., xiii, 19f, 33
wonder, 19–30, 168f, 252–54
Wordsworth, William, 186

Zen, 19, 24f, 58, 70, 81, 84, 87, 96f, 100, 250
Zen-Existentialism, xxi, 81–90
Zimmer, Heinrich, 231